MW00889925

HEAVEN!

SAM CHESS

© 2023 by Samuel E. Chess

Published by:

PANTHERA PUBLISHING
PANTHERAPUBLISHING.COM
STUART, FLORIDA

First Printing – May 2023

Printed in the United States of America

ISBN: 9798393255329

DEDICATION

This book is dedicated to Don Chess.

My Dad, Donald Eugene Chess, went to Heaven to be with Jesus May 15th 2021. When I say, "went to Heaven," I don't mean "ducked in past Saint Peter at the Pearly Gates." My Dad was a Saint in every sense of the word. He lived his life with an intense focus on honoring God with every action, reaction and attitude.

My dad "wasn't a scholarly type" by his own admission but dug his way through a bachelor's degree in music. My dad wasn't an up-front kind of person, yet he and my mom Nancy traveled in music evangelism. When my dad lost his singing voice, he went to meat-cutting school and faithfully worked to support his family. But Dad never lost his ministry desire, and I watched him serve every local church he was ever in right up until his old age. If you look up the word "faithful" in the dictionary, you should probably find an inserted picture of Don Chess. He learned to play multiple instruments, and even with a croaking singing voice, he would lead crowds of several hundred waving the slide of his trombone.

Up until he went to be with Jesus, he would faithfully read my books. He read *Unmasking Revelation* in the early days from front to back and said, "That's really good." *(It wasn't!)* That first book went through 18 revisions and every time I reprinted it, he would read it through again and say, "That's really good."

My attempt in this my third book is to try to draw word pictures that let me/us see what Don Chess *(and your loved ones)* are experiencing right this moment. He'll never read this new book. I'll never hear him say, "That's really good." But my guess is that what he is actually experiencing, right now, will make my best written pages in this book seem like infant scribbles.

They are the best I could do. I'll see you soon, dad, in God's home!

Table of Contents

HEAVEN: Part I

INTRODUCTION

Introduction

Are you looking forward to Heaven?

What does the Bible actually say about Heaven? We all want to go there when we die, right?

To be honest, few of us are looking forward to "the dying part" to get there! Everybody wants to go to Heaven; nobody wants to die! The United States Marines use that phrase as a call to wade into fierce battle.

But this book isn't going to be so much about the "dying part" as the "Everybody wants to go to Heaven" part. "I'm going to go to Heaven when I die," we say. "I'm going to live with Jesus forever and ever," we say. <u>What does that even mean</u>?

If we were to go to every church in your town, pull out two people at random, line them up in the front of an auditorium and ask them to explain Heaven to us – we would probably hear a whole lot of pausing and stuttering! Why is that?

In the New Living Translation of the Bible the word Heaven is used 913 times! That's huge! Very few of our key Biblical theologies include that many verses.

The power-packed word – GRACE, which is so central to the Gospel message, is used just 95 times in the whole Bible.

The word Heaven is used 9.6 times more often! Clearly Heaven is a really important topic to God. The things that are super-important to God *(one would imagine)*, he would have seen fit to include the most often in inspired Scripture!

So let's ask ourselves a logical *(theo-logical)* question: If we know the subject of "Grace" is so critical to the Word of God and to our faith *(and it is)*, what would cause God to discuss Heaven almost 10 times more often in the Bible? *(Note! Not all of the uses of the word "Heaven," in the Bible, are talking about God's present home and our future home – we'll get to that.)* But hundreds and hundreds of them are!

Let me also add this: Those 913 verses are just the references that actually use the word "Heaven." My personal habit when I set out to teach on a new subject – is to pull out every single reference in the Bible. I lay them all out on a conference table and categorize them all, trying to see a pattern that will help me *(and others)* see how those eternal truths unfold.

When I first pulled the passages that use the word Heaven *(with their surrounding contexts)*, they initially filled 150 pages single spaced! You often hear preachers and writers say *[I'm afraid I've been one of them]* that the Bible really doesn't have much to say about what is coming when this life is over. They/we are dead wrong!

In addition to all the hundreds of Scriptures that unfold the realities of Heaven *(we'll be looking at many of them!)*, there are many more verses that teach us about Heaven – without actually using the word.

- When I put both of those sections together, there are more verses in the Bible that talk about Heaven than there are using the name – Jesus. *(1447 times in the NLT.)*

- Yet if I asked each of us to talk about Jesus, we would still be talking an hour later. If I asked us to talk about Heaven – most of us would run out of things to say after three minutes. Why?

I'll try hard not to make this boring. I'm going to write things in just this introduction that will make some of you say, *"Oh my goodness, you can't be serious! Really?"* I think you will have that reaction many times over as you study through the next 28 chapters!

Our first big collective challenge

Thirty three of the 39 Old Testament books talk about Heaven! Twenty one of the 27 books in the New Testament do as well. Jesus himself mentions Heaven 70 times in the book of Matthew alone – yet a lot of Christians, not only don't know very many facts about Heaven, they are not even quite sure they want to spend an endless eternity there!

Randy Alcorn in his book titled *"Heaven"* writes:

A Pastor once confessed to me *(A Pastor!)*, "Whenever I think about Heaven, it makes me depressed. I'd rather just cease to exist when I die." *Why? Randy asked.* "I can't stand the thought of that endless tedium. To float around in the clouds with nothing to do but strum a harp – it's all so terribly boring." *Alcorn asked*, "How could a Bible-believing

Seminary trained Pastor get such a view of Heaven? It was certainly not from the Bible!" [1]

Isaac Asimov, a professor of biochemistry *(now a long dead author of over 500 books),* used to write a lot of "science fiction" before it really became a thing and wrote about "robots" before they much existed. When it came to Isaac's view about Heaven, he wasn't much of a fan. His famous quote is: "I don't believe in an afterlife, so I don't have to spend my whole life fearing hell, or fearing heaven even more. For whatever the tortures of hell – I think the boredom of heaven would be even worse!" [2]

Boredom? What boredom? The Bible presents Heaven as the exact opposite of boring! Where did the common shallow misconception come from that Heaven involves sitting on a cloud strumming a harp? I have zero interest in that myself! I'm not a harp-strumming kind of person.

And the idea of being "afraid" to go to Heaven is something most of us would never say out loud, but it might actually be in the back of some of our minds.

Randy Alcorn also records receiving a written response from another woman who wrote him saying: "I've been a Christian since I was five. My teacher when I was seven told me that when I get to Heaven, I won't know anyone from this earth or remember anything from this life. I became terrified of going to Heaven. It's been hard for me to grow in my Christian walk because I'm still so afraid of going to Heaven and spending all of eternity there!" [3]

That sounds a whole lot different than "Everybody wants to go to Heaven – but nobody wants to die," doesn't it?

Perhaps everybody <u>doesn't</u> want to go to Heaven! Why would you want to leave what you are so familiar with here to go to somewhere you know little or nothing about, with a bunch of strangers?

The Marine who walks into sniper-fire because "nobody wants to die" surely needs to be asking, "What does come on the other side of this battle if I don't come out alive?"

We humans are amazingly uncurious! How many people do you know who are older and statistically approaching death yet seem to not have the slightest thought about what happens "one earth minute after they die."

- How many funerals have you been to where the pastor or priest puts the "dearly departed" safely into Heaven, regardless of how they lived, and what they did or did not believe in?

- And the majority of other people sitting in the room, many of whom are also approaching the final ribbon, are far more interested in the party following the funeral than they are in what just happened to the deceased.

- I've officiated lots and lots of funerals. I have learned to capture the moment because it is the one time when people get the closest to asking themselves, "Is there really more to this life – than this life?!"

Perhaps you, like myself, have had people close to you recently breathe their last breath. My own Father *(who this book is dedicated to)* died just a few months ago. We've had several dear Saints in our church die, and even local Pastors who were close friends died – several because of Covid-19.

13

So when I was sitting in those memorials, or you were sitting in the final service of the one you so loved – what were we thinking about where those departed loved ones were?

When you were sitting and reminiscing and the waves of grief were washing over you for the one you so loved, what was going through your head about what had happened to them? Where are they right now? What are they doing?

Jerry Katzmann, a retired navy pilot, in our church that we all respected as a mighty man of God died early in 2021. I asked our whole church this probing question: "What is Jerry doing right now?"

 I put this picture of an aircraft carrier up at his memorial, because he used to land planes on aircraft carriers – so we talked about "his final approach" in this life and "his final landing."

My question to you today is: What would you imagine my friend Jerry has been doing since his earthly departure? I am purposely raising questions that we will try to answer (biblically) as this study unfolds.

John Eldridge in his book, The Journey of Desire says: "Nearly every Christian I've spoken with has some idea that eternity is an unending church service. We have an image of the never-ending sing-along in the sky, one great hymn after another, forever and ever, amen. And our heart sinks.

Forever and ever? That's it? That's the good news? And then we sigh and feel guilty that we are not more 'spiritual.' We lose heart and turn once more to the present…" [4]

Are we really all looking forward to a never-ending church service in the sky?

Revelation 4 really is a snapshot of "the mother of all church services in the sky." When we get further into this book, I will show us a vivid high-definition gaze, from the pages of Scripture, right into a worship service going on in the Throne Room of God that you, as a Believer, will certainly one day attend. There is indeed going to be amazing worship going on in Heaven – that makes what is going on here seem like muted stutters.

> **Revelation 4:8-11: "Each of the four living creatures had six wings and was covered with eyes all around, even under its wings. Day and night they never stop saying: 'Holy, holy, holy is the Lord God Almighty,' who was, and is, and is to come.** *(Those are angelic praisers, that's their job – we'll talk more about them.)* **Whenever the living creatures give glory, honor and thanks to him who sits on the throne and who lives for ever and ever,"** *(That is what the "Serafim" angels seem to be doing.)*
>
> **"The twenty-four elders fall down before him who sits on the throne and worship him who lives for ever and ever. They lay their crowns before the throne** (*the crown always refers to redeemed humans*) **and they say: You are worthy to receive glory and honor and**

15

power, for you created all things, and by your will they were created and have their being." *I presented the view, in my book Unmasking Revelation, that I have come to believe that these "24 Elders" represent all the Saints (O.T. 12 Tribes/ N.T. 12 Apostles – Church) who have gone before us.*

This would include Jerry Katzmann and all the other Saints in our church, your church and all around the world who have died over the last few months/years – in fact, since the beginning of time. Are they all now worshipping, praising, and "laying down their crowns"? Yes!

- But is that all they are doing? Has my saintly Dad, Don Chess, since he graduated into Heaven May 15th, 2021, been falling down in the Throne Room of Heaven "laying his crown" before God?

- Yes! I believe he has– but surely that's not all he's been doing! And in spite of his musical skills, I seriously doubt he has taken up harp playing!

This is a real valid probing point. God gives us all an intensely varied life here on this planet. He gives us intelligence and skills to do all kinds of creative things. He helps us to stretch our brains and develop new ideas, and build new things that didn't exist before, and to search for even more knowledge to do even more and more. We're designed by God to be expanding, growing, and developing as we live in this world. Does all that stop when we arrive in Heaven?

This may sound a little unspiritual *(even sacrilegious)*, but to most of us the idea of kneeling in the Throne Room of God "casting our crowns before him" for ever and ever doesn't seem eternally inviting, does it? So if that is not all we will be involved in for all of eternity, what else will we be doing? *(Please don't hear me minimizing worship in Heaven, but there is more to our eternal future than that!)*

That last phrase catches in my throat if I try to say it. My fingers pause over the keys as I write it.

- Because when we do finally find ourselves in Heaven "one moment after we die," and the curse of sin has completely fallen away, and the pain and the tears, and the fears, and the confusion of this sin-soaked life has faded from view… *(There is still more!)*

- When we for the first time walk into the Throne Room of God – and from deep in the depths of our soul, a praise begins to rise joining in unison with million/billions of other "Saints" along with millions/ billions of angels – worshipping in ways we can only get the briefest glimpse of now.

- One "heavenly hour" of worship on that level will make all the traumas of this life seem worthwhile!

- But that all said there is still more to our future in Heaven than just that amazing future glory!

Let's jump, Scripturally, to the extreme other end of this study for just a moment and let ourselves catch a glimpse through the curtain of what is waiting on the other side:

2 Timothy 2:11-12: "Here is a trustworthy saying: If we died with him, we will also live with him; if we endure with him, we will also reign (συμβασιλεύω,

symbasileuo, reign over, become rulers) with him."
You/me reigning, ruling with Jesus! When? Over whom?

Whatever that "reigning with Jesus" means – it's probably not going to be happening while we are kneeling inside the Throne Room of God!

> **Revelation 5:9-10: "And they sang a new song, saying: 'You (Jesus) are worthy to take the scroll and to open its seals, because you were slain, and with your blood you purchased for God people from every tribe and language and people and nation. You have made them to be a kingdom and priests to serve our God, and they will reign on the earth.'"** *(βασιλεύσουσιν)*

This is clearly not talking about this present age. It's after the end of "this age" as we know it, and at the beginning of eternity to come. Revelation 5 tells us, **"You purchased for God persons from every tribe and language and people and nation. You have made** them *(the purchased people)* **to be a kingdom and priests to serve our God, and** they *(we/us)* will reign on the earth."** Again, that has to be something other than kneeling in God's Throne Room. It's a future activity requiring an expanding of all the experiences you learned to use in this life! *(We'll get back to that.)*

> *Paul:* **1 Corinthians 6:2-3: "Don't you realize that someday we Believers will judge the world? Don't you realize that we will judge** *(evil)* **angels?"**

Can't you imagine the Believers that this was first written to in Corinth reading that for the first time saying, *"What? What'd he say? We're going to do what? When?"*

The thing is, if you were to run those same phrases by many, many Christians today, they would say – I've never heard that before in my life! As it turns out, it's been right here in the book of 1 Corinthians for the last 1965+ years!

Here's one more passage, three chapters from the Bible's end:

> **Revelation 20:3-4: "The angel threw him *(satan)* into the bottomless pit, which he then shut and locked so satan could not deceive the nations anymore until the thousand years were finished."**
>
> **"<u>Then I saw thrones, and the people sitting on them had been given the authority to judge</u>. And I saw the souls of those who had been beheaded for their testimony about Jesus and for proclaiming the word of God during the Tribulation. They <u>all</u>** *(not just the martyrs)* **came to life again, and <u>they reigned</u> (ἐβασίλευσαν) <u>with Christ for a thousand years</u>."**

Did you know that was going to be part of your future?

INTRODUCTION

Chapter 1

Building a framework for our thinking.

We've got a lot to construct here, but we first need to clear the brush and mark out where our structure is going to set, and get some feel for what it is going to look like. So let's spend a chapter walking around the property envisioning what we are about to build. Then we will begin, in the next chapter, constructing a biblical foundation for how, and what, and why, and where Heaven is.

Jesus made it a point to leave us with the truth that one of His primary activities after His resurrection, and before His glorious Second Coming – was going to be leaving earth "for a while" – to prepare "a place" for us.

> **John 14:1-3 NKJV: "Let not your heart be troubled; you believe in God, believe also in me. In My Father's house are many mansions/rooms; if it were not so, I would have told you. <u>I go to prepare a place for you</u>. And if I go and prepare a place for you, I will come again and receive you to myself; that where I am, there you may be also."**

We know, for sure, that when Jesus first arrived on this earth, he came here <u>from</u> Heaven. Then when he left to "prepare a place for us," he went back <u>to</u> Heaven. How do we know that? Because, the Bible tells us so!

> **John 6:33, 38, 41-42, 51: "The true Bread of God is the one who <u>comes down from heaven</u> and gives life to**

the world. <u>For I have come down from heaven</u> to do the will of God who sent me, not to do my own will. Then the people began to murmur in disagreement because he had said, "I am the bread that came down from heaven." They said, "Isn't this Jesus, the son of Joseph? We know his father and mother. How can he say, "I came down from heaven"? '<u>I am the living bread that came down from heaven.</u>'"

So, again, just to be sure: Where did Jesus come from when he came to earth? Heaven! And where did Jesus go back to when he left earth to "prepare a place for us"? Heaven! How do we know where he went back to?

Luke 24:50-53: "Then Jesus led them to Bethany, and lifting his hands to heaven, he blessed them. While he was blessing them, <u>he left them and was taken up to heaven.</u> (οὐρανός – ouranos) So they worshiped him and then returned to Jerusalem filled with great joy. And they spent all of their time in the Temple, praising God."

Acts 1:9: "After saying this, he was taken up (ἐπαίρω) into a cloud while they were watching, and they could no longer see him."

The two primary words for Heaven in the Bible are:

O.T; Hebrew: *shamayim* – which means "the heights"

N.T; Greek: *ouranos* – "that which is raised up"

It's a good thing to allow our minds to ask questions. In some cases, our questions are going to be unanswerable until we arrive on the other side of this life. In some cases we can dig through the 913 uses of the word Heaven/heavens and find an answer, or at least some very helpful clues. In some cases, after we immerse ourselves in all the following scriptural material on Heaven, we can actually make "informed speculations" that will likely turn out to be very accurate. Here's a sampling based on the passages we just read:

Q: Acts 1:9 says, Jesus was "taken up into a cloud." How do we know he went on through the clouds to a "far off place," the same far-off place from which he will one day return? Because Luke 24:51 clearly says he went up to Heaven.

Q: When Jesus said he "went to prepare a place for us," How do we know that is somewhere far beyond the visible stars? Is Jesus actively involved in preparing a real physical place – "a mansion/room" for us, right now? Yes, yes he is, because that's the place Revelation 21-22 describe in detail. Your "mansion" is housed inside a much larger place called the "New Jerusalem"! *(We'll look, keep reading!)*

Q: We can see a long way into space right now and the "New Jerusalem" that the last two chapters of Revelation says is eventually coming down here to earth – is not visible. Why hasn't that massive "Holy City" shown up on the Hubble Space Telescope? The new James Webb Space telescope is three times bigger than the Hubble. It's peering out across the universe – If there was a Holy City being prepared by Jesus out there, shouldn't it be visible? *(No, no it shouldn't! We'll talk about why.)*

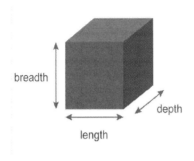

Some people believe *(me included)* that there are actually more than our familiar three dimensions. If angels *(good and bad)* are often present in our lives and we usually can't see them, does that not mean there is at least another dimension beyond our familiar three? *Yes!*

Some suggest that all of Heaven right now sets just outside the realm of our normal three dimensions. It's somewhere right off the end of your fingers! *(I doubt that!)* The Bible defines Heaven as a real already-existing place, and the "New Jerusalem," *(the part of Heaven that Revelation 21 and 22 describes)* will one day come down to Earth. It's an actual visible place. People, who were born and lived and died, in our familiar three-dimensional earth are already in Heaven right now doing the same things we are going to one day do!

- We'll soon see in this book that the Bible states over and over – Heaven is where God is! Right now!

- Heaven is where Jesus is right now! Jesus is not a spirit. He is in a glorified human body.

- Heaven is where your Redeemed loved ones are right now!

- Heaven is God's Tabernacle. It is his Sanctuary. It is his Home.

- Heaven is where the Throne Room of God is – at least for now.

Heaven is *"up there and out there" somewhere right now*. Often when Jesus prayed to the Father, the Bible says he lifted his eyes "up" toward heaven.

Heaven – all of it, wherever it is "up and out there," is a massive place, the home of God, housing for now the New Jerusalem and the Throne Room of God – along with millions, billions of angels, and millions of already dead Saints. It is not a small place!

Let me show you this next *illustration* as a mind stretching exercise. I'm not trying to prove that the following is where Heaven is, but it will help us grasp a bigger picture than most of us ever tend to think about. This report is from *Science.com,* but was first published in the *Astrophysical Journal.*

"The universe has a huge hole in it that dwarfs anything else of its kind. The discovery caught astronomers by surprise. The hole is nearly a billion light-years across. It is not a black hole, which is a small sphere of densely packed matter. Rather, this one is mostly devoid of stars, gas and other normal matter, and it's also strangely empty of the  mysterious 'dark matter' that permeates the universe. Other space voids have been found before, but nothing on this scale. Astronomers don't know why the hole is there. 'Not only has no one ever found a void this big, but we never even expected to find one this size,' said researcher Lawrence Rudnick of the University of Minnesota.

Rudnick's colleague Liliya R. Williams also had not anticipated this finding.

'What we've found is not normal, based on either observational studies or on computer simulations of the large-scale evolution of the universe,' said Williams, also of the University of Minnesota. The universe is populated with visible stars, gas and dust, but most of the matter in the universe is invisible. Scientists know something is there, because they can measure the gravitational effects of the so-called "dark matter." Voids exist, but they are typically relatively small.

'This gargantuan hole was found by examining observations made using the Very Large Array (VLA) radio telescope, funded by the National Science Foundation. The region had been previously dubbed the "WMAP Cold Spot," because it stood out in a map of the Cosmic Microwave Background (CMB) radiation made by NASA's Wilkinson Microwave Anisotopy Probe (WMAP) satellite.'

'Although our surprising results need independent confirmation, the colder temperature of the CMB in this region appears to be caused by a huge hole devoid of nearly all matter – 6 to 10 billion light-years from Earth, and **a billion light years across'**, Rudnick said." [5]

So, there is at least one massive place in the universe that our largest telescope can't see into. *And it is beyond huge!* <u>One billion light years across</u>!

Just for reference:

Our sun is "eight light-minutes" away from us.

Our whole solar system, from our Sun to Pluto *(doubled)*, is only 660 "light minutes" across.

Our entire galaxy is <u>100,000 light years wide</u> *(100 – 400 billion stars)*.

So, out there somewhere is an area 1,000,000,000 light years across that we can't see into at all! <u>It's one thousand times larger than our whole galaxy</u>!

- Is that where Heaven is right now? We can't possibly know, but I'm suggesting it is somewhere like that!

- Is it somewhere like that where Jesus went "to prepare a place for you"? Perhaps! Yes! Probably!

- Is that where your "saintly" relative is right now along with Saints from back in the Old Testament? Has your mom or grandma sat in a huge cosmic sanctuary and listened to Moses tell his adventures firsthand?

Here's what I can surely tell you is going to one day happen because it is right here in the Bible.

Revelation 21:1-2: "Then I saw a New Heaven and a New Earth, for the old heaven and the old earth had disappeared. And I saw the Holy City, the New Jerusalem, coming down from God out of Heaven like a bride beautifully dressed for her husband."

1) One of the things that makes the 913 NLT passages a bit hard to sort out – is because the Bible uses the same Hebrew and Greek words to described **the First Heaven** *(our atmosphere – with breathable oxygen, about ten miles high).*

2) **The Second Heaven** – The vast universe with galaxies of stars and planets. And,

3) **The Third Heaven** – The Highest Heaven *(Home of God Most High - El Elyon)* King Solomon called it "God's dwelling place."

At the "End of the Age" – When Jesus returns, the first two heavens are going to be completely "remodeled," including the earth we live on, removing all traces of sin and the curse. The Highest Heaven, God's dwelling place, will then expand and absorb them – so much so that Heaven, God's home, shows up here on Earth! *(We'll unfold this in great detail in the pages ahead.)*

Revelation 21:2-5: "And I saw the Holy City, the New Jerusalem, <u>coming down from God out of heaven</u> like a bride beautifully dressed for her husband. I heard a loud shout from the throne, saying, 'Look, GOD'S HOME IS NOW AMONG HIS PEOPLE! He will live with them, and they will be His people. God Himself will be with them. He will wipe every tear from their

eyes, and there will be no more death or sorrow or crying or pain. All these things are gone forever.' And the one sitting on the throne said, 'Look, I am making everything new!'"

Revelation 21:16-17: "When he *[the angel]* **measured it, he found it was a square, as wide as it was long. In fact, its <u>length and width and height were each 1,400 miles</u> [12,000 stadia]. Then he measured the walls and found them to be 216 feet thick."** (I do find it interesting that the 1400 mile footprint of the Holy City is about the same length and width as the original Promised Land given to Israel in Genesis 15! *We'll look at that!*)

And don't forget, this coming Holy City is also 1400 miles high.

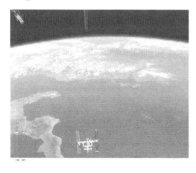

By comparison: the International Space Station is orbiting 205 miles above the earth, so this city will extend seven times higher than the space station in orbit. Imagine if your "mansion" is going to be on the 1300th floor!

Is this what Jesus is right now preparing for you? Yes. Yes! Wherever that Holy City is right now, that is where the Throne Room of God is! But instead of it just staying "up there" somewhere, Revelation 21 says it will descend "out of heaven" and come here! Very clearly, *(we will see)* this is where the promised "reigning with Jesus" will happen. *(What's that?)*

- Clearly we are supposed to draw the conclusion that Saints from both Old and New Testament times will live in that city. *(Jews and Gentiles)*

- It is entirely possible that you will have a room right next to one of the Children of Israel who trudged through the wilderness.

- He can tell you what it was like when his shoes never wore out, and you can explain how many sets of tires you burned up on your cars in 40 years!

The original sinless Heaven *(the Third Heaven, the Highest Heaven)* is still going to exist wherever it is right now!

REVELATION 22 : 3

AND THERE BE NO MORE CURSE, BUT THE THRONE OF GOD AND OF THE LAMB SHALL BE IN IT. AND HIS SERVANT SHALL SERVE HIM.

But it will *(once the sin-curse is gone)* expand to include all the rest of the universe – becoming part of God's "New Heavens and New Earth." The vastness of the newly remodeled universe will apparently be your "stomping grounds" for all of an endless eternity. *("I don't understand all that Sam." Hang on, you will!)*

No more sin, no more pain, no more dying, no more sorrow!

And you will be living in the loving presence of God, not just while you are worshipping in the Throne Room, but everywhere you travel to the extreme ends of the universe!

- God's undiluted, unfettered presence will be with you,

- And we will all be involved in "eternal occupations" that will make whatever we did here on earth seem like playing in a sandbox! *(IMO)*

Let's unfold this – piece by piece

CHAPTER 1

Chapter 2

"The Scripture you've just heard has been fulfilled."

If I were to ask each of you where you will be one minute after you breathe your last breath on this earth most of you would instantly respond – I'll be in Heaven! O.K., what exactly will you be doing in Heaven, wherever that is?

David Berg: "A lot of people think Heaven is sitting on a cloud playing a harp all day, doing nothing except being holy – and they don't find it very appealing! Thank God that's not what Heaven is like!" [6]

If you know who David Berg was, you are perhaps shocked that I would use him in a quote. He founded the "Children of God" cult back in the late 1990's. They did some really bad things in the name of God. His followers thought he was Moses returned back to earth.

But you have to admit, his quote was spot on. We're not just going to be playing harps – "Thank God that is not what Heaven is like!" The problem is, at that point Berg just started making up stuff about what he projected Heaven would be. I mean, after all, if you are "Moses back from the dead," who's going to doubt you?

But isn't that kind of what many other people have done too, including even sometimes sincere Christians? In the absence of studied knowledge we do often just fill in the gaps in our minds from our imaginations.

• I told you I pulled out every Scripture that uses the word Heaven, and there is not one single verse that says we, Believers, are going to "become angels" when we die, or get a pair of wings, or sit on a cloud, or play a harp. And yet if I were to visit every church in my area and announce a sermon on Heaven, a lot of those very images would pop up in people's minds. *Why?*

• Surely there is a logical, *(theological)* systematized *(systematic)* theology that applies to teachings on Heaven, just like there is a logical, systematic theology that applies to salvation, or sin, or the doctrine of the Church? What kind of mess would evangelical Christianity be in if we all just made it up as we go on the doctrines of sin and salvation?

It is one thing for me to preach the "Gospel" message year after year and assure people that repenting of our sins and embracing Jesus' death on our behalf, means we will not spend eternity in hell. That's certainly true! "Not perishing" Jesus called it in **John 3:16 – "Whoever believes in me will 'not perish', but will have everlasting life!"** *We'll have everlasting life where? Doing what?* If you escape eternal punishment and receive a promised eternal reward – what does that even mean? If there are hundreds of verses in the Bible on the subject, and we have all studied them – shouldn't we all be teaching basically the same thing?

In the Adventures of Huckleberry Finn, Atheist Mark Twain, *(who didn't believe in God or Heaven)* presented it like this: *(As a kid I remember pouring over these pages many times, reliving the adventures of Huck Finn and Tom Sawyer.)*

Christian Miss Watson is talking to Huck: "She went on to tell me all about the good place. She said all a body would have to do there was go around all day long with a harp and sing forever and ever. So I didn't think much of it. I ask her if she reckoned Tom Sawyer would go there, and she said "not by a considerable sight!" I was glad of that because I wanted him and me to be together." [7]

What if instead of Miss Watson telling him that nonsense, she had told him some of the points from our introductory chapter; that Heaven is a real place, the home of God, and that Jesus, God incarnate, came from there – came down to this earth to die for and forgive our sins. And that this same Jesus, after his resurrection from the dead, went back up to Heaven to "prepare a place for us."

What if she'd told him that there was coming a day when God was going to say, "That's enough," and he will finally pour out his wrath on sin and satan, and the curse? What if she had added that Jesus would soon "rapture" the bodies of the dead Saints and all the remaining living Saints from this earth – and we all will enter Heaven with our newly glorified bodies! And then, soon after, all the Saints will return with Jesus in his Glorious Second Coming. And Jesus himself *(with all of us piling in behind him)* will finally wipe out satan's power on this planet once and for all! <u>What if Miss Watson had said that</u>?

And, she could go on to say *(Peter says)* that the sin-cursed earth and the heavens above will be renovated and all traces of sin and the curse will be gone forever.

2 Peter 3:10-13: "Then the heavens will pass away with a terrible noise, and the very elements themselves will disappear in fire, and the earth and everything on it will be found to deserve judgment. Since everything around us is going to be destroyed like this, what holy and godly lives you should live, looking forward to the day of God. But we are looking forward to the New Heavens and New Earth he has promised, a world filled with God's righteousness."

What if Miss Watson had told Huck Finn that Heaven would expand from wherever it is now and consume all of the newly renovated cosmos?

- And she might have added, the Throne Room of God in the New Jerusalem would actually descend out of Heaven down here to earth. *(Revelation 21-22)*

- And Jesus and his Saints will reign from right here on this newly renovated curse-free earth for all of eternity!

- And that the New Heavens, which then includes the entire vast universe, now all a part of Heaven *(God's Home)* could become the place where Huck Finn and Tom Sawyer and all the rest of us could explore in an eternal adventure forever and ever! *What if she had told him that?*

- What if she had just read the first few verses of Revelation 21 to him?

Revelation 21:1-5: "Then I saw a new heaven and a new earth, for the old heaven and the old earth had disappeared. And I saw the Holy City, the New

Jerusalem, coming down from God out of heaven like a bride beautifully dressed for her husband. I heard a loud shout from the Throne, saying, 'Look, God's home is now among His people! He will live with them, and they will be His people. God Himself will be with them. He will wipe every tear from their eyes, and there will be no more death or sorrow or crying or pain. All these things are gone forever.' And the one sitting on the throne said, 'Look, I am making everything new!'"

If you are a bit fuzzy on all those details, don't feel bad, so are millions and millions of other Believers!

I have made it my task to <u>buy every single significant book written about Heaven</u>. Several I found used because they were out of print. How many books do you think I found written about Heaven in the last 100 years that I could find anywhere available to purchase? Now I'm not talking about books where someone says they died and visited Heaven. I'm talking about books that actually unfold what inspired Scriptures say Heaven is like. Do you think I was able to buy 100 books, 150? <u>My grand total as of this printing is 26 books! Just 26 books</u>! I promise you, any other Bible topic and you would be able to find dozens, to hundreds of books. Not this one! Why? Why do so few people want to write about Heaven?

And, to be honest, I was a little stunned as I was reading from some of the great *(now dead)* writers of the past. The verses some of them referred to – and what they had to say about them sometimes flowed together in what I've affectionately begun to call a "stew." The eternal New

37

Jerusalem is often stirred in with the same "intermediate" Heaven where Moses and David are right now. The seven visions looking right into the Throne Room – given to us by Moses, Isaiah, Daniel, Ezekiel and John are often ignored completely – even though they, amazingly, give us five detailed descriptions of the Heavenly Father sitting on his Throne, and two high definition descriptions of the risen Jesus in Heaven. *(We'll look!)*

Is it even possible for us to sort through all that the Bible says – and then lay it out in a logical *(theo-logical; theos-logos; God-logic; God-reason)* systematic way that we can all understand and learn? Yes, I certainly believe so!

Some of you reading this, at some point in your lives, decided to migrate from your birthplace – leave your country of origin and move here to the United States. One would imagine before you came here, you attempted to find out all you could about the place you were coming to.

Can you imagine NASA getting ready to send the Apollo astronauts to the moon and for the scientists and the astronauts not to have researched every tiny little detail they possibly could before they first set foot inside the rocket? It would be illogical not to! Yet we have millions of Christians in this world who are approaching the end of their life, and if you ask: "Where are you going when you die?" They will respond, "To Heaven!" But the follow-up questions, "Where's Heaven? What are you going to do when you get there?" – might bring a blank stare! Why? That doesn't have to be true!

- I can't promise how good a job we are going to do over the remaining chapters in digging out everything we can find in the Bible on Heaven and putting it together into a logical *(theo-logical)* pattern of thought, but I can promise you this; we are going to try!

- We can't possibly study hundreds of verses in the Bible on Heaven *(plus all the other ones that talk about Heaven without actually using the word)* and not start to sense that our mind is expanding and our focus is clearing, and we are starting to "fix our eyes on the realities of Heaven" as Paul admonishes in Colossians 3.

Here's part of our present-day lack of knowledge about Heaven, and the more I discovered the problem, the more frustrating it became. Great theologians in the past just flat-out ignored the subject of Heaven.

John Calvin; *(famed reformer, and avid commentary writer)* I was assigned to read all of Calvin's unabridged <u>*Institutes of the Christian Religion*</u> in Seminary. *(540 pages!)* Calvin wrote deeply and at great length on virtually everything in the Bible – but he seldom ever mentioned Heaven! Why?

- Why would John Calvin write so powerfully about the sinful state of humanity, our great need of a Savior, the wonderful gift that God provided through Jesus' death on a cross?

- Why would he detail so much biblical truth about this life up until the moment of death, and then largely ignore the life to come? *(I'll provide an explanation later in the book.)*

- Understand, John Calvin, in my mind, was much, much farther up the spiritual road than I will ever will be, but I do have this one "bone to pick" with him. The lack of teaching on the eternal Heaven to come surely couldn't have been because he thought the Bible had nothing to say on the subject!

- And John Calvin was not alone in ignoring the topic: Randy Alcorn, in his book titled "Heaven" provides the following list on pages 20-22; [8]

  1) Theologian Reinhold Neibuhr's in-depth *The Nature and Destiny of Man*. 684 pages – and there is <u>not one word</u> in it about Heaven. *("Mr. Neibuhr, you used the words 'destiny of man' in your title!")*

  2) William Shedd's *Dogmatic Theology*. (992 pages) There are 87 pages on hell – but only two pages on Heaven!

  3) A Pastor who has become something of a hero to me – Martyn Lloyd-Jones (EFCA) *Great Doctrines of the Bible* (928 pages) devotes a whopping two pages to Heaven!

4) Louis Berkhof's classic Systematic Theology. (*I used to have a friend in Bible College who would carry his Berkhof around with him.*) 737 pages long! –and there's <u>one whole page on Heaven</u>! *Why?*

These guys were smarter in their little finger than I am in my whole brain, but I can't help getting a little smart-mouthed with them. What were you thinking guys? We're on this earth for a few dozen years. Then we're going to be in Heaven for all of eternity. How about turning a little of that brainpower into helping us understand Heaven? Was it because there was nothing to say? No! Quite the opposite! (*Again, there is a reason why these guys chose to not tackle the Biblical teachings on a literal "future home" in Heaven, but before I tell you what it is, we first need to study through some of the massive amounts of Scripture they were choosing to ignore.*)

I actually issued an apology to our church when I began truly studying all that Scripture has to say on this subject, and trying to teach it in an understandable way:

1) I apologized that I was 43 years into preaching before ever seriously taking on the topic of Heaven to preach a whole series of sermons.

2) I apologized that I had always parroted what I heard other people say and what I was taught instead of digging into the Scriptures for myself.

3) I was sorry that I had made the statement that: "There isn't all that much in the Bible to teach us about Heaven. God has chosen to leave the subject

rather vague." That was a completely unlearned statement!

4) I taught that the people in the Old Testament knew little about an afterlife – thus they knew little about the possibility of there being a Heaven. False and false again!

5) I had stated that there is really no way to define much of anything about Heaven until we get at least to Jesus' words in the Gospels or even on into the Epistles. Who knew there were <u>hundreds of verses</u> about Heaven in the <u>Old</u> <u>Testament</u>? *(I probably should have actually looked that fact up earlier. Years earlier – decades earlier!)*

Chapter 3

"The Scripture you've just heard has been fulfilled..."

Let me show you something we would possibly never catch, unless we systematically studied everything the Bible has to say about Heaven and tried to put it all together into a logical, theo-logical pattern. *(theology = theo-logos = God logic/reason)*

Way back with ancient Abraham – as he is completing God's test of faith on Mt. Moriah:

> **Genesis 22:10-17: "And Abraham picked up the knife to kill his son as a sacrifice. At that moment the angel of the LORD called to him from heaven, 'Abraham! Abraham!' 'Yes,' Abraham replied. 'Here I am!' 'Don't lay a hand on the boy!' the angel said. 'Do not hurt him in any way, for now I know that you truly fear God.'**

> **"Then Abraham looked up and saw a ram caught by its horns in a thicket. So he took the ram and sacrificed it as a burnt offering in place of his son. Abraham named the place Yahweh-Yireh (which means 'the LORD will provide').**

> **"Then the angel of the LORD called again to Abraham from heaven. 'This is what the LORD says: Because you have obeyed me and have not withheld even your son,**

your only son, I swear by my own name that I will certainly bless you.'"

An angel from Heaven: We may look at Abraham as a fresh-out-of-paganism Bedouin "dweeb" who didn't have any Bible yet, and assume he couldn't begin to understand the deeper things of God that we as New Testament Believers so clearly understand today. But I'm telling you, the old boy had picked up an awful lot in his few years as a God-follower:

#1) He understood that he was supposed to obey God even when he didn't quite understand why.

#2) He understood that God was his Source, his Supreme provider, in the most impossible of times.

#3) He understood that <u>angels</u> *(from Heaven)* <u>were playing a major role</u> in his life and in the lives of his family.

- Angels played a huge active role in the Old Testament and again in the New Testament.
- Many modern Believers have little concept of the role of angels in our daily lives.
- The idea that angels accompany you in life's tasks seems almost weird to most of us.
- We're not going to be able to talk about Heaven without talking about angels *(from Heaven)*, so put on your seatbelt.

#4) Abraham didn't only hear the angels when they spoke to him, he didn't seem to have any problem chatting back with them.

#5) And he seemed to know instinctively that when the angels spoke to him some were "speaking to him from Heaven."

How in the world did somebody with no Bible at all, figure out that the angels were communicating with him from a place called Heaven? I don't know, but I'm telling you; he knew a whole lot more than many "enlightened" Christians seem to know today.

Watch this, as he is sending his "Chief of Staff" out to find a wife for his son Isaac:

Genesis 24:3, 7: "Swear by the Lord, the God of heaven and earth, that you will not allow my son to marry one of these local Canaanite women. For the Lord, the God of heaven, who took me from my father's house and my native land, solemnly promised to give this land to my descendants. He will send his angel ahead of you, and he will see to it that you find a wife there for my son." Who knew we could build a beginning theology of Heaven *(and angels)* by reaching way back here to Father Abraham?

#1) He seems to understand clearly that God is the "Lord of Heaven" and dwells there.

#2) In fact, he seems to understand that the Lord is God of both Heaven and Earth – and that they are two completely different places.

#3) He also seems to understand that the same "Heaven-ruling God" is sending out angels across the universe with specific divine tasks.

Now wait a minute Sam, you said in Chapter one that the same Hebrew word is used to describe all three levels of Heaven in the Old Testament. The atmosphere above the earth is the "shamayim." That's the <u>first level</u>.

The <u>second level</u> is the cosmos with stars and planets and meteors and black holes. **Genesis 1:1, 14: "In the beginning God created the heavens *(ha-sham-a-yim)* and the earth. Then God said, 'Let lights appear in the sky to separate the day from the night.'"**

The <u>third level</u> is what the Bible literally calls "the third Heaven," "the Highest Heaven," "the abode of God." That is not found in the earth's atmosphere, and it's not even part of the cosmos. Wherever Heaven is right now – it is separate from the rest of the universe. It is the dwelling place of God. <u>But it is also called the "Shamayim"</u>!

That is the place from which Jesus is going to return to Earth. And it's the same place where Abraham thought God was – and Moses, and David, and Solomon did too. *(I'll show you.)*

- Sam, you're giving way to much credit to Ancient Abraham. He was a camel riding Bedouin. He lived in moveable rawhide tents.

- He had no Bible or any other books that we know of.

- He, like anybody else on a dark night, could only see about 2000 of the stars in our galaxy out of the billions that are actually there. And he knew nothing about a billon more entire galaxies beyond our own.

- What could he know of a special place beyond the stars where God himself dwelled and sent out angels to care for him and his family?

In Abraham's Hebrew language – couldn't God have been dwelling just behind the moon, in the first or second heaven, (*shamayim*) and couldn't the angels have been living just behind the clouds? Perhaps, except for this treasured piece of Scripture from Hebrews 11 – we call the "Faith" chapter!

Hebrews 11:8-10: "It was by faith that Abraham obeyed when God called him to leave home and go to another land that God would give him as his inheritance. He went without knowing where he was going. And even when he reached the land God promised him, he lived there by faith—for he was like a foreigner, living in tents. And so did Isaac and Jacob, who inherited the same promise. Abraham was confidently <u>looking forward to a city with eternal foundations</u>, a city designed and built by God."

Did you see that? Abraham, the Bedouin living in tents, was looking forward to a city that God was going to build! Not just one with foundations, *(unlike his tent)* but one with eternal foundations. <u>One that God himself would be the architect and the builder of</u>! Abraham saw this before there ever was a David or a Solomon or a Stephen or a Paul!

Abraham was looking forward to the very city that Jesus would say he was going back to Heaven to prepare for us! The same one we read earlier that is coming down to earth in Revelation 21-22! The God of Heaven was going to be building that city and he, Abraham, would one day live in it! So will you! Jesus has now been in Heaven, "preparing that city" for the last 2000 years. While some of our great Bible commentators can't seem to find the words to express much of anything about Heaven, the ancient patriarchs didn't seem to have any trouble.

Abraham's grandson Jacob, amid all his deceiving, had a vision. And it wasn't a vision of how he was going to get a lot more camels, or a vision of how he would be victorious over his enemies. When God wanted to show himself and his presence to Jacob, he gave him a mental picture – of what?

> **Genesis 28:12, 17: "As he slept, he dreamed of a stairway that reached from the earth up to heaven. And he saw the angels of God going up and down the stairway. But he was also afraid and said, 'What an awesome place this is! It is none other than the house of God, the very gateway to heaven!'"**

Again, Jacob was a man who is presented as very faulted in Scripture – but even in the early parts of his stumbling relationship with God, he was able to form some basic theology.

- There is a Heaven!
- Heaven is not on earth!
- Heaven is "up there"!

Turns out from the beginning book of the Bible, angels are God's ministering messengers who He deploys in human lives to achieve his divine ends. *(And the "flawed" patriarchs knew it!)* When God opens the "gateway to heaven" even just a crack, we can get a brief glimpse into just how amazing Heaven is one day going to be – for us!

Solomon also got to peer through the crack: As we all know, he was a faulted sinful human being too. As he got older he strayed further and further from his relationship with God.

And that's really hard to imagine – after an experience with God like Solomon had after finishing the temple. He finally got a place built so that "the presence of God could dwell with his people." Solomon did seem to understand that "housing the presence of God" was like trying to put the whole ocean in a small bottle.

> **1 Kings 8:22-23, 27, 30: "Then Solomon stood before the altar of the Lord in front of the entire community of Israel. He lifted his hands toward heaven, and he prayed, 'O Lord, God of Israel, there is no God like you in all of heaven above or on the earth below. You keep your covenant and show unfailing love to all who walk before you in wholehearted devotion. But will God really live on earth? Why, even the highest heavens cannot contain you. How much less this Temple I have built!**
>
> **"May you hear the humble and earnest requests from me and your people Israel when we pray toward this place. Yes, <u>hear us from heaven where you live</u>, and when you hear, forgive.'"**
>
> **1 Kings 8:49, 54: "'Then hear their prayers and their petition from <u>heaven where you live</u>, and uphold their cause...'" When Solomon finished making these**

prayers and petitions to the Lord, he stood up in front of the altar of the Lord, where he had been kneeling with his hands raised toward heaven."

2 Chronicles 7:1 *adds:* "When Solomon finished praying, fire flashed down from heaven and burned up the burnt offerings and sacrifices, and the glorious presence of the LORD filled the Temple." *Wow!*

We have just barely started to scratch the surface of what the Old Testament teaches us about Heaven. There are hundreds of verses! Not to mention hundreds more verses in the New Testament. This is not the kind of thing *(IMO)* one should want to leave completely out of Bible commentaries – or that Pastors should never preach any sermons about. *(Ouch!)* This is our eternal future we are talking about!

- Everything we've looked at so far in just three Old Testament chapters place Heaven outside the realm of the normal cosmos. It is clearly in existence right now as you are sitting somewhere reading this book.

- God is there. The Throne Room is there, for now. Jesus is there until he returns to come back here.

- The New Jerusalem is being prepared there, for now.

- Those who have died and gone on before you are there, for now. *(We'll establish that fact.)* We will all be joining them soon either by death or by the Rapture.

1 Thessalonians 4:13-14, 16-17: "And now, dear brothers and sisters, we want you to know what will happen to the believers who have died so you will not

grieve like people who have no hope. For since we believe that Jesus died and was raised to life again, we also believe that when Jesus returns, God will bring back with him the Believers who have died. For the Lord himself will come down from heaven with a commanding shout, with the voice of the archangel, and with the trumpet call of God. First, the believers who have died will rise from their graves. Then, together with them, we who are still alive and remain on the earth will be caught up in the clouds to meet the Lord in the air. Then we will be with the Lord forever."

Immediately after the above described "Rapture" ends, this event in Revelation 7 follows *(IMO)*:

Revelation 7:9-10: "After this I saw a vast crowd, too great to count, from every nation and tribe and people and language, standing in front of the throne and before the Lamb. They were clothed in white robes and held palm branches in their hands. And they were shouting with a great roar, 'Salvation comes from our God who sits on the throne and from the Lamb'!"

I want us to look at those verses and think these thoughts. That's me! I'm going to be there as part of that vast newly "raptured" crowd! I'm going to hear that great roar – and then I'll realize my voice is roaring right along with the rest!

I'm praying something starts to stir inside of us all. Most of us Christians tend to live our lives with an image in the frontal lobe of our minds of all that has to be done today, tomorrow, and the next day. But what if right behind that, buried in the God-infused center of our minds, there was a vivid picture of that mind-bending meeting in the Throne Room of God that we are going to be part of one day?

When Paul, himself, started to catch on to that truth, he wrote: **Colossians 3:1-4: "Since you have been raised to new life with Christ, set your sights on the realities of heaven, where Christ sits in the place of honor at God's right hand. Think about the things of heaven, not the things of earth. For you died to this life, and your real life is hidden with Christ in God. And when Christ, who is your life, is revealed to the whole world, you will share in all his glory."** If this really is our future, somehow it's going to have to come to consume more of our present! Isn't it?

Author E.M Bounds *(Edward McKendree Bounds)* really had a tough life. Many of us have read his books on prayer. None of those were even published until after he died.

- He had studied to be a lawyer, passed the bar, then ended up sensing a call to be a Pastor. He no more than started pastoring before the civil war broke out.

- The North demanded that he sign an oath of allegiance and pay a $500.00 fee. He didn't have $500.00, and wanted to pastor without politics, so he ended up being arrested and put in prison for 1 ½ years.

- When he got out, he'd been branded a Confederate. He just wanted to be a pastor! But then while trying to serve as a chaplain to the wounded he ended up as a prisoner of war until the war ended.

- That's not exactly what anyone would plan for their life, but what he learned during those hard years was <u>how to pray</u>! His prayers were powerful, sometimes three hours a day, sometimes all day. His books on prayer have changed lives all over the world, including mine! *(But he never got to know about any of that!)*

- He wrote a long out-of-print book on Heaven that I managed to acquire. Unlike his books on prayer, it's not particularly well written. His "theology of Heaven," is in my opinion, a bit of a "stew."

- But what I heard him saying particularly as he aged was:

*God wants our hearts to be
fixed on Heaven!*

1) You have to live in this life – but figure out how to "put your heart in heaven."

2) It will change dramatically how you view what is going on here, on this sin-soaked earth!

CHAPTER 3

Chapter 4

"Jesus... in the last hours before his trial, crucifixion and resurrection told his disciples:

John 14:1-6: '"Don't let your hearts be troubled. Trust in God, and trust also in me. There are more than enough rooms in my Father's home. If this were not so, would I have told you that I am going to prepare a place for you? When everything is ready, I will come and get you, so that you will always be with me where I am. And you know the way to where I am going.' 'No, we don't know, Lord,' Thomas said. 'We have no idea where you are going, so how can we know the way?' Jesus told him, 'I am the way, the truth, and the life.'"

Typically, we pastors excitedly preach a message at that point *(and not wrongly so)* about Jesus' pronouncement that he is the only way to Heaven. That's true and very important, but we often don't pause and ask the obvious follow up questions:

- Where is Jesus, right now, as he is getting your future home ready? Where in this vast universe is a place that the omnipresent Creator God calls home?

- What does it mean that he is "preparing a room" for us "in his Father's home"? That was Jesus' home too,

> before he came to this Earth to pay our sin penalty, and it's his present home again now!

We seldom stop to get upset over Thomas' statement that he didn't have any idea where Jesus was going. That's not just a doubting statement Mr. Thomas – that's just flat false!

We might not know it was a false statement if we hadn't been digging through the Old Testament Scriptures about Heaven. Hundreds of the verses on Heaven in the Bible are in the Old Testament <u>which was Thomas' Bible at the time</u>. If he had been reading his Bible at all, he would have known exactly where Jesus was going!

> We saw in the last chapter that Abraham's knowledge about Heaven was far deeper than most imagine: **Hebrews 11:10: "Abraham was confidently looking forward to a city with eternal foundations, a city designed and built by God."**

How in the world could pagan Abraham have figured out there was a place called Heaven and inside that Heaven, a city with eternal foundations whose architect and builder is God? He must have found it out from what God told Adam! How?

You have, perhaps, seen charts like the following one from the *WiderBible*. The word-of-mouth distance between Adam and Abraham was far shorter than we tend to imagine:

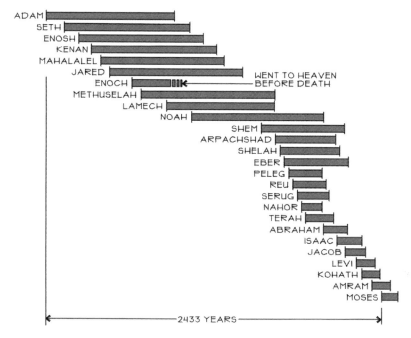

Here's the nutshell: Adam was still alive for years after Methuselah was born. Methuselah was alive for 100 years after Noah's son Shem was born.

After the flood, Noah's son Shem was still alive two hundred years into Abraham's life. So whatever God had told Adam and Eve in the Garden only had to pass from Adam to Methuselah to Shem and straight to Abraham! Those ancient Patriarchs weren't as ignorant of God's plan as we sometimes imagine they were.

> *Jacob* – **Genesis 28:12, 17: "As he slept, he dreamed of a stairway that reached from the earth up to heaven. And he saw the angels of God going up and down the stairway. 'What an awesome place this is! It is none**

other than the house of God, *(he said)* the very gateway to heaven!'"

Moses – **Deuteronomy 4:39: "So remember this and keep it firmly in mind: The Lord is God both in heaven above and on the earth below, and there is no other!"**

Deuteronomy 26:15: "Now look down from your holy dwelling place in heaven and bless your people Israel."

Solomon temple dedication - **1 Kings 8:27,33: "Why, even the highest heavens cannot contain you. How much less this Temple I have built! May you hear us from heaven where you live, and when you hear, forgive."**

"That's just a tiny fraction of the verses the Old Testament Patriarch's and Matriarch's had to say about Heaven – "Mr. Doubting-Disciple Thomas!" Don't say you didn't know where Jesus was going to! You had mountains of Biblical evidence about Heaven!

Question #1: So one of the questions we will have to define is – where exactly did Jesus go back to? He said he had to return there, so that he could "send his Spirit" to live in and through us on this earth, until he returns to take us all to "be where he is."

Question #2: If I could pull back a curtain and let us all have a brief glimpse inside, what would we see?

That's what I am going to try to do, *(from Scripture)* particularly when we get to parts five through seven of this book. But let's not be in a hurry to get there. We're trying to build a whole structure of systematic biblical understanding – so that when someone asks you to describe what is coming when this life is over, you will not under any circumstances "pull a Thomas" on them.

We're trying to raise not only our awareness of what Heaven is like now – but also a spiritual hunger that starts to make Heaven seem more desirable – than this sin-cursed earth. **Colossians 3:1-2: "Since** *we* **have been raised to new life with Christ,** *we are setting* **our sights on the realities of heaven, where Christ sits in the place of honor at God's right hand.** *We are going to be increasingly thinking* **about the things of heaven, not the things of this earth."** *(Revised)*

But that is not easy to do! Most of us reading this book have been "raised to new life with Christ," but our sights are still firmly planted on the things of this earth. Let's be honest, the vast majority of our daily thoughts are not about Heaven!

If we weren't studying this subject right now, how many of us *(including me)* would make it through the whole week – and all of our focus, all of our prayers, all of our plans and ambitions, even all of our church activity would be centered around how we are going to live out the next few hours, days, and years here on this planet? I'm not trying to make any of us feel bad – it's the human condition.

- How in the world are we supposed to "think about the things of Heaven" when all we really truly understand are the things of this earth?

- Thomas took the easy way out by just saying, "I don't know nothin' 'bout any of that."

- But with 900+ verses in Scripture, we're supposed to know something *(many some-things)* about Heaven!

- In fact, Paul says we are supposed to focus our hearts on the realities of heaven! Or as E.M. Bounds said, "put your heart in Heaven"!

The only way I know to do that is to keep building on more and more of the information about Heaven we have in the Bible and try to paint word pictures – until it sparks something in our minds. That's what we're going to try to accomplish here, and we have just scratched the surface.

More Old Testament leaders erupted with statements about God in his Heavenly home, often right in the middle of teaching other subjects. But we can actually track how much the ancients Saints knew about Heaven based on what had been written at the time in which they lived.

> *David*: **Psalm 11:4: "But the Lord is in his holy Temple; the Lord still rules from heaven. He watches everyone closely, examining every person on earth."**

> *Asaph*: **Psalm 82:1: "God presides over heaven's court; he pronounces judgment on the heavenly beings."**

> *Descendants of Korah*: **Psalm 84:1: "How lovely is your dwelling place, O Lord of Heaven's Armies."**

> Micaiah: **1 Kings 22:19: "Then Micaiah continued, 'Listen to what the Lord says! I saw the Lord sitting on his Throne with all the Armies of Heaven around him, on his right and on his left.'"**

Anonymous: **Psalm 102:19: "Tell them the Lord looks down from his heavenly sanctuary. He looks down to Earth from Heaven…"**

- Taking into consideration Solomon's stated problem with housing an omnipresent God in a single place – After all, "all of God is everywhere, all of the time!"

- The universe that He created came "out of his being" *(all matter, all energy)* which means God has to be bigger than the entire universe he created.

That said, God himself targets a single place in the universe as his home, his Heavenly sanctuary, the place where his Throne Room is. It's the place where Jesus our risen Savior "sits at the Father's right hand."

You might ask, Jesus sitting at God's right hand is figurative, Sam – isn't it? Is the worship going on around the Throne in the Throne Room of God figurative? Or is that actually happening right now? Is the Heavenly City that Jesus said he went there to prepare for us, that Ancient Abraham is looking forward to – is that figurative? No, and no to the above questions!

- The Bible leaves not one shred of doubt that this Heaven we are talking about actually exists! It is a real place! It is the home of God!

- That fact should raise some additional questions in our minds. When did Heaven become the home of God? <u>Was it already in existence when God created the earth and the universe around us</u>?

Just assume with me, for the sake of discussion, that there is a place *(up there)* called Heaven. All of the Bible uses the words "up" to Heaven and "down" from Heaven. The earth, of course, rotates on its axis but "up there" is perhaps only in one direction.

I'll bring this illustration up again. Some may have found it surreal in Chapter 1, but it helps create "word pictures in our minds"! My mind doesn't function well unless the words get turned into pictures. That's probably true of many of us. That's why television and commercials are so addicting. We like pictures! Each picture is "worth a thousand words."

 This is another picture of the Bootes Void. We already read that this is a massive hole in space that our telescopes simply won't penetrate. This is not a black hole, they are relatively small. This "hole" is <u>a billion light years across,</u> and either there is absolutely nothing in it or we <u>simply can't see inside</u>. You can tell from the photo that we have a perfect view of millions of stars all around it – but then zip - nothing!

- The Bootes Void is an area <u>1000 times bigger than our entire Milky Way galaxy</u>.

- Is Heaven presently found in this massive void or another one like it? Your guess is as good as mine –

but somewhere out there is, definitely, a place that simply doesn't match the rest of the universe!

Let's answer another valid question. <u>How long has Heaven been there</u>? Did God create his Throne Room the same day he created cows and camels here on this earth? No!

I did another big study a few years ago, where I pulled every use of the words "eternal, ever-lasting, eternity," and the very first thing we determined from Scripture was that – God is eternal, God is everlasting. He had no beginning, and he will never end. The Bible says so, over and over!

So where was an eternal God "living" before our vast universe was created? Was he just floating around in a massive void? Or has Heaven, God's home, his sanctuary, existed for millions or billions or trillions of years before the earth and universe were created? Possibly. <u>Probably</u>!

Everybody always comes back to the same argument, but **Genesis 1:1 says, "In the Beginning God created the Heavens and the earth." Yes? Right!**

- But in the beginning of what? Not God! In the beginning of – TIME!
- What does God not live in? Time!
- What do the last two chapters of Revelation say we will no longer be living with in Heaven? Time!

<u>There's no time in Heaven</u>! There is "time" for us on earth now. We're stuck with the sun-rising thing, and an earth taking exactly one year to revolve around the sun. God made it that way, for now. He made "a sun to rule the day and a moon to rule the night" so we could look up and say,

"I believe it's time to get up," "I think it's time to go to bed." But God doesn't live inside of the time he created for us – so there is clearly no passage of time as we know it, in God's home, in his sanctuary – in Heaven.

Light itself is a function of time. A man named Einstein toyed with all of that. You can't move faster than light which always travels the same speed. The closer you move toward the speed of light the more time slows down. When you reach the speed of light – time stops?

Could that explain why we can't see inside the massive Bootes Void? There is no time there? That's speculation, of course, but as you stare at the picture imagine for a moment that beyond your possible gaze there really is a one billion light year wide "Home of God" inside that void (or one like it). Just imagine, for the moment, that you can't see in because time doesn't exist there!

Now, imagine that invisible void existing before any of the rest of the picture existed. From inside of Heaven, God created first the Earth and then the massive universe around it. (That view isn't in any of the natural science books on this planet – but that is the way Genesis describes the process.) God created the universe from Heaven starting with this earth!

Genesis 1:1-5: "In the beginning God created the heavens and the earth. The earth was formless and empty, and darkness covered the deep waters. And the Spirit of God was hovering over the surface of the waters. Then God said, 'Let there be light,' and there was light. And God saw that the light was good. Then he separated the light from the darkness. God called

the light 'day' and the darkness 'night.' And evening passed and morning came, marking the first day."

That's not just the creation of this planet and all the other planets, and the billions of stars around us. That's the creation of time itself – for us to exist in. *(Do we see that?)* And that "time" will continue right up until Revelation 21:

Revelation 21:1-3, 23-25: "Then I saw a new heavens and a new earth, for the old heavens and the old earth had disappeared. And <u>I saw the Holy City, the New Jerusalem</u> *(the place Jesus said he was going to Heaven to prepare for you),* **<u>coming down from God out of Heaven</u> like a bride beautifully dressed for her husband. I heard a loud shout from the <u>Throne</u>, saying, 'Look, <u>God's Home is now among His people!</u>' … And the city has no need of sun or moon, for the glory of God illuminates the city, and the Lamb is its light. The nations will walk in its light, and the kings of the world will enter the city in all their glory. Its gates will never be closed at the end of day because there is no night there."** *(Time, as we know it, no longer exists.)*

Do we see that Heaven *(wherever it is now)* will enlarge itself to fill the whole "newly-renovated-from-the-curse" universe? And at least in part, Heaven arrives right here on this newly un-cursed Earth. That may sound like science fiction, but remember this was written long before there was such a thing as science fiction!

Revelation 22:3-5: "<u>No longer will there be a curse upon anything</u>. For the Throne of God and of the Lamb will be there, and his servants will worship him.

And they will see his face, and his name will be written on their foreheads. And there will be no night there—no need for lamps or sun—for the Lord God will shine on them. And they will reign forever and ever."

We'll talk about that more in the chapters ahead. But let's go back to God standing on the edge of eternity, before time, saying those famous words "Let there be"!

"It's too bad there were no other beings there to watch him fling out billions of stars and planets." Whoa, not so fast! Who said there were no other beings present when God created the earth? Watch this:

God is having a "come-to-Jesus" moment with Job, who was getting a little smart-mouthed with his Creator over his deep trials. We can pick up something in God's response that might change our pre-creation mental mindset.

Job 38:4-7: "Where were you when I laid the foundations of the earth? Tell me, if you know so much. Who determined its dimensions and stretched out the surveying line? What supports its foundations, and who laid its cornerstone as the morning stars sang together and all the angels (*ben Elohim, sons of God*) **shouted for joy?"**

God wasn't alone at Creation! He had already "created living beings" capable of <u>shouting for joy</u> as the universe sprang into existence. Sometime in the "eons" before God created the world, his timeless Heaven was already filled with the company and the voices of other beings.

- Those (*ben Elohim*) joyous beings *(angels)* had to have been there before the earth was formed and the stars were flung into space.

- How long before we don't know – but God was using the "pre-creation time" to get them ready to become the extensions of his power and purpose, *(usually invisible, but sometimes visible)* extensions of His Almighty hands, and messengers of His eternal words.

As we branch into including angels in our study of Heaven for a few chapters, it is important that we understand – angels are not the source of their own power. Angels function in the power of God and only in the power of God! They function in the knowledge of God and only in the knowledge of God! They are not the source of their own divine messages – they carry only the words of God. We do not pray to angels! We do not ask angels for deliverance. We do not command angels to obey us. Our deliverer is Jesus! Our Savior is Jesus! The angels do exactly what he tells them to do. Their tasks are quite specific. *(We'll talk about that.)* We've reduced angels down to little fat-winged figures that we cast out of cheap metal and wear around our neck. *(We need to correct that image.)*

When Jesus was agonizing in Gethsemane before his crucifixion and Peter tried to fight off the advancing soldiers, Jesus said: **Matthew 26:53: "Don't you realize that I could ask my Father for more than twelve legions of angels to protect us, and he would send them instantly?"** More than 72,000 angels were poised breathlessly just to monitor the events in the Garden of Gethsemane that evening and make sure that they happened exactly as God planned.

Angels are not actually inhabitants of earth. They don't have a home address here. God's home is their home. It "always" has been! They arrived here on earth, from Heaven, to announce the birth of Jesus.

> **Luke 2:13-15: "Suddenly, the angel was joined by a vast host of others—the armies of heaven—praising God and saying, 'Glory to God in highest heaven, and peace on earth to those with whom God is pleased.' When the angels had <u>returned to heaven,</u> the shepherds said to each other, 'Let's go to Bethlehem!'"**

Angels have existed in Heaven since before Creation, they exist outside of time and have done so since before "earth time" began.

In whatever days, or years, or eons the angels existed before creation, *(It's a bit hard to talk about, because I'm using measures of time to describe the timeless.)* I would imagine God was getting them all ready for the big task ahead. They couldn't really understand the task ahead because none of them had one second of actual experience with humans *(or salvation).* But all of the angels were there, including Lucifer and the one-third who would eventually rebel against God. So, how many angels were actually there? Daniel's later "end-times" look into Heaven matches almost exactly what John sees in Revelation:

> **Daniel 7:9-10 ESV: "As I looked, thrones were placed, and the Ancient of Days took his seat; his clothing was**

white as snow, and the hair of his head like pure wool; his throne was fiery flames; its wheels were burning fire. A stream of fire issued and came out from before him; <u>a thousand thousands served him, and ten thousand times ten thousand stood before him</u>; the court sat in judgment, and the books were opened." That's 101,000,000 *(101 million)* angels before the rebellion. Other passages indicate the total number across the universe might be even higher.

So, what <u>would have caused a massive uprising among God's created angels in the timeless paradise of Heaven</u>, in the very home of God?

- The 101 million+ angels were clearly all on the same page on the first day of Creation when the morning stars sang together, and <u>all</u> the angels shouted for joy.

- Ezekiel 28 indicates that <u>Lucifer was perhaps an Archangel and/or Cherub</u> and was possibly responsible for leading the heavenly hosts in praise.

If that is true – then when God was creating all the matter and energy into a vast new universe and forming the earth with all kinds of unheard new life forms, Lucifer's voice must have been louder than all the rest – as he whipped 100 million+ angels into a perfect chorus of God-honoring praise!

- But then came day six of creation – and the pre-incarnate Jesus *(that John 1:3-4 says created everything and everybody)* arrives on this newly formed earth and gently fashions out of the dust of the ground two new-never-before-seen beings, and lovingly breathes into their nostrils his own "breath of life."

- Lucifer and company's curiosity turns to concern, and then into panic, as they start to catch on to the fact that God has just formed this new life-form exactly in "his own image and in his likeness." This must have been a cosmic-sized shock to Lucifer and his cohorts.

Here's the prophet Ezekiel's inspired take on what happened:

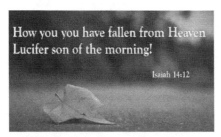

How you you have fallen from Heaven Lucifer son of the morning!

Isaiah 14:12

Ezekiel 28:14-17: "I ordained and anointed you as the mighty angelic guardian. You had access to the holy mountain of God and walked among the stones of fire. You were blameless in all you did from the day you were created until the day evil was found in you... you sinned. So I banished you in disgrace from the mountain of God. I expelled you, O mighty guardian, from your place among the stones of fire. Your heart was filled with pride because of all your beauty. Your wisdom was corrupted by your love of splendor." *(You may want to look at the addendum at the back of the book entitled, "Four Key Passages on satan in the Bible." – Addendum A)*

- "Heart filled with pride, evil found in you" – This is unthinkable in Heaven – in the Sanctuary of God, the Home of God.

- "Corruption" found among the angelic beings that God himself created to minister as his extended arms of grace.

- Those angels, at the highest level, rejected God's plan not just because of their pride, but because they thought they themselves were God's favorites!

- And now God creates these *new "dirt-people"* and lifts them to a level in his love and affection that exalts them above even his most trusted Archangel.

It's hard to think about the Heaven we are all headed toward that the Throne Room of God is in with all the pictures of intense worship we earlier read about – and then imagine a "revolution" in Heaven between good and the newly minted evil. God wasn't surprised of course. It was part of his larger plan to use the rest of the angels to forge his Church – which would transform their world and then reign with him for all of eternity. *(But I'm getting ahead of myself…)*

- As Jesus is beginning to forge his Church on Earth and is just starting to give his power to the new growing Believers, he reminds them – that there had been a war in Heaven! *(Revelation 12)*

- We seldom think about God getting to the seventh day of creation where he "rests" – and then immediately launching into a full scale "war" right up in his Sanctuary with his top "Archangel" and millions of others following him – right at the end of the seven days of Creation – perhaps on day 8!

Try to get your mind around that momentous day for just a moment. The angels have been created, then prepped to serve God in an upcoming role that he has impressed on them has eternal consequences.

" Are not all angels ministering spirits sent to serve those who will inherit salvation? "

Hebrews 1:14NIV

For the majority of the angels, when they see their Creator on the newly formed Earth lovingly fashioning humanity and "breathing into their nostrils the breath of life" – they would have <u>instinctively known that their whole reason for existence had just been created. God had fashioned his final masterpiece!</u> In fact he had created the planet earth, and the entire universe above, just to house these "in-his-image" humans!

The majority of the angels are not only rejoicing about the wonders of Creation – but they are rejoicing that their Heavenly Father has created another set of elevated beings. Imagine the horror in two thirds of angels as satan starts a "war in heaven," predictably loses, is cast down to earth the very planet God just placed the new humans on! And then in short order he tempts the humans, and they fall flat on their newly formed faces!

I imagine utter confusion and angst in the remaining angels in Heaven. They were primed to be "ministering spirits to serve those who will inherit salvation." *(Hebrews 1:14)* They didn't even yet know what that meant – but they were primed to do their part. Instead Adam and Eve are driven from the Garden, one of the good angels is charged with keeping them out, and sin begins to rage across this planet.

They didn't yet understand what "serving those who would inherit salvation" might mean because they didn't yet understand the concept of a "Savior." <u>They couldn't possibly imagine that God himself would visit earth again – this time not to create humanity, but to save humanity</u>!

They didn't yet know that many/most of them would become part of "Heaven's Armies" and they would follow the pre-incarnate Jesus into spiritual battle as their "Lord of Hosts" – the Lord of Heavens' Armies. They would come to know it well!

- They didn't know that many of them would get to be part of a massive choir that would announce the incarnate arrival of God in human form to solve humanity's sin problem. *They did!*

- They didn't know they would one day get to see the look on satan and his minion's faces when he and they suddenly realized – that the God they used to serve in Heaven was here on earth, in human form, to defeat their power over mankind – and was promising not only to defeat them all, but to assign every one of them to an eternal lake of fire. *They found out!*

- They didn't realize that one of them would one day get the mission to bind Lucifer himself with a massive chain and put him forever into the Abyss. *He would!*

Please keep reading, as we discover more things *(from Scripture)* about angels – some of which are brand new to me. We are going to get to know these angels well.

They know you better now, than you know them, because they are serving you unnoticed without any thought or thanks!

But one of these days you will be in the Throne Room of Heaven with them, and they can share with you how they saved you and your family from driving into the path of the semi – and you can thank them in person!

HEAVEN: Part II

Sam, It sounds like you are starting to drift off into talking about angels – and even Lucifer and his demons. I'm reading this book to understand Heaven. <u>I want you to take me inside of Heaven</u> and explain where I am going after my last breath!

<u>I am, I will, I promise</u>! But a vital part to understanding your eternal future, is understanding the "history of Heaven," and how that led to what is now happening in "Heaven-present," and how that will eventually lead into "Heaven-future."

Lucifer was once *(perhaps)* the worship leader in all of Heaven. He is now your greatest opponent on this earth. Why? How? We'll move closer to seeing inside of Heaven in Part V and dramatically inside in Part VI and VII, but <u>please don't skip part II</u>!

I will say *(scriptural)* things in the following pages that I have never thought of before *(and quite honestly never read anywhere else before)*. Our understanding of why there was a "war in Heaven," and what God's initial and ultimate defeat of satan means to your future – is critical knowledge for us, as Believers, to understand.

Please turn your attention to the next page and dive in. I promise I will get you "gazing inside the Pearly Gates" soon!

CHAPTER 4

Chapter 5

Understanding the History of Heaven!

In the last chapter, we tipped our toes into the topic of angels who apparently, like God, call Heaven their home. I'd like us now to take off our shoes and jump into an even deeper end of that subtopic again (*figuratively speaking* ☺ - *you can leave your shoes on*).

1) When did angels arrive in Heaven?

2) What have they been doing there?

3) Why do they seem *(now)* to leave Heaven and regularly visit earth?

4) When did that practice start, and why?

I've been scouring through the pages of Scripture for answers, and I'd like to try to form a running narrative in our minds that, of course, will lead us right back to the centerpiece of history – that is the death and resurrection of Jesus, the only solution to our sin problem here on this earth! But I'd like us to try to look at the event through the eyes of the angels!

We saw something in the last chapter that may have startled a few. Let me take some time to build up to that.

Question: How long has God himself existed?

Psalm 106:48: "Praise the Lord, the God of Israel, who lives from everlasting to everlasting! Let all the people say, 'Amen!' אָמֵן Praise the Lord!" *(Halelu-jah)*

I stated in the last chapter that I had pulled out every passage in the Bible on *eternity, eternal, everlasting.* I was startled to find over 500 verses! I told you I've been teaching for over 40 years that the Old Testament Saints knew little about Heaven. I've also been teaching for over 40 years that the Old Testament Saints knew little about eternity. I was wrong twice – because over three hundred of those passages on eternity – are in the Old Testament!

So, in line with our topic, the Old Covenant Saints had enough Biblical facts to put "Heaven and eternity" together and figure out some very important truths. And so, of course, do we today!

עַד - AD – ADAH – continual existence, eternal, forever, forevermore, perpetual.

Psalm 10:16: "The Lord is king forever and ever! *(Ad-Adah)* The godless nations will vanish from the land."
"Forever" in the Bible is not just forever going forward – it is forever going backward too!

When Isaiah prophesied the coming of Jesus 700 years before his birth, he wrote the famous words we use every Christmas season. **Isaiah 9:6: "For a child is (*will** *be*) **born to us, a Son is (***will be***) given to us. And he will be called: Wonderful Counselor, MIGHTY GOD, (***the baby child will be God!***) EVERLASTING FATHER, Prince of Peace!"**

The coming baby JESUS <u>is</u> the EVERLASTING FATHER – *in Hebrew the Abba/Father; Abba Ad*/continual existence, eternal, forever, forevermore.

<u>Not only has God existed forever and ever, so has Jesus *(who is God!)* </u> "In the beginning" when God created the Heavens and the Earth – we understand that wasn't the beginning of God! And that wasn't the beginning of their Throne or their rule!

It was the beginning of TIME, and our earth, and our universe, and us Humans. We did, however, find one group of living beings who already existed with God before the "beginning of time" *(There is a bit of review here – review is good. And <u>wait till you see where it takes us</u>!)*

> **Job 38:4-7: "Where were you when I laid the foundations of the earth? Tell me, if you know so much. Who determined its dimensions and stretched out the surveying line? What supports its foundations, and who laid its cornerstone as the morning stars sang together and all the angels** (*ben Elohim*) **shouted for joy?"**

Remember from the last chapter. God had already created living beings capable of shouting for joy as the universe sprang into existence. Those *(ben Elohim- sons of God, angels)* had to have been there before the earth was formed, and the stars were flung into space. Here is where the narrative taking us up to Jesus' birth, crucifixion, and resurrection, needs to begin.

Where did the pre-creation angels come from? God made them! In fact, the same Mighty God, Everlasting Father →Jesus, who would arrive here on earth as a baby in a manger – created them!

> **Colossians 1:15-17: "The Son is the visible image of the invisible God, He existed before anything was created and is supreme over all creation, For in him all things were <u>created: things in heaven and on earth, visible and invisible, whether thrones or powers or rulers or authorities; all things have been created through him and for him. He is before</u> all things, and in him all things hold together."**

Jesus the baby *(who would one day lie in a manger then die on a cross)* – created the angels. When? Why? The "when" part is unknown. It had to be before day one of creation if they were singing in joyful excitement as Jesus flung the stars into place.

And everything before day one of creation moves "outside of time" so it's hard to pinpoint. A million years would have seemed like a day. It will be so in our eternal future as well.

But my sometimes logical mind says it must have been a prolonged period of time. These "newly-minted angels" had to come to know and understand their God. They apparently were all created with free-will – so they had the option to embrace their Supreme Creator – or not!

- Several places in Scripture paint a mental snapshot of masses of angels bowing before the Throne of God in worship. When did that start? Probably back before "day one" of creation, perhaps millions of "earth years" before!

- If the Angels were all tuned-up in unison the first day God flung the stars, planets, and comets into place, chances are *(IMO)* they didn't come into existence a few earth hours earlier.

Lucifer, of course, grabs all of our attention. I doubt he was created five days before Adam and Eve, cast down to earth two days later, and was tempting them on day nine earth time.

Lucifer *(helel)* means to "shine" or to "bear light." Isaiah referred to him as "the son of the morning." He perhaps reflected the radiance of God's majesty. He must have been in that role for some time. There is, by the way, a reason Lucifer is sometimes referred to as "the possible worship leader of Heaven."

> **Ezekiel 28:12-17 NKJV: "You** *were* **the seal of perfection, full of wisdom and perfect in beauty. <u>The workmanship of your timbrels and pipes was prepared for you on the day you were created</u>. You** *were* **the anointed cherub who covers;** *(cacak – the same word as the covering on the eventual Ark of the Covenant)* **I established you; you were on the holy mountain of God; You walked back and forth in the midst of fiery stones. You** *were* **perfect in your ways from the day you were created, till iniquity was found in you. So I**

cast you as a profane thing out of the mountain of God; and I destroyed you, O covering cherub, from the midst of the fiery stones. Your heart was lifted up because of your beauty; You corrupted your wisdom for the sake of your splendor." *(If you see this passage as simply talking about an earthly king who walks "on the Holy Mountain of God" as an "anointed cherub" I invite you to study Scripture Addendum A.* This is not an earthly king – this is Lucifer*!)*

Again, Lucifer *(IMO)* didn't start filling the above role two days after Jesus created him! *(Leading the whole of Heaven in the worship of God – reflecting the very radiance of God's majesty.)* He had probably been at that for a long period of time, long before the universe was created. But then came his arrogant ruin!

Revelation 12:7-9: "Then there was war in heaven**. Michael and his angels fought against the dragon and his angels. And the dragon lost the battle, and he and his angels were forced out of heaven. This great dragon—the ancient serpent called the devil, or satan, the one deceiving the whole world—was thrown down to the earth with all his angels."**

Some would suggest that because this is found in the middle of the Revelation prophesy, there is still some future coming "war in Heaven." As someone who has spent a great deal of time studying the "kai eidons" and "meta tauta eidons" *(Greek chronological time stamps)* in Revelation – I am more sure than ever that this chapter is a flashback by John to the beginning of time. *(a parenthetical insert)*

While we don't know how long Lucifer led the multi-millions strong band of still "all righteous angels" in worshipping their Creator God and while we don't know how many uncountable eons, outside of time, passed by – we can pinpoint exactly (*IMO – within a few hours*) when satan and 1/3 of the angels fell!

1) satan clearly couldn't have been thrown down to earth before the earth was created!

2) In fact, Lucifer was possibly still leading the outburst of joyful praise as Jesus directed the stars and planets to explode into existence!

3) There is only one event (*IMO)* that could have made satan and a third of the angels so enraged – even/especially the lofty archangel who most radiated God's glory.

4) There is only one logical event that could have led to the rebellion – and that had to be when the God of Heaven (*probably the pre-incarnate Jesus himself)* personally went down to the newly formed earth, and lovingly fashioned two new humans "in the very image and likeness of their Creator!" (*Something the angels are not!)* And then God carefully breathed his own breath into their nostrils making them (*Nephesh)* "living beings" existing at a higher level than all of the angels themselves.

5) And, then, God began pouring out his love, and his grace onto his new "masterpiece," something the Bible never says about the angels. Satan is furious – he rebels and is cast to earth.

6) Now, satan clearly had to be on this earth when he began to tempt Adam and Eve in the Garden. We don't know how much later that might have been, but the Bible seems to paint it as a relatively short time.

7) The evil one has now been stripped of the "reflected glory" he had been experiencing in Heaven, stripped of the honor and power he had enjoyed – second only perhaps to the power of God himself. He had been stripped of the very presence of God, trapped in the skin of a lowly snake crawling on his belly.

8) Imagine going from basking in the immediate, intense presence of a holy God, filled up to the fullest, to then being completely, hopelessly empty of God's presence!

9) Satan's only retaliation against the God whom he now hated was to go after the "in-his-image, objects-of-God's-love" humans that God had created – and he sure wouldn't have waited a long time to try!

Amazingly, satan tempts – and Adam and Eve bite, in more ways than one! And the evil one gains an earthly foothold that will last for more than 6000 years.

Satan begins to organize his fallen angelic minions. He is clearly convinced he can still beat God! How can he be so stupid? God still controls all of the eternal Heaven outside the universe. God is omnipresent *(everywhere present – all of the time)* across the vastness of space – satan is not! *(Notice, I always use small case letters, satan doesn't deserve upper case!)*

The "evil one" can only be in one place at a time, and he is largely stuck on this one tiny planet. *(Job 1 says satan presented himself before God" – it doesn't say where that took place.)* He has a large but limited number of fallen angels. Why in the world does he still think he can beat back God's eternal plan?

- I'll tell you. *(He still believes it by the way.)* He is trying tooth and claw-nail to foil God's great divine plan right at this very minute!

- How can satan be so dense as to believe that he can beat an infinite God? Because he quickly figured out – on that first week of creation something that is still completely true today.

- All God's plan is centered around one thing! God's timeless Heaven, his creation of this earth, and the vast universe around it – his creation of all the angels to start with. All of those amazing things center around one thing. And that one thing is the masterpiece of his creation – Humanity – Us!

It seems almost inconceivable that not just from the beginning of time, but from the timeless eternity before time, that God's plan of the ages was to create us! We're the ones Jesus plans to forge into "the body of Christ," his Bride, his Church.

We're the ones Jesus plans to return for, then with, when he sets up an eternal reign over the entire universe from right here on this planet! The earth really is the center of the universe as far as God is concerned! This is the only planet where God himself came to die for the sins of his beloved Creation. This is the only planet he is going to return to, with all his angels and all of the Redeemed.

This is the only planet where the New Jerusalem will be with the Throne Room of God in it, *(the place Jesus went to prepare for us).* This is the only planet that the Holy City is going to come down to *(Revelation 21-22),* and where God will finally say:

"Now I will live among my people."

Here's another huge question: When did satan and all the other angels figure out that God's ultimate plan wasn't really about them? God hadn't created all of timeless Heaven, and the whole universe around the earth, just so they could consume all of God's focus as he consumed theirs.

Hebrews 1:14NIV

This famous passage in Hebrews 1:14, defines why angels were even created to start with. They are "ministering spirits sent to serve those who will inherit salvation"! Yes, they also worship God. But that is not why Jesus actually formed them.

So when did the angels figure out that their entire existence wasn't really about them or their closeness to God? At what point did God set them all down *(all 131 million of them ☺)* and say, "Just a heads up. Your future role is to serve the humans I have made in my image."

I'm imagining that conversation happened on the evening of the sixth day of creation!

- The angels had finished bellowing joyful praises the evening before.

- God shocks them all on day six by personally forming these "dirt people" and breathing his breath into them.

- I'm guessing the joyous bellowing turned into hushed wonder and confusion.

- God returned to wherever the angels were doing their praising from and said:

"Those people I just formed are going to become the entire focus of your future!"

For my "image and likeness" children – you all are going to devote the rest of eternity to being their "ministering spirits," starting with you Lucifer! Perhaps some brave angel spoke up and said, "What does it mean that we will serve those who will inherit salvation?" "What's salvation?" "You'll find that out soon enough," Jesus *(might have)* said.

Perhaps it was at that point that Lucifer first stated out loud – "I'm not buying into this at all!" What if that's when some of the rest of the "free-will" angels began to grumble about a future that looked very different than what they had envisioned. Maybe that first Sabbath day, as God was peacefully "resting," some other parts of Heaven were not quite so peaceful!

Revelation 12:7-9: "<u>Then there was war in heaven</u>. Michael and his angels fought against the dragon and his angels. And the dragon lost the battle, and he and his angels were forced out of heaven. This great dragon—the ancient serpent called the devil, or satan, the one deceiving the whole world—was thrown down to the earth with all his angels." *Again some people imagine Revelation 12 to be a future event yet to come. There is (IMO) no theological way that can be true! <u>Evil can never again get into Heaven</u>!* This is a flashback describing Lucifer's battle with God.

But did you notice: John seems to describe all of the angels as getting involved. The relationship between two parts of God's created angelic host is about to take a sudden turn. I assume God, perhaps Jesus himself, finalized the victory and tossed satan and his minions out on their ears.

- But imagine that you were one of the remaining good angels. I used the word in the last chapter, *shock*. Surely they were shocked out of their heavenly minds.

- Some of you practical types might theorize: "There must have been a buildup of negative campaigning where an unhappy satan was working to get more and more angels onto his side." Possibly.

- Luring another angel away from the God they had been 100% focused on for timeless eons would have been no small task.

But it so strikes me that these angels weren't created on a "war footing." Their training *(for how many ever eons)* had been on how to worship God more and more effectively, and how to fly without tangling their wings – and suddenly *there is war in heaven!*

Satan then arrives in exile on earth and promptly deceives God's new "image-people" almost without breaking a sweat.

What wasn't a war footing becomes one! God's angels have already been organized for *(perhaps)* a huge chunk of eternity past. We see that because of how some are eventually described in Scripture.

Without question, the evil one sets out to organize his forces against God. Because of his exile, he can't take God on in Heaven or out in the vastness of the universe – but only on Earth and in the "Heavenlies" above the earth. God's righteous angels, however, can move from Heaven to earth or as Jacob's vision sees it, "He saw angels going up and down a stairway into Heaven." Satan and his demons are locked onto this planet and are focused on one thing only – to bring down God's beloved human creation.

Note the organizational names given by the Apostle Paul to the angelic hosts in Colossians 1 and Ephesians 6 below:

Colossians 1 vs. Ephesians 6:12

1) Thrones
2) Dominions
3) Principalities ----------------------- 1) Principalities
4) Powers ------------------------------ 2) Powers
                                                    3) Rulers of Darkness
                                                    4) Spiritual Hosts

Perhaps the above indicates that the "higher level angels" did not fall. But what it certainly does indicate is that the "heavenlies" had entered into a cosmic spiritual warfare mode.

Any thoughts of angels being cute little chubby adolescent cherubs, flitting around the universe is clearly not accurate. Angels are not strumming harps or shooting love arrows.

And let me emphasize one more thing again, many modern people are told that their departed relative has gone to Heaven and become an angel. There is absolutely zero Biblical basis, for saying that any human being ever becomes an angel!

1) Trust me you don't want to become an angel! They don't get to experience salvation. They don't get to develop a love relationship with Jesus as their Savior. <u>They don't have a Savior</u>! The good ones aren't ever going to sin, and the bad ones can never repent!

2) They aren't ever going to be part of Jesus' Church. They will return with Jesus along with millions of departed Redeemed Saints – but while the Redeemed take their place "reigning with Jesus," the angels will forever be "ministering spirits sent to serve those who inherit salvation."

3) And as far as right now goes – the angels of God are in full-out "war-mode" to make sure you who "inherit

salvation" have available every drop of grace that God extends in your direction!

4) There are those who say the angel's tasks on earth ended with Jesus' resurrection. There is zero biblical evidence that is the case. It flies in the face of the angels continued actions in Acts and the Epistles. It directly contradicts the whole stated purpose for their existence – to be ministering spirits for Jesus' redeemed people. And it negates the large number of prophetic references about the role angels will play in the End Times and on into eternity.

All that said imagine the good angels trying to regain their footing after the fall of Lucifer. God would have explained, to them, very clearly what their role was going to be.

We've already seen their early actions with Abraham, and Hagar, and Jacob – but did you ever notice this: When God arrives on top Mount Sinai to give Moses the Law – that will begin to unfold to the Jews *(and then the whole world)* what God's salvation was going to be:

> **Deuteronomy 33:1-2: "This is the blessing with which Moses the man of God blessed the people of Israel before his death. He said, 'The LORD came from Sinai and dawned from Seir upon us; he shone forth from Mount Paran; <u>he came with ten thousands of holy ones, from his right hand went a fiery law for them</u>.'"**

> **Psalm 68:17: "The <u>chariots of God are unnumbered thousands, even thousands of angels</u>: the Lord is among them, <u>as in Sinai</u>, in the holy place."**

How many of us knew that when Moses received the Law on Mount Sinai, God came surrounded by an "unnumbered thousands" of angels? I didn't! Three more times in the New Testament that same exact point is made. *Who knew?*

We often don't realize the significance and seriousness of the cosmic battle that is going on in a "fourth dimension" outside our familiar three dimensions, but God's righteous angels were sure catching on.

Watch this: Joshua is scouting out Jericho. He sneaks in toward the city. There appears in front of him a "mighty warrior" like none he's ever seen. "Are you for us or for our enemies," Joshua asks. "I am the commander of the army of the Lord," the mighty warrior responds. Joshua throws himself on his face in humility. "Take off your sandals, you are standing on holy ground." Now take your forces on into Jericho.

Something very vivid has happened to the millions of angels who spent timeless eons worshipping God and preparing for the unknown to come. Some of them are still involved in perpetual worship – some of them have become divine messengers, but many of them, perhaps most of them, have become "warrior angels" *(at least for the moment).* Pre-creation Heaven didn't need "warrior angels," but a fallen, sin-cursed earth sure does! You can literally watch the change take place in the pages of Scripture.

This is startling: Starting in 1 Samuel, exploding through the historical books, and heavy in the writings of David – a new phrase shows up:

1 Samuel 17:45: "David replied to the Philistine, 'You come to me with sword, spear, and javelin, but I come to you in the name of <u>the Lord of Heaven's Armies</u>— the God of the armies of Israel, whom you have defied.'"

2 Samuel 5:10: "And David became more and more powerful, because <u>the Lord God of Heaven's Armies</u> was with him."

2 Samuel 7:26: "And may your name be honored forever so that everyone will say, '<u>The Lord of Heaven's Armies</u> is God over Israel!' And may the house of your servant David continue before you forever."

Yahweh tsaba – army, war, warfare;

צְבָאוֹת יְהֹוָה shows up – 267 times!

1 Kings 22:19: "Then Micaiah continued, 'Listen to what the Lord says! I saw the Lord sitting on his Throne with all the armies of heaven around him, on his right and on his left.'"

There are hundreds more examples we could look at unfolding in the Old Testament. The cosmic battle between good and evil, between God and satan, between angels and satan's minions – is <u>led by the Lord of Heaven's Armies</u>! Who in the world is the Lord of Heaven's Armies? There is only really one logical *(theo-logical)* candidate. That is the pre-incarnate Jesus, long before he arrives on earth as a human embryo – He is leading the heavenly battle against sin and satan!

- Then one day, the Lord of Heaven's Armies, leaves his position of honor and makes his way back to earth.

- The One out of whom came the command, "Let There Be," and all the matter and energy in the universe sprang into existence. The same one who breathed into humanity the "breath of life." *(John 1:1-4)*

- The same "Commander" who took out the entire Egyptian army with a wave of his hand.

- The "Lord of Hosts" who sent a single angel to wipe out 185,000 top Assyrian elite military who were threatening to destroy Jerusalem.

<u>That Commander</u> headed back to earth, and this time it was not to create humans. "The Mighty God, the Everlasting Father," left behind *(some of)* his divine nature and climbed into a tiny human embryo, just as Isaiah had prophesied. When he was born in Bethlehem, a huge number of his own Army of Angels were dispatched to announce his arrival!

- The "angels of the Lord's Army" then watched the "Commander of the Lord's Army" take massive grief at the hand of satan's minions and their human followers.

- They watched them bring him to trial. They watched him be beaten mercilessly.

- He could have "called twelve legions of angels." They were waiting, they were ready! Any single one of them could have wiped out all of the Roman army. They were poised to rescue him.

- They must have turned to the Father – "Do we save him Almighty, Abba Father. Do we rescue him from the clutches of satan?" "<u>No! No we don't, let him die</u>!"

But Abba Father, our task is to be "ministering spirits to those who will inherit salvation." If anybody needs ministering to right now, it is the Creator of the World, the Commander of the Lord's Armies, who is being slaughtered by the very people he came to save!

"Let him die," his Father said, "it's his death that will save them!"

"How, Abba Father, how?"

"This is what salvation is all about," the Father replies.

"This is what all of your 'ministering' has been leading humanity toward."

"Let him die, Angel Armies" – and they did – and he did!

He died, for the Roman soldiers who killed him, for the Jewish leaders who set up his death, and for every one of us reading this today!

CHAPTER 5

Chapter 6

Soon we will be looking at the parts of this study you might most want to hear.

1) Where are those seven pictures inside the Throne Room of Heaven that you said the Bible describes?

2) Are our departed, believing loved ones there right now?

3) Is there a "rapture" coming *(There is!)* that will take the remaining Redeemed to join the already-departed Redeemed in Heaven? Yes? Then what comes next?

4) What is this time called the "Marriage Supper of the Lamb" that Revelation 19 talks about that seems to take place with Jesus and all of the Believers in Heaven?

5) Explain the event where Jesus returns to this earth, with all his angels and <u>all</u> the Redeemed, to finally wipe out the power of sin and satan once and for all!

6) What is this New Jerusalem coming down out of Heaven to Earth with the Throne Room of God in it? *(Described in the last two chapters of the Bible.)*

7) What does it mean that we will "reign with Jesus" forever right here on this Earth and presumably, across the vastness of the whole universe?

Clearly there is a lot to unfold. You are now through the first 20% of all we need to unpack. What we have gotten deeply into now are the parts of this topic that we often skim over – and they really are critical to the understanding of our faith!

Much of this is taught as Bible stories to children. *(Adam and Eve in the Garden and the fall of humans into sin.)* And we just assume that it's all true without asking why – or how.

These are the very underpinnings on which the entire Bible rests. If we don't understand these often-ignored truths, it will leave cracks all the way down the line in our thinking.

Let me bring this image back so we can advance to a really momentous point.

עַד - AD – ADAH – continual existence, eternal, forever, forevermore, perpetual.

1 Timothy 1:17 KJV: "Now to the King eternal, immortal, invisible, the only God, be honor and glory for ever and ever. Amen."

We used this in chapter five to establish that God is eternal. God never had a beginning, and God will never have an end! That fact alone is mind blowing! But if we are not watching closely, we will have missed something else here. God is not the only thing in those verses that is eternal:

- God's throne is eternal too!
- God's kingship is eternal!

We all assume that will be true going forward, but we often have a more serious problem with those truths looking back. When did God's kingship start? It never did! His throne is forever!

- What does being a King imply?
- What must a king have to be a king? *A kingdom!*
- What is absolutely necessary for a king to have a kingdom? There has to be s*omebody to reign over!*

"The Lord is King forever and ever!" ← *backward and forward* → *(Psalm 10:16)* If God's Throne existed a billion years ago, long before there was an Earth with humans on it, clearly God's <u>whole eternal focus was on what he was getting ready to do</u>!

Did we ever pause and consider that even God's personal characteristics *(attributes)* of love, and mercy, and faithfulness, goodness, and justice – *assume that there had to eventually be somebody for him to love, and be merciful and be faithful to!*

The Everlasting God was getting ready to create somebody, not something – SOMEBODY!

Living Beings that he could/would rule over – but it was going to be more intense than that. He could "rule over" the angels. He was getting ready to create beings that he could also love, and be faithful to, and be good and gracious toward. God was already in that mode a billion years ago! *(But then, after all, a billion years is like a day to God. He exists outside of time!)* So God does, as he had carefully planned for infinite eons, create two distinct groups of "living beings."

1) Group #1: Angelic beings – We discovered that God made angels before humans, perhaps a long time before humans, because on day one of creation, Job 38 says they were shouting in unified amazement at what they saw taking place as God exploded the stars and planets into existence.

Ezekiel said top-tier Lucifer was **"the radiance of God's presence."** That's pretty heady stuff! But here is a point that is brand new to me – and it begins to explain so much:

God created angels with a lot of power and knowledge, but they were only extensions of God's power and knowledge. The Bible never says God loves them or that they ever revel in his grace. Angels were not created to experience God's forgiveness and soul cleansing. They don't have a soul. Even the good angels who have ministered in your life this week can't quite grasp what we are going to be talking about before this chapter is over.

> **1 Peter 1:12 TLB: "Now at last this Good News has been plainly announced to all of us. It was preached to us in the power of the same heaven-sent Holy Spirit who spoke to them; and it is all so wonderful that even the angels in Heaven would give a great deal to know more about it."** (TLB)

In addition to not understanding or experiencing salvation – there is one more thing the angels were never ever supposed to do.

- The angels were never created to "<u>rule</u>" over anything. They were created to enhance, carry-out, serve in, and minister in the eternal rule of God.

- God's eternal Throne in Heaven is where all of their marching orders come from. Always have – always will!

Here is where we should start to get an "A-HA moment" on what happened. God made Lucifer, with great power and beauty, reflecting God's glory. But God specifically made him to serve and only to serve! *(In fact to serve us!)* If we line up the famous passage in Hebrews 1:14 with the famous passage in Isaiah 14:12-14 on what misfired inside Lucifer, we immediately begin to understand what happened.

 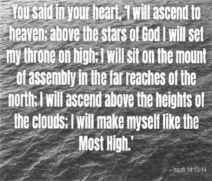

Ezekiel wrote about Lucifer's beauty tripping him up, but remember Lucifer was just reflecting the radiance of God's glory.

What catapulted Lucifer to the next level *(without any doubt in my mind)* <u>was his desire to rule over a kingdom</u> – in fact, God's kingdom. That was the bonfire that 1/3 of the angels piled on to as well. *(IMO)* But let me show you something that I didn't quite understand.

We asked earlier, what could have been the trigger that actually led to "a war in Heaven"? I have suggested that it was on day six of creation when the God Lucifer had been serving so faithfully, the God whose radiance he was reflecting – the one who Isaiah would eventually call Mighty God, Everlasting Father, the Son, the second person of the Trinity, the Creator of the Earth *(John 1:1-4)* that God personally came down to the newly formed Earth and personally fashioned a brand new set of beings "in-his-own-image."

2) Group #2: Human beings – The massive angel choir and Lucifer himself pause their singing, watching intently as the Creator bows down on the newly formed earth, scoops up some of the dirt, and fashions the new "Adam." Adam becomes the common Hebrew word for "man." It probably comes from adamah – earth, soil, dirt, red. *("The dirt people")* Why in the world did God do that? God didn't make anything else out of the dirt! He didn't fashion angels from dirt. There wasn't even dirt yet to fashion them from. He didn't fashion animals from dirt. Why didn't he use "star dust" like the atheist Carl Sagan used to say?

- For some reason, God considered it very important that he himself visit the new planet *(as opposed to simply issuing a command from Heaven).*

- So he gets down here, *(not sure in what kind of body)* perhaps kneels down as millions of angels watch in fascination. He reaches his hand *(if he had one)* into the new soil and molds the dirt into the first human body.

It's almost like he was saying to the watching angels – I can't take this any lower than I'm demonstrating to you right now. I'm not making this being the way I made you. I spoke you into existence and you came instantly from out of my being just like the whole universe did. But this being I'm forming from the lowest elements possible.

And then he apparently "breathed," the Bible says, into the **new human's nostrils – the breath of life**. *(neshamah)* No angel was functioning with the Breath of Life in them. Lucifer was reflecting God's glory, but he was doing it without any infilling "breath of life" from his Creator. But then God did something else that was huge – literally it defines all of the rest of human history.

When God created humans in his image, **Genesis 1:26 KJV says: "He gave them 'dominion' over the earth." Psalm 8:6 NIV says "God put everything under Adam and Eve's feet."** And once the "war in heaven" ended badly for Lucifer, and he/they got tossed to Earth now that "dominion" apparently included satan and his rebellious fallen angels.

If we are looking for a trigger of what caused satan and 1/3 of the angels to declare war on God, we probably just found it! Lucifer must have had building for some time a desire to graduate from simply reflecting God's glory to *being like God.* There had to have been a growing dissatisfaction with him spending all of the rest of eternity just serving God. At some point God must have said something like: "Oh by the way – you are now also going to be serving these newly created beings that I have fashioned in my image!"

"And, by the way, while I have ordained that you will never actually 'rule' over anything ever, not in Heaven, not throughout the universe, and definitely not on earth – I am putting these newly created beings in a place of exalted honor as the 'governors' over the new planet! You will serve them just as you now serve me!" I'm imagining – it's right about there that the pot boiled over in Heaven!

- Satan and 1/3 of the angels fall and get confined to earth and as Psalm 8 said – they find themselves "under the feet of Adam and Eve." *(Under their rule!)*

- Remember, satan's huge desire was undoubtedly to rule, to have a kingdom, to have subjects. *(Please see Appendix A to study "Four key passages on satan in the Bible.")*

- He's here on a new planet where God's "in-his-image" creation has been appointed the new "rulers," and he has gone from second place under God – to being ruled by God's "adamah's" *(people of the red dirt).* Imagine the humiliation!

Somewhere along the line there had to be a strategy meeting where the other fallen angels said, "Thank you very much Mr. Lucifer for your fine leadership that got us in this mess! What exactly do you intend to do now?" And the plan satan came up with literally defines the rest of human history!

We read the story of Adam and Eve and their fall in the Garden like it is a cute little Bible story about two people, a snake, and an apple – it's not! When satan goes after Adam and Eve, he's not just trying to stick a hate-filled finger in the eye of God. <u>He's going after the dominion/rulership of the world</u> that God gave them!

- What did Isaiah 14 say satan most wanted, but couldn't have, in his exalted position in Heaven? <u>Rulership</u>! So now, the completely evil heart of satan is fixed on that singular goal!

- Now that satan has lost everything – revenge is all he thinks about day and night. Corrupting God's beloved children becomes the laser focus of his mind, and we need to always remember – it's not just about revenge against God – <u>rulership is satan's ultimate goal</u>!

If Adam and Eve will rebel and transfer their allegiance to satan, the "dominion" of the earth slips out of their hands into his. That's what the "two people, a snake, and an apple" is really all about!

In order to establish a "kingdom," satan had to have subjects over which to "rule." *He could not create beings himself!* The only way to become a "king over a kingdom" was to persuade those subjects God had made to join him in his rebellion. He did that. First with a third of the angels but more importantly in his battle against God, he convinced God's beloved "masterpiece" humans to join him too. Amazingly, the bait that satan used to tempt Adam and Eve was perhaps the only lure satan could come up with in his now sin-crazed mind – and amazingly, it worked!

1) Humans could be their own "sovereign"!
2) They could rule their own life!

3) They would become like God!

4) They could directly disobey the orders of their King and try to become "kings" themselves.

5) And just like that – the "governors of the earth," became the governed!

6) Satan becomes "the god of this age," "the ruler of this world," "the prince of the power of the air." – Apostle Paul

Do we ever think about the fact that satan actually got what he had been longing for? He now had a kingdom! He had taken control of the earth, and also now controls the "masterpieces of God's creation." The only ones in all of infinite eternity that God ever gave "rulership" to – had now transferred that rulership to satan!

- The only ones who had the very breath of God breathed into them had become sin-filled subjects to satan's rule in his new kingdom.

- The only living beings in the universe that God loved with an infinite love had spurned him and thrown that love back in God's face.

- Satan seems to have won! Satan seems to have beaten God! Humans had, by their own choice, "died" spiritually! (*Don't underplay how critical this is!*)

Genesis 2:17 NIV: "You must not eat from the tree of the knowledge of good and evil, for when you eat from it you will certainly die." (*They did! Spiritually, and then physically.*) **Romans 6:23: "For the wages of sin is death!"** *It was and it still is!*

Humanity had just transferred their membership in the kingdom of God – to membership in the kingdom of satan!

Sam, that's just a bunch of theological babbling. No it's not!

That's exactly how the Bible paints the totally depraved condition that sinful humans found/find themselves in! Instead of becoming our own sovereign – humanity was brought under the dominion of a new and evil king! Mankind was/is completely incapable of "rescuing" himself/herself. Satan's "kingdom" seemed complete. A third of God's angels, and all of the broken-image humans are now filling the entire earth as the evil one's now "cursed" kingdom! Nothing short of supernatural divine intervention could save humanity! *(And that is just exactly what happened 4000 years later!)*

> **Colossians 1:12-14: "He has enabled you to share in the inheritance that belongs to his people, who live in the light. For he has rescued us from the kingdom of darkness and transferred us into the Kingdom of his dear Son, who purchased our freedom and forgave our sins."**

That's the whole unfolding of the Bible from Genesis 3 until the crucifixion and resurrection of Jesus! What we often see as disconnected Bible stories are actually the unfolding of the "conflict of the ages." God's plan is to rescue fallen humanity from satan's kingdom of darkness and transfer us securely into his eternal kingdom. Satan's plan is quite the opposite!

You say, Sam, the whole concept is absurd. Satan was just a created being. He wasn't and isn't infinite in power. <u>God is</u>! God was/is still God of all of Heaven. God's Throne is quite secure. Satan is powerless over it! God's rule extended to all the vast universe. Satan was stuck on this one planet and his power, while great over fallen humanity, was limited.

- It seemed ridiculous for satan to imagine that he could ultimately win the "conflict of the ages" over the one true sovereign God of the Universe!

- Yes, but he did think that! He still does! And we can figure out exactly what satan's war plan was.

- In satan's mind he didn't have to take over Heaven. He couldn't! He had tried that back when he had a lot more power and failed miserably.

- His war plan didn't include taking over Heaven. That was off his strategy list.

- He didn't even have to exert any control over the vast universe. That didn't matter anymore.

All he had to do to beat God was completely control the minds and hearts of God's "Beloved, Breath of Life, Dirt People," and <u>in satan's mind</u> <u>God's eternal plan was over</u>! And as distorted as satan's sin-choked mind often tends to be – that logic wasn't too far off!

1) What good is God's "heavenly kingdom" if there are no beloved "image" people for God to rule over?

2) What good are millions of righteous angels flying from Heaven to Earth if they were created to be "ministering spirits" – and there is nobody to minister to?

3) What good is a planet that God intended for his "in-his-image" humans to rule over if those humans are now under the chokehold rule of satan?

4) This was exactly satan's logic as the Bible unfolds. Satan's intention was to crush God's plan – by crushing God's people!

God had warned satan immediately after the fall: **Genesis 3:15 NIV: "And I will put enmity between you and the woman, and between your offspring and hers; he will crush your head, and you will strike his heel."** We may think that is just a stray verse, but it is the lynchpin on which the rest of the Bible rests. We now call it the *"proto-evangelium,"* the first presentation of the Gospel – but satan surely didn't understand that.

He just knew that the Almighty God of the Universe had warned him that One was coming who would deliver to his head a devastating blow – and Lucifer/satan is fanatically determined to beat God before God beats him!

He and all his minions are determined to stop this "Redeemer of humanity" from showing up. When "God-rejecting Cain" decides to kill his "God-following" younger brother Abel, that wasn't a tiff between two siblings. Who did satan believe Abel was? He thought he was the Redeemer! Bible stories take on a whole new significance when we see them through the lens of the "Conflict of the Ages."

Adam's third son Seth is born whose name literally means: "the substitute." It's as if God is saying – You take one out, I will provide another! You are not going to win! You are going to get your head crushed! If we can see the first 11 chapters of the Bible as something other than just a few cute Bible stories, we will realize that the world for the first 2000 years after the fall of Adam was a cosmic divine war zone.

Genesis describes the earth as filled with violence and corruption. Satan is putting every drop of his energy into stopping the plan of God. We might even let ourselves stray into the "usually-skipped-over" four verses at the beginning of Genesis chapter 6.

> **Genesis 6:1-4: "Then the people began to multiply on the earth, and daughters were born to them. The sons of God saw the beautiful women and took any they wanted as their wives. Then the LORD said, 'My Spirit will not put up with humans for such a long time, for they are only mortal flesh. In the future, their normal lifespan will be no more than 120 years.' In those days, and for some time after, giant Nephilites lived on the earth, for whenever the sons of God had intercourse with women, they gave birth to children who became the heroes and famous warriors of ancient times."**

We tend to think that one of the common views in theology – that evil angels actually somehow mated with human women is weird and extreme. Oddly, both Peter and Jesus' kid brother Jude seemed to write something about that into their inspired New Testament books. *(2 Peter 2:4; Jude 1:6)* What we do know is that whatever was happening on this sin-drenched planet, it was awful.

> **Genesis 6:5-6: "The LORD observed the extent of human wickedness on the earth, and he saw that everything they thought or imagined was consistently and totally evil. So the LORD was sorry he had ever made them and put them on the earth. It broke his heart."**

And the very next verse begins the story of Noah and the flood where God takes out every human on the planet except for eight "righteous" people! But why didn't God save the dear sweet grandma next door to Noah's house? There apparently wasn't a dear sweet grandma living next door to Noah's house. That's how seriously satan pursued making *"every intent of every heart evil all the time"*!

Just two generations after the flood evil again begins to rear its head. Satan has a lot of demons unemployed and only a handful of people to tempt. It's only a hundred years later that humanity is already straying far, far from God. All of the world's population is bunched on the same few square miles of real estate. They all speak one language and are feeding evil into each other – again! They are building a tower into heaven on the Shinar plain. RULERSHIP – again! Sound familiar? It's satan's ancient playbook!

But one day Shinar Fred said to his friend Shinar George. "Good morning, How are you doing?" And suddenly nobody had any idea what the others were saying. Those who found they spoke the same new language migrated to the same new part of the Middle East and throughout the earth.

It's not just a cute Bible story. It was part of the "Conflict of the Ages." Satan says, "I got God this time," and God would say "check" again! One day, by the way, God will say "Check-mate," and the "Conflict of the Ages" will be over once and for all. *It's all coming in the chapters ahead!*

It's just 100 years after the Tower of Babel that God shows up just a few miles south of the plain of Babylon and calls Abraham and tells him, "I promise I'm going to bless the whole world through you."

- As you study your way through the Old Testament, you can literally see satan making his moves on humanity.

- The world turns evil *(again)* and sexually perverted "as it was in the days of Noah." God worship is replaced with idol worship.

- Idol worship turns evil and bizarre where humans are being sacrificed, and people are even sacrificing their own children.

- Abraham's descendants get sucked in! God reaches in and extracts them! That's the story behind the story in the Old Testament.

- Satan tries to take out vast chunks of the Jews to stop the still-coming Redeemer. Pharaoh tried to take them out. God took Pharaoh out instead. Haman tried to take them out in Esther's time. God took out Haman instead. God sends prophet after prophet saying, "The Redeemer is still coming!

Can you imagine the evil one's consternation when the Army Angels of Heaven show up in the sky announcing the arrival of a Savior?

Satan kicks his efforts up several more gears. Imagine the huge knot in satan's evil stomach when he begins to realize that the Redeemer who arrives on earth is actually the Creator God, the same one he used to lead worship toward, the same one whose radiance he once reflected. The Redeemer is actually the Lord of Heaven's Armies! God is here on Earth, but satan imagines he is here in a weakened human form!

Satan has a handful of chances to stop whatever God had planned – and clearly God had something planned! Satan tries to kill him with Herod's goons. He tries to have him thrown off a cliff in Nazareth. Every single time Jesus eludes him. He meets him one-on-one and offers him of all things, *(get this)* **rulership of the earth**!

He finally convinces the evil religious leaders and a satan-filled disciple to arrange Jesus' death. He holds his breath hoping he can pull it off without the Redeemer escaping. The Redeemer doesn't even try!

CHAPTER 6

And as his last breath is escaping from his body, and satan and his minions are starting their celebration – Jesus *(the head-crusher)* squeaks out three more words:

It is finished!

"What is finished," satan wonders?

"What is finished," satan screams!

What did the Lord of Heaven's Armies just finish?

I beat him! I beat the Creator once and for all.

What does he think he <u>finished</u>?

Chapter 7

"He will strike your head!"

God said to satan in Genesis 3:15: "One of Eve's offspring will one day 'strike/crush your head'!"

- The evil one had quickly convinced Cain to murder his righteous brother Abel – because satan thought Abel was God's promised "head-crusher." Thus, the Conflict of the Ages began!

- God finally chose Abraham in Genesis 12. Remember this was all happening in front of the wide-eyed angels of Heaven as they tried to grasp the unfolding plan of God. But it was also happening in front of the now evil hearts of satan and his minions as they tried to figure out a way to stop God.

When God shows up in Ur of the Chaldees and promises Abraham that out of him will come a great nation of people, and through his offspring *(which are also Eve's offspring)* "all the nations in the world will be blessed," satan begins to realize that his task just got a lot bigger – because now he

has to figure out which person out of a "great nation" God would one day send to "crush his head."

We could spend the next two chapters, going through one Bible story after another in the Old Testament, discovering that they are all part of this "conflict of the ages" where God is systematically unfolding his plan to redeem humanity. And satan and his minions are scrambling wildly to try to stop the divine plan of Almighty God! Let me bring up one familiar story here and then I want to move on to something I never noticed before.

- Imagine God unfolding the mighty history of Joseph made Prime Minister of Egypt, and how he saved all of Israel from the starving fate that the evil one had planned.

- Then satan seemingly flips the tables by raising up a godless, satan-controlled Pharaoh who enslaves God's children.

- God counters by sending the unlikely stuttering Moses as a deliverer. Satan counters by hardening Pharaoh's heart.

- God responds with 10 plagues and somewhere along about there, not only does Pharaoh start saying something like, "Uhhh Ohhh" – when God sends just one of his mighty warrior angels to take out every firstborn Egyptian – satan must be saying something profound like, _oops!_

- But soon all of Israel is racing across the sand, with the vast Egyptian army behind them, and they find themselves trapped against the Red Sea.

Satan is undoubtedly thinking, "All I have to do is wipe them out right here, and I will have stopped any possibility of God sending his 'redeeming deliverer' through any of them."

And then satan watches in horror as the Red Sea rolls back, all the Israelites make it through on dry ground, and all the Egyptian army is drowned, and satan is left saying something like drat, drat, drat. *(censored)* But all the good angels are screaming and shouting with joy!

Can you see the Great Conflict unfolding in Scripture?

Let me show you something else here that satan must have had his eye constantly fixed on which had to be extremely unsettling to him. This is actually a huge deal throughout the Old Testament in this Conflict of the Ages.

Watch this:

1) Hagar, Abraham's cast off "maiden" gets a visit from an angel.

> **Genesis 16:7, 11, 13: "The angel of the LORD found Hagar beside a spring of water. And the angel also said, "You are now pregnant and will give birth to a son... Thereafter, Hagar used another name to refer to the LORD, who had spoken to her. She said, 'You are the God who sees me.'** *(El-roi)* **She also said, 'Have I truly seen the One who sees me?'"** *What just happened there?* Who was that "angel"? Why did Hagar seem to think she was talking directly to God? Could the

reference to an "angel" actually be a reference to God himself in this case?

2) Now climb up Mt. Moriah with Abraham. He is about to bring his knife down on his son Isaac lying on a altar.

> **Genesis 22:11, 16-17 NIV: "But the angel of the LORD called out to him <u>from heaven</u>, 'Abraham! Abraham!' 'Here I am,' ... 'I swear by myself, declares the LORD, that because you have done this and have not withheld your son, your only son, I will surely bless you and make your descendants as numerous as the stars in the sky and as the sand on the seashore.'"** *(Descendants, remember, that God was going to send his Redeemer, Deliverer, Head-Crusher through.)*

I am completely convinced that there were a whole lot more than one angel in attendance that day, trying to figure out what in the world was happening, and how this all fit into God's plan.

I am also convinced that satan would not have missed this event. He knew what God had promised Abraham. He would have been stalking him! But who else is also there that day speaking directly to Abraham enforcing his promise of many descendants? Reread the text above. Clearly God himself was speaking directly to Abraham! *Was the angel actually God?*

3) Another example: Jacob is camping late one night along the Jabbock river. He had already sent his family and belongings across the river:

Genesis 31:11 NIV: "The angel of God said to me in the dream, 'Jacob.' I answered, 'Here I am.'"

Genesis 32:24, 27-30 NIV: "Jacob was left alone and a *man* wrestled with him until daybreak. The man asked him, 'What is your name?' 'Jacob,' he answered. Then the man said, 'Your name will no longer be Jacob, but Israel, *(struggles with God)* because you have struggled with God and with humans and have overcome.' Jacob said, 'Please tell me your name.' But he replied, 'Why do you ask my name?' Then he blessed him there. So Jacob called the place Peniel, *(face of God)* saying, 'It is because I saw God face to face, and yet my life was spared.'"

What is going on here?

Are these people really having conversations with God? Is it possible that not only do we have throughout the Old Testament satan and his minions scrambling around trying to thwart the plan of God, and angels *(the righteous ones)* flying to and fro – ministering the plan of God to God's in-his-image humans – but could it be possible that God himself is here, personally, as part of the Conflict of the Ages?

- We tend to think of God as creating the earth from Heaven then coming here on day six of creation to scoop up some dirt and breathe in the breath of life.

- We tend to think of God walking with Adam and Eve in the Garden. Then after the fall, we wait patiently for 4000 years for God to reappear on this planet as an incarnate baby human. <u>What if that's not the way it all actually happened?</u>

4) Here's one last example and there are more, Moses is herding sheep near Horeb, the mountain of God:

> **Exodus 3:2, 4 NIV: "There <u>an angel of the Lord</u> appeared to him in flames of fire from within the bush... <u>God called to him</u> from within the bush."**

> **Exodus 3:14-16: "God said to Moses, 'I AM WHO I AM. This is what you are to say to the Israelites: "I AM has sent me to you." God also said to Moses, "Say to the Israelites, The LORD, (YAHWEH) the God of your fathers—the God of Abraham, the God of Isaac and the God of Jacob—has sent me to you. This is my name forever, the name you shall call me from generation to generation. Go, assemble the elders of Israel and say to them, The LORD, the God of your fathers—the God of Abraham, Isaac and Jacob—appeared to me and said: I have watched over you and have seen what has been done to you in Egypt."'"**

- It's a *theophany* we say, the visible appearance of God on the earth. It's a theophany!

- Wait a minute! Isn't this Moses the same guy who in Exodus 33 would say: "God I want to see you!" And didn't God say, "No way, no person can see me and live!"

- The same God that Jacob said, "I saw God face to face and lived," is saying to Moses here:

Exodus 33:18-20: "Moses responded, 'Show me your glorious presence.' The LORD replied, 'I will make all my goodness pass before you, and I will call out my name, Yahweh, before you... <u>But you may not look directly at my face, for no one may see me and live.'"</u>

If the one Daniel calls the "Ancient of Days" that we only get to see through a handful of visions in the Bible – If he did not ever come here to earth because one glimpse of him would overwhelm us humans – <u>then who in the world kept showing up here</u>?

I know where our minds may be going on this. I hope so! It is really important that they do – and I've come to see how critical this is to our present discussion. You are perhaps thinking that it was JESUS coming to earth communicating with the Patriarchs and Matriarchs?

- You may be thinking that long before Jesus came here as a baby Savior, he came to form human beings from dirt and breathe into their nostrils, and now you are thinking that he may have actually come back – over and over to personally shape our spiritual ancestors, in how to overcome satan and live righteous lives. Yes?

- How could you possibly be sure that is true? Where is your proof? Before this study I couldn't answer that question. Now I can! Straight from the pens of Moses and the Apostle Paul.

As the Children of Israel are following God's Pillar of Fire:

Exodus 23:20-21 KJV: "Behold, <u>I send an angel before you</u> to guard you on the way and to bring you to the place that I have prepared. Pay careful attention to him and obey his voice; do not rebel against him, for he will not pardon your transgression, <u>for my name</u> (SHEM- character – my attributes) <u>is in him</u>."

Question: Who was the "angel" guiding the Children of Israel? Thank you Paul for a definitive answer. And this answer tells us so much more about what was really going on in the Old Testament. *Watch this:*

I Corinthians 10:1, 3-4: "I don't want you to forget, dear brothers and sisters, about our ancestors in the wilderness long ago. All of them were guided by a cloud that moved ahead of them, and all of them walked through the sea on dry ground. All of them ate the same spiritual food, and all of them drank the same spiritual water. For <u>they drank from the spiritual rock that traveled with them, and that rock was Christ</u>!"

We preach from that verse that we should all "drink from the living water" that is Jesus, he is the "rock of our salvation."

No, no, no! Look what it says: It says <u>Jesus was traveling with the Israelites in the wilderness</u>!

1 Corinthians. 10:4: "For they drank from the spiritual rock that traveled with them and that rock was Christ."

ἀκολουθούσης πέτρας ἡ πέτρα δὲ ἦν ὁ Χριστός

traveled with the rock and that rock was the Christ

There is no way to say that other than exactly what it says. The pre-incarnate Jesus traveled with the Children of Israel! The pillar of cloud and fire displayed his presence, yes – but when that water split across the Red Sea it was undoubtedly Jesus, the Creator, pushing the water out of the way. *Do we see that?*

I'll tell you who else saw that – *satan and his minions!* What in the world is the second person of the Trinity, Jesus, the Son of God doing rushing all over this planet teaching his children here and delivering his children from satan there – in the Old Testament?

He's probably the One who delivered Israel from annihilation in Esther's time. He is possibly/probably the one who held off God's enemies as Nehemiah rebuilt the fallen walls of Jerusalem. This is undoubtedly where this whole Old Testament concept comes from, in 2 Samuel that we looked at earlier. *(IMO)*

> **2 Samuel 7:27: "O Lord of Heaven's Armies, God of Israel, I have been bold enough to pray this prayer to you because you have revealed all this to your servant."**

Yahweh tsaba – army, war, warfare
267 - צְבָאוֹת יְהוָה times!

God's "righteous angels" have become a "mighty army of angels" warring against the evil one and his minions here on earth as God unfolds the Plan of the Ages! Without any doubt in my mind – **JESUS is the LORD OF HEAVEN'S ARMIES** long before he ever arrived here as a baby in a manger!

As that birth event approaches, there is angst in satan's camp. In fact, virtually nobody on earth then seems to understand this next point. The prophets present the coming Deliverer, Redeemer, Savior – in two opposing ways:

#1) He will be a suffering Savior who will die to pay the human sin penalty!

#2) He will be a glorious King who will establish the Kingdom rule of God over this earth forever and ever.

> Isaiah the prophet in Chapter 53 NIV says that **"it is the Lord's will to crush him** *(v. 10)* **and cause him to suffer, and his LIFE WILL BE MADE AN OFFERING FOR SIN."**

> The same exact Isaiah, in the same exact book in **Isaiah 9:6-7 says that a human baby boy will be born to a virgin girl. He will actually be the Mighty God, the Everlasting Father, the Prince of Peace.** The "baby God" will eventually set up a Throne on this earth that will never ever end!

> - Satan has to be running these opposing facts through his distorted mind. The good angels are looking on with confusion. The humans who receive the messages are practically clueless. I'm not sure if even the prophets understood what they were writing.

- <u>How could God himself come to earth, die, then still reign on that same earth forever</u>?
- The prophets called him the Anointed One, the Messiah. Daniel called him the Messiah Prince and predicted right to the year when he would come. He also prophesied that he would die!

Daniel 9:25-26: "Now listen and understand! Seven sets of seven plus sixty-two sets of seven (483 years) **will pass from the time the command is given to rebuild Jerusalem until a ruler— the Anointed One** (the Messiah Prince)—**comes. After this period, <u>the Anointed One will be killed</u>, appearing to have accomplished nothing."**

Now, what again was the trigger that caused satan to rebel against God? **Rulership!** What did satan wrestle away from Adam when he fell? **Rulership!** What is God promising the coming Messiah is going to do for ever and ever? **<u>Rulership!</u>**

It may seem like I'm just cutting through fine hairs, but I really believe we are taking a look inside of satan's confused mind.

By the time we approach the end of the Old Testament, there is probably no doubt in satan's mind (there shouldn't have been any doubt in anybody's mind) which person of the Godhead was planning to come to this earth. It's the same part of God (IMO) that had been interacting with human beings all through the Old Covenant.

I don't know if satan and his minions had access to Mary's room when the angel Gabriel showed up with a message. If

125

he did, it would have exploded the throbbing vein in his evil neck. *(If he has veins?)*

> **Luke 1:30-33: "'Don't be afraid, Mary,' the angel told her, 'for you have found favor with God! You** *(a virgin)* **will conceive and give birth to a son, and you will name him Jesus. He will be very great and will be called the Son of the Most High. The Lord God will give him the throne of his ancestor David. And he will reign over Israel forever; his Kingdom will never end!'"** I don't know what unbelievers today may or may not think about those verses, but I can tell you what the "ultimate professed unbeliever" thought.

Every word was like a dagger in satan's evil heart.
There could only be one possible interpretation!

I don't know if satan had one of his minions keeping track of every prophecy from every God-following prophet – but if he had compiled a list of them all, he would have run down the list, check, check, check, check – going clear back to Genesis 3:15. This baby fulfilled every single prophecy!

- THIS WAS GOD'S "HEAD-CRUSHER!" The rest of the world was confused about who he was, but the evil minions sure weren't!

> **Luke 4:33-34: "Once when he was in the synagogue, a man possessed by a demon—an evil spirit—cried out, shouting, 'Go away! Why are you interfering with us, Jesus of Nazareth? Have you come to destroy us? <u>I know who you are—the Holy One of God!'"</u>**

How did the demon know who he was? Because at one time that demon had been "a good angel" worshipping Jesus in Heaven! As we have already stated – satan had a strategy all through the Old Testament of stopping the Redeemer from making it to this earth. That strategy failed! And now, without question – the seed of Eve that God planned to crush "the evil one's" head with, had arrived.

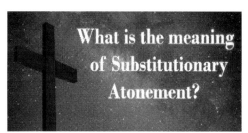

Satan had all the information he needed to know that this Deliverer was prepared to die! And Isaiah 53 alerted the world that Jesus' death would be a "substitutionary atonement." Satan had all the information he needed to put two and two together – but his head-long rush to kill Jesus shows us that he didn't understand the implications of Jesus' death. The evil one is often presented by well-meaning teachers – as if he is almost as "all-knowing" as God – the truth is, he really isn't the sharpest knife in the drawer!

Jesus, the Creator God – the Lord of Heaven's Armies, came here planning to die in the place of every sinner – to break them free from satan's power!

Hebrews 2:14: "Because God's children are human beings—made of flesh and blood—the Son also became flesh and blood. For only as a human being could he die, and <u>only by dying could he break the power of the devil</u>, who had the power of death."

This is the thing the good angels watched in fascination because they just couldn't quite figure it all out. **"Even Angels long to look into these things!"** *(1 Peter 1:12 NIV)* Obviously, if the good angels were struggling with the theology of salvation – the evil angels were all but clueless.

But somewhere in satan's sin-addled brain was enough theology for him to understand that he had to stop the substitutionary atonement! If Jesus died voluntarily, on God's timeline, his death would pay for all humanity's sins! Satan knew he had to stop Jesus! He may not have grasped the full plan of God, but he knew he had to stop it! Satan, *(whether he understood it or not)* was walking a fine line. He would try three strategies:

#1) He sets out to kill the Savior before he can voluntarily give up his life. We talked about Herod trying to kill the babies. Jesus' townspeople try to throw him off a cliff when he claimed to be the Messiah. The religious leaders, the ones who should have been most excited to see him, were constantly pronouncing him "a fraud and a blasphemer" and were sitting in some back room trying to plot how they could kill him.

#2) Satan attempts to convince Jesus to accept the rulership of the world – from him. He promised Jesus "all the Kingdoms of the world" if he would bow down and worship him. Jesus' path to "world rulership" would have included satan ruling over him! It was an absurd offer to make to the Creator of the Universe – but like I said, satan's not the sharpest knife in the drawer! If Jesus had given in –

every single one of us would have still been part of "satan's kingdom."

John 14:30 ESV: *Jesus:* **"I will no longer talk much with you, for the <u>ruler of this world</u> is coming. He has no claim on me!"** *(It sure wasn't for lack of trying!)*

- As satan's minions approach Jesus with the Jewish religious leaders and Roman soldiers as their pawns, they are still convinced that this may be their last chance to kill him before he can voluntarily lay his life down.

- They know he is the Creator God that they themselves worshiped in Heaven, but he is trapped inside a fragile human body! If they can just <u>kill the human body</u>, they will have won their war against God!

#3) Satan's minions pour their efforts into convincing the Jews to reject Jesus as their long-awaited Messiah. If Jesus kept preaching the Jews might believe – that's why he had to die! But, satan overstepped his skis again.

John 12:23-24, 27, 31-33: "Jesus replied, 'Now the time has come for the Son of Man to enter into his glory. I tell you the truth, unless a kernel of wheat is planted in the soil and dies, it remains alone. But its death will produce many new kernels ... Now my soul is deeply troubled. Should I pray, "Father, save me from this hour"? No, this is the very reason I came! <u>The time for judging this world has come, when satan, the ruler of this world, will be cast out</u>. And when I am lifted up

from the earth, I will draw everyone to myself.' He said this to indicate how he was going to die."

Don't you think at some point one of satan's lackeys should have approached him and said, "Do you think we should pull in the dogs? He keeps telling people he is getting ready to die. He just told a group of people that he was a single kernel of wheat getting ready to fall into the ground and that the death of his single kernel would bring massive life to many others.

- "Isn't that what we've been so afraid is going to happen?"

- "He even said that the time for judging the world is here, and he is going to cast out the 'ruler of this world!' Satan, that's you!"

- Irrationality! It's satan's mode of operation! *(He lies all the time – even to himself!)* The "satanic Bible" describes Jesus as "incompetence hanging on a tree, the lasting foulness of Bethlehem, the fugitive and mute god, the vile and abhorred pretender to the majesty of satan."

- It describes satan as "the Lord of light with angels cowering and trembling in fear, prostrating themselves before him, while he sends the gates of Heaven crashing down!" Really? [9]

I have news for these satanists. Satan has no majesty! He was just reflecting God's majesty – but he lost it all! There has never been the briefest moment when the righteous angels have prostrated themselves before satan! They are in a "full-court press" to bring about his final doom. They are the Warriors of the Heavenly Armies! The day is coming when satan will be chained and bound into the abyss. Do you remember how many angels *(Revelation 20:1-3 says)* it takes to finally do that job? <u>ONE</u>!

Satan isn't crashing down the gates of Heaven. He can't get anywhere near Heaven, he's stuck on this earth! And the one they call "incompetence hanging on a tree" – his death and resurrection have utterly transformed the lives of you reading this book, thousands in my own Treasure Coast region, thousands more in whatever region you are living in, millions in your country, and billions on this earth!

As our Savior was dying on the cross, he screamed out the words, "Father, forgive them" – then finally gasped, "It is finished!"

- **He was <u>talking to his Father</u>, that is clear. "I have finished the plan of redemption."**

- **I think he was <u>talking to good angels too</u>. "It's done! The plan of the Ages is accomplished!"**

- **He was <u>talking to the people who were listening</u> that day. Some would record his exact words.**

- **And I'm so sure <u>he was talking to satan</u>. "It's done. You tried every weapon in your arsenal to stop me, and you failed. Your doom is set, your days are limited, your power still exists – but only for one more season."**

It is finished! You are finished satan! And as usual satan didn't believe him. (He still doesn't.) But one day he will!

We can't possibly imagine what happened those next three days. The whole idea that Jesus was personally carrying the sins of every wretched human being when he died, that when he screamed *"It is finished,"* and the last of his lifeblood was draining out of his body – he was finalizing the payment for every sin you would ever commit, and me, and Mother Teresa, and Osama bin Laden!

Derek Prince used to say that when Jesus poured out his blood, "the life of God was released into the universe." I think I agree even though I'm not sure what it all means. What must that have meant for the One who **Hebrews 1:3 says: "sustains everything by the mighty power of his command"?** How vulnerable, how teetering on the edge was this whole universe at that moment – when the One who is the very glue that holds the molecules together poured out his last drop of blood?

I don't know what satan was doing at that moment; probably not sipping a cup of tea. He knew that the "glue" that was holding the universe together *(Hebrews 1:3)* had just died. I imagine satan was holding his breath and watching to see if the cosmos would implode. It didn't – not yet!

I think about how the evil one and his minions probably went into full party mode. I imagine the whole "Jesus descending into hell" thing that the Apostle's Creed talks about, and Jesus taking on satan and the power he held over fallen humanity, and the "ripping off the gates of hell." *(whatever that means)* Jesus did say in Revelation 1:18 – I hold the keys of death and Hades! I wrote in my book <u>What Scares Demons</u> about how terrified the demons were in the presence of Jesus on earth. Imagine how terrified the demons became when they thought they had killed Jesus – and he shows up on their own turf, in hell!

Then comes his rising back through the darkness of death, settling back into the tomb, flipping his lifeless eyes back open, throwing aside a two ton rock, and exploding back onto the earth – alive once again!

- I'm convinced we can't even begin to imagine the shock waves that hammered through the universe. On the surface, the Bible says, there were massive violent earthquakes! Don't forget the disciples were watching laser-focused! The angels were watching stunned, the demons were watching, horrified! The sun went pitch dark.

- I like to think that one of the disciples, maybe John, said something like: "Well whatd' ya know? It seems Jesus setting up his promised eternal kingdom actually meant him staying up there on the cross, dying for our sins, and then rising back to life – just like he said?"

Just then, somebody comes running from the Temple with astounding news:

 Matthew 27:51-52: "At that moment the curtain of the temple was torn in two from top to bottom. The earth shook and the rocks split. The tombs broke open and many holy people who had died were raised to life."

Something huge just happened. You can sense the power of the resurrected Jesus spreading across the planet. You can sense the power of satan over humanity letting loose!

Hebrews 2:14: "Only as a human being could Jesus die, and <u>only by dying could he break the power of the devil</u>, who <u>HAD</u> the power of death." *(<u>HAD</u> the power of death!)*

*Jesus did it! satan blew it! It was finished!
Jesus won – satan lost!*

Chapter 8

The most massive miscalculation of all time!

 In the most massive miscalculation of all time – satan brings Jesus to death on a cross, the very thing Jesus had planned to do from the beginning of time, to pay the sin penalty for all of humanity.

Three days later, Jesus conquers death and rises victorious over death and the grave – victorious over sin and satan and hell! We can't begin to humanly grasp the immensity of what just happened, right there in this raging Conflict of the Ages.

- Satan was "out over his skis," *(again)* and became an unwilling and unwitting pawn in God's great plan to redeem us all from sin!

- When Jesus then rose from the dead, satan and his minions should have known their "goose was cooked."

- But don't underestimate the raging hatred satan had/has for the God he once served and worshipped.

- And don't overlook how utterly narcissistic satan is *(to his core)* believing completely in his own warped abilities. *(He is the father of lies – lying even to himself!)*

- And remember how insanely frantic he is to bring God's Plan of the Ages crashing to a halt! Here's the Biblical reality of what was happening as Jesus died on the cross:

Colossians 2:13-15: "You were dead because of your sins and because your sinful nature was not yet cut away. Then God made you alive with Christ, for he forgave all your sins. He canceled the record of the charges against you and took them away by nailing them to the cross. In this way, <u>he disarmed the spiritual rulers and authorities. He shamed them publicly by his victory over them on the cross</u>."

1) Disarmed the powers – ἀπεκδύομαι – stripped them of their weapons.
2) Shamed them publicly – δειγματίζω – made a visible mockery of them.
3) Triumphing over them – θριαμβεύω – public procession of victory. That sure sounds like Jesus completely defeated satan and his fallen lackeys by his death and resurrection, doesn't it?

Hebrews 2:14-15: "Because God's children are human beings—made of flesh and blood—the Son also became flesh and blood. For only as a human being could he die, and <u>only by dying could he break the power of the devil</u>, who had the power of death. Only in this way could he set free all who have lived their lives as slaves to the fear of dying."

You say, Pastor Sam when I look around at the in-our-face toboggan slide of morality on this planet right now – the open promotion of things the Bible clearly calls evil, and the mocking rejection of the things the Bible calls good,

> 1) I can't see hard evidence that Jesus "made a public spectacle of satan triumphing over him by the cross"!

> 2) How exactly did Jesus' death disarm the evil powers and authorities?

> 3) Did the New Testament Early Church believe satan had been defeated by the cross, stripped of his weapons, publicly paraded as a loser?

We all know many of those early Believers died violent martyr deaths at the hands of very sinful pagans. Did they die saying, "Jesus you won, we won! I'm on my way to Heaven right now." Yes! But remember, the earliest Early Church didn't have the Colossian and Hebrew passages you just read. In fact, they didn't have any parts of the New Testament for 15 more years, and then these books appeared slowly up until Revelation was written 50 years later.

Many of them would be long dead before Jesus would reveal in the final New Testament book his plan to defeat satan once and for all. *(He did, you know!)* By the end of inspired Scripture, satan is prophesied to be completely defeated and destroyed, and the Jesus followers are reigning with him in Heaven for all of eternity. *(We'll get there!)*

- I dug through every passage that details the Conflict of the Ages in the life of the Early Church in the First Century. I'm going to give you the condensed version.

- But Sam, you just said Jesus won the Conflict over satan on the cross – He did! So why did the conflict between satan and God rage on? *(And it still is!)* Let's peel back the layers so we can understand what God is thinking, what satan and his minions are thinking, and what Jesus followers on earth are thinking – as the Conflict of the Ages unfolds and careens toward its explosive prophesied end.

- There is no other pathway to eternal life in Heaven than the one that includes us as Believers living inside the Conflict of the Ages between God and satan.

- And this New Testament pathway to Heaven is not some second or third try attempt on God's part after satan threw a wrench in God's first try!

This "conflict of the ages" was included in God's plan of redemption from the beginning! <u>Why else would God have exiled satan to the very same planet that he had just created humans on</u>? God expected spiritual conflict – and out of that conflict would come our divine, eternal rulership in Heaven!! *Let me show you…*

Let's briefly hit the reverse button for just a minute: Jesus, in his three years of ministry, is constantly being attacked verbally by the human agents of satan. It amazes me how many times we find that they accuse Jesus of being demon-possessed! Even when he was casting out demons, sinful people said he could only do it because he himself was filled with demons!

Many people paint Jesus as soft-spoken, always preaching tolerance. He wasn't! He responded with statements like, "You are calling me demon-possessed because you yourselves belong to your father, the devil!" *(John 8:44)* He is a murderer, he is a liar, he steals what isn't his. So do you!

Your "<u>paternity</u>" defines your <u>eternity</u>! That's still true!

But notice some key phrases that Jesus kept using. It seemed to go right over the disciples head, but probably was like a dagger *(maybe a whole sword)* in satan's eye!

John 12:31: "The time for judging this world has come, when satan, the ruler *(ἄρχων – holds significant sway)* **of this world, will be cast out."** *(ἐκβάλλω – ekballo – thrown out, driven out, thrown overboard, completely removed!)* Jesus is acknowledging that satan holds power, but is prophesying his complete doom. The Early Church didn't need the book of Revelation to know, at least in part, what was going to happen to the devil!

John 14:30: "I don't have much more time to talk to you, because the ruler of this world approaches. He has no power over me." *(He thinks he does – he's going to be proven very, very wrong!)*

What appeared to be the greatest defeat in all of history, as Jesus died on a cross, turned out to be the most massive, monumental victory over satan in all of time – as the evil one's hold over humanity is severed! Jesus promised the new Believers that after his death he is leaving earth – but he will be sending his own Spirit to infill them and guide them!

John 16:8-11: "When he (*the Holy Spirit*) **comes, he will convict the world of its sin, and of God's righteousness, and of the coming judgment. The world's sin is that it refuses to believe in me. Righteousness is available because I go to the Father, and you will see me no more. Judgment will come <u>because the ruler of this world has already been judged</u>."** (Κρίνω – *krino; satan's plan is completely naked before me.*)

Jesus: "Satan is already in a state of defeat, a state of judgment by God – even before I go to the cross! satan is just so miscalculating that he doesn't yet realize that he is already disarmed, shamed, and triumphed over!" When Judas schemes to betray Jesus, John says "satan entered him." Jesus simply says to him at the Last Supper – Get this over with! What you are going to do, do it quickly. You and your new father, the devil, can bring on the battle. I'm ready for it!

But there were more clues the disciples should have had locked in their brains:

Jesus had taught them to pray: **Matthew 6:12-13: "Forgive us our sins, as we forgive those who sin against us. Don't let us yield to temptation, but <u>rescue us from the evil one</u>!"**

In Jesus final prayer to the Father he prays: **John 17:14-15: "I have given them your Word, and the world has hated them because they are not of the world, just as I am not of the world. I do not ask that you take them out of the world, but that you <u>keep them from the evil one</u>."**

Imagine the disciples trying to wrestle with what Jesus was planning. In one setting he is saying, **"the time for judging this world has come, when satan, the ruler of this world, will be cast out."** A handful of days later he is praying: "I'm not asking you Father to **take my followers out of this world, but that you keep them from the evil one"** while they are living in this world!

Jesus was going to 1) disarm the powers of satan – strip them of their weapons, 2) shame them publicly, and 3) triumph over them by his death on the cross and his victorious resurrection. But the truth was/is: the distance between Jesus unwrapping satan's claws from around our throats so that we could be set free and redeemed from our sins – the distance between that and the point where satan will be bound eternally and thrown forever into the lake of fire – is the distance in the Bible from John 12:31 to Revelation 20:10.

In earth years that's already been a period of *(at least)* 1991+ years! Why God – why?

Why did you go away to prepare a place in Heaven for us and then stay away for 1992+ years?

Why did you defeat satan on the cross and then leave him here to continue his "conflict of the ages" with us?

Remember this, we're not suffering through God's plan B or C because his first plan didn't work out. This is plan A! There is something eternal to be gained by us not being "taken out of this world," but by us being "kept from the evil one" while living in this world! Paul in Philippians 3:20 would call it: "Being Citizens of Heaven" right now, while we are living here! God's "Plan of the Ages" is not off track in the slightest!

Clearly there is more to God's plan than what we have seen so far! There is a large chunk of the Bible that comes after the resurrection, and before the return of Jesus to set up His eternal kingdom – but if we don't know this point, it needs to lock in right about here.

- Revelation 11 is a turning point in the last book of the Bible, it's a turning point in all 66 books of the Bible – in fact, it's a turning point in all of redeemed human history.

- Saying that Jesus disarmed satan, shamed him, and triumphed over him on the cross is obviously not the same thing as saying that Jesus "took charge of the earth" reducing satan to utter impotence. That has not happened yet – but it will!

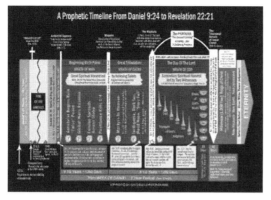

When? When will that happen, Sam? When will Jesus finally take complete charge of this earth? Jesus can't reign forever on this earth, and us reign with him – while satan is in all-out war with him and us. That's true! The answer is detailed right here in Revelation 11: *(You can download this color chart free at samchess.com)*

> **Revelation 11:15-17 NIV: "The seventh angel sounded his trumpet, and there were loud voices in heaven, which said: 'The kingdom of the world has become the kingdom of our Lord and of his Messiah, and He will reign for ever and ever.' And the twenty-four elders,** *(representative of Believers who have gone on before us)* **who were seated on their thrones before God, fell on their faces and worshiped God, saying: 'We give thanks to you, Lord God Almighty, the One who is and who was, because you have taken your great power and have begun to reign.'"** *(The divine sovereign hammer finally falls!)*

The "seventh trumpet" unloads the famous "bowl judgments" which come crashing down onto this earth. Not on Believers, they have been raptured up to Heaven with Jesus! *(We're coming to that!)* The bowl judgments come crashing down on satan and the antichrist and the willfully rebellious. Then *(big white arrow)* Jesus returns with all of us

143

Saints in Revelation 19. He wipes out the amassed demonic armies of the earth, and one angel binds satan into the bottomless abyss!

It is so important to remember: <u>Revelation is not about punishing Believers</u>; it is about punishing sin and satan! Revelation is the story of the eternal salvation of Believers and the eternal destruction of satan, the antichrist, sin itself, and all the effects of the curse of sin on this earth!!

Revelation is the story of eternal triumph for God and for all who chose to follow Him! Imagine its electrifying effect on the late Early Church when they finally read it. They began to understand that satan was not going to win the Battle of the Ages. He loses!

But the earlier Early Church didn't have that perspective at all. As I lined up the passages that they did have, I was fascinated to see what God revealed to them – and what he revealed to them, he was also revealing to us. It was electrifying to them! It should be to us too!

Hit the reverse button back to the book of Acts. The fledgling Church is telling everybody they meet about the crucified Jewish Messiah who was "God in the flesh." Who after being dead for three days, came back to life and then went back to Heaven to prepare a place for all who would repent and believe!

The Church was not confused about whether Jesus' death and resurrection wiped satan and his minions off the planet.

They instantly found themselves persecuted "even unto death" by satan's followers.

- They came up against demon-possessed people and found themselves having to cast out demons, just like Jesus did.

- The murderer, turned Apostle, Paul, tried to visit the newly formed churches, and says he was slowed down because "satan blocked his way." *(1 Thessalonians 2:18)*

> My prayer is not that you take them out of this world but that you protect them from Satan, the evil one.
>
> John 17:15

The seven sons of Sceva try to pretend they are Believers, and all hell breaks loose. *(Or better yet, all Heaven breaks loose! Acts 19: 13-16)*

The Church remembers that they are "living in this sinful world," but they are actually "citizens of Heaven." *(Philippians 3:20)*

The Believers are "in this world," but "they are not of this world" *(as Jesus prayed)*, and they are being protected from the evil one! *(John 17:11, 14-15)*

Try to put yourself in the place of those first Christians. They didn't have a New Testament yet. They didn't have a church on every corner. They passed by lots of pagan temples where other human beings were being sacrificed to idols.

They didn't live in a country where their Declaration of Independence offered everyone "life, liberty, and the pursuit of happiness" – where everyone was "created equal through inalienable rights from God." *(Like the U.S.*

Constitution) They, and their families, were increasingly being imprisoned and even executed by people whose "father was the devil." The very first inspired New Testament letters they get – are 1 and 2 Thessalonians in your Bible:

> **1 Thessalonians 4:16-18: "For the Lord himself will come down from heaven with a commanding shout, with the voice of the archangel, and with the trumpet call of God. First, the believers who have died will rise from their graves. Then, together with them, we who are still alive and remain on the earth will be caught up in the clouds to meet the Lord in the air. Then we will be with the Lord forever. So encourage each other with these words."**

That encouraged them! But they didn't have the slightest idea if that would happen in the next year, or in 100 years, or in 1991+ years. They were still surrounded by the evil one and his minions – who seemed to be raging the "Conflict of the Ages," out of control.

The beginning of the Church on the Day of Pentecost, and the outpouring of the Holy Spirit to infill and indwell believers brought enormous spiritual benefits – but it did one more thing that we almost never notice. It focused satan's attention like a laser on stopping the explosive growth of that specific group of redeemed people. Because satan instinctively knew that this growing Church was the focus of God's redemptive plan from the very beginning of time! Satan's hatred of God turned into a hatred of Jesus' Church! We see them being chased down like rats to be exterminated. But God increasingly unfolded his plan in newly revealed Scripture – and the new Church begins to catch on and understand their role in it all.

1 Corinthians 15:22-25: "Just as everyone dies because we all belong to Adam, everyone who belongs to Christ will be given new life. But there is an order to this resurrection: Christ was raised as the first of the harvest; then all who belong to Christ will be raised when he comes back." *(That part we notice and talk about all the time – this next part we don't…)*

"After that the end will come, *(there is going to be an end)* **when he** *(Jesus***) will turn the Kingdom over to God the Father** *(the one he has built here on earth using his Church!)***, having destroyed every ruler and authority and power."**

(That's not talking about Adolph Hitler and Saddam Hussein, it's talking about satan!) **"For Christ must reign until he humbles all his enemies beneath his feet."**

The Corinthians may not have had the book of Revelation in those early days – but they now knew "an end" was coming!

And somewhere along the way, God's enemy, their enemy, satan and his minions were going to finally get their clocks cleaned!

2 Corinthians 4:3-4: "If the Good News we preach is hidden behind a veil, it is hidden only from people who are perishing. (Not from you the Church – satan doesn't have the right to hide the truth from you. (2

Corinthians 2:11 tells us that —we know his schemes! If he manages to hide the truth from you, it can only be by deception. Don't let him do it! Don't fall into his traps! You have been brought out of his kingdom of darkness into God's kingdom of light! Live it out!)

"Satan, who is the god of this world, has blinded the minds of those who don't believe. They are unable to see the glorious light of the Good News. They don't understand this message about the glory of Christ, who is the exact likeness of God."

But you do! Spread the Word! Push back against his puny Kingdom of darkness! That's your task! You are the only ones who can do it! I've filled you for the task! Go after the ones who are blinded by satan – lead them into the light! You, my Church, are the ones I have ordained from the beginning to do that job. It's part of your "Training for Reigning" in Heaven for all of eternity!

The New Testament letters begin to pile in with increased speed through the late 50's to early 60's A.D. and the language gets stronger and stronger, and more and more exciting! Watch in this letter to the Romans. Let me put some unwritten words in their mouths.

The Roman Church responds: "But Jesus. What you are asking is so hard. We're right here in Rome in the stinking armpit of the evil one. satan is raging against the Church through those who call him their father!" *Watch what God tells them:*

Romans 8:18, 25, 35, 37-39: "What we suffer now is nothing compared to the glory he will reveal to us later... And we believers groan, even though we have the Holy Spirit within us as a foretaste of future glory, for we long for our bodies to be released from sin and suffering... But if we look forward to something we don't yet have, we must wait patiently and confidently. *But, but, but Jesus, It's just so hard! "Listen to me, my dear child:"* **Can anything ever separate you from my love? Does it mean I no longer love you if you have trouble or calamity, or are persecuted, or hungry, or destitute, or in danger, or threatened with death? No, despite all these things, overwhelming victory is yours through Christ Jesus, who loved you!"**

Read this with me like it is really your personal truth! It is!

"And I am convinced that nothing can ever separate me from God's love. Neither death nor life, <u>neither angels nor demons</u>, neither our fears for today nor our worries about tomorrow — <u>not even the powers of hell can separate me from God's love</u>. No power in the sky above or in the earth below — indeed, nothing in all creation will ever be able to separate me from the love of God that is revealed in Christ Jesus my Lord!"

This had to be like a huge shot of adrenaline in the spiritual arms of the Early Church! "Do you hear what I'm saying to you, my dear children, in my growing new Church? Satan can't and won't ultimately win! He can lie himself into believing all he wants to, right up to the 'end of the age,' but, Jesus says, I already defanged him on the cross!

1) I disarmed the powers – ἀπεκδύομαι – *stripped them of their weapons*

2) I shamed them publicly – δειγματίζω – *made a visible mockery of them*

3) I triumphed over them – θριαμβεύω – *a public procession of victory*

4) Now – "neither angels nor demons, not even the powers of hell – can separate you from my love!" (*Romans 8:38*)

Now go into the battle! Use your weapons of the Word of God and prayer! You are the Overcomers – more than conquerors! I have commissioned you to build up my Church right from out of those who are presently in the kingdom of satan! Push back the powers of darkness in your family, your church, your community, your state, your country, and your world! I've called you to it!

I'm fascinated by how the book of Romans ends. This would be a great "declaration" for us all.

Romans 16:20: "The God of peace <u>will soon crush satan under your feet</u>. May the grace of our Lord Jesus be with you." *Here's how that can happen:*

Ephesians 6:10-14: "A final word: Be strong in the Lord and in his mighty power. Put on all of God's armor so that <u>you will be able to stand firm against all strategies of the devil</u>. For we are not fighting against flesh-and-blood enemies, but against evil rulers and authorities of the unseen world, against mighty

powers in this dark world, and against evil spirits in the heavenly places.

"Therefore, put on every piece of God's armor so you <u>will be able to resist the enemy </u>in the time of evil. Then after the battle you will still be standing firm. Stand your ground..." *(This is your Divine-calling!)*

CHAPTER 8

HEAVEN: Part III

CHAPTER 8

Chapter 9

Please Sam, I can't wait for this study to take us into Heaven itself!

We are going to start to make that transition in this section. Parts 4 -7 will increasingly be all about that topic. But there are parts to this puzzle we still need to fill in.

I've read some authors who cautioned that Heaven is going to be so supremely different than anything we have ever seen or experienced, anything we could ever hatch up in our wildest imaginations – that trying to study Heaven would be like an earthworm trying to grasp what you do each day at work! Your job is bigger than an earthworm's brain! And Heaven, they say, is bigger than our tiny finite brains can envision. *Eye has not seen, ear has not heard, the things God has prepared for those who love him.* It's too hard to understand – so let's move on to another more earthly subject!

By the time you get done with this book, I hope you will see what utter nonsense the "so let's move on" part is. As I studied the material you are getting ready to read, my own tiny mind expanded on this subject, more than I ever imagined – and I pray you will have the exact same experience!

To start with, the "eye has not seen" verses are often misquoted. **1 Corinthians 2:9-10** actually says, "**That is** what the Scriptures mean when they say, 'No eye has seen, no ear has heard, and no mind has imagined what God has prepared for those who love him.' *(Quoting Isaiah 64:4)* **But** <u>**it was to us that God revealed these things by his Spirit**</u>**. For his Spirit searches out everything and shows us God's deep secrets."** *(Did you catch that?)*

Just because Heaven is a lot bigger than our puny brains doesn't mean we are not going to try to see through a crack in the curtain! **"Fix your eyes on the things of Heaven," Paul said.** *(Colossians 3:2)* **"We fix our eyes not on what is seen, but on what is unseen, since what is seen is temporary and what is unseen is eternal!"** *(2 Corinthians 4:18 NIV)* We can't do that if we have no idea what we are looking for! I told you I found 76 dozen verses in the Bible on Heaven! It's not like we have nothing to work with!

The more clarity on Heaven in our minds – the less interesting the things of earth become!

1 Peter 1:3-4: "It is by his great mercy that we have been born again, because God raised Jesus Christ from the dead. Now <u>**we live with great expectation, and we have a priceless inheritance—an inheritance that is kept in heaven for you,**</u> **pure and undefiled, beyond the reach of change and decay."** Keep reading and in the pages ahead, that priceless inheritance will appear sharper and more compelling!

These verses, right at the end of Jesus' earthly sin-atoning life are so important:

John 14:2-3 NIV: "**My Father's house has many rooms; if that were not so, would I have told you that I am going there to prepare a place for you? And if I go and prepare a place for you, I will come back and take you to be with me that you also may be where I am.**" *(Jesus is going to prepare a place– then he's coming back!)* The same Jesus, who came from Heaven to this earth and was born as a human baby to die on a cross to save you from your sins – in his last moments of earthly life;

> **Acts 1:9-11 NIV**: "**Was taken up before their very eyes, and a cloud hid him from their sight. They were looking intently up into the sky as he was going, when suddenly two men dressed in white stood beside them. 'Men of Galilee,' they said, 'why do you stand here looking into the sky? This same Jesus, who has been taken from you into heaven, will come back in the same way you have seen him go into heaven.'**"

This same Jesus, who died for your sins, has been in Heaven "preparing" for almost 2000 years – preparing a future home for you. That's a big deal to your future as a Believer! That same Jesus is going to return to earth again, not in a "first coming," but in a promised "second coming" where you will then be with him for all of eternity!

Clearly not everybody believes that. Dr. Stafford Betty, professor of religious studies at California State University says that 32% of atheists and agnostics say they believe in life after death. They say they don't believe in God – but they still say this life is not all there is. A Pew Research Poll found that 37% of atheists and agnostics and people with no identifiable religion say they believe in a Heaven, and 27% of them say they believe in a hell. [10]

Meanwhile, church attendance numbers are falling off at an alarming rate. The numbers of people who believe exactly what the Bible teaches in the exact way it is taught is declining – something that Jesus said would happen before his "Second Coming."

Oddly the only "spiritual part" of what seems to be growing in our increasingly agnostic "western" world is a belief in an after-life. David Jeremiah in his book, *Revealing the Mysteries of Heaven,* [11] offers an example of why that may be true. *(I'm adapting his illustration for our study.)* "We 'in-God's-image' humans are not dogs or frogs who don't think beyond today – or imagine living on after our last breath."

If I said to my dog *(my wife's dog),* "you only have two weeks to live," she would attempt to lick my face, then go wagging her tail across the room.

But, if your doctor or I sat you down in our offices and said "you only have two weeks left to live" – nobody would be blissfully happy about that! It would kick open all kinds of questions in our human minds!

That may explain why so many people reject everything the Bible has to say about a Savior, the salvation that Savior says he offers, the place in Heaven he said he left here to prepare for you – and yet they still want to hang onto the illogical belief that there is something "good" waiting for them when this life is over.

I have officiated a large number of funerals in the 34 years of our church's history. We've had several Saints die recently including my own Father. The question that is almost always on every family member's mind is what is going on with my loved one right now? Where is he? What is she doing right now? Not very many people actually imagine their loved one having just blinked off into "black oblivion."

And those aren't new questions. The people living in New Testament times were just as concerned with those questions as we are! And I'm not putting words into their mouths. It's actually a topic of discussion in the New Testament. The Apostle Paul writes out inspired answers to those very same questions. We'll get to some of those verses in a few minutes.

First, let's try to put ourselves into the heads of the early Believers for a moment.

Think about those brand-new Christians after the day of Pentecost. Acts 2:41 says that 3000 people were converted that first day – Jewish people, from all over the world, who had travelled there for the Feast. They had embraced their long-expected Messiah.

And then non-Jews *(Gentiles)* started to embrace Jesus as their Savior too. The number of newly converted quickly grew from 3000 to many, many thousands. But by Acts 8, persecution from non-believing Jews is already raging, illustrated with the stoning of Stephen. Christians were forced out of Jerusalem – and by Acts 20, wherever the Believers ended up they were getting together in houses for worship on the first day of the week. *(The Lord's Day, they called it, the day of Jesus' resurrection.)* So now there are suddenly hundreds of new house-churches meeting every week, with the number growing by dozens and dozens every month.

- So Sunday morning, after people in 1000 small house churches sang a couple of songs, and then a few people testified about the power of God in and through them that week, and after they introduced the new people that had just come to Jesus that week – *What did they then talk about?*

- Did some guy get up and say: "Turn to the Gospel of John and we'll read John 3:16." No, my no! John was only in his late teens or early 20's, when Jesus rose from the dead! He wouldn't write his Gospel *(the fourth book in your New Testament)* for five decades! The very first New Testament book didn't show up for 19 more years!

- They did have the Old Testament Scriptures, and they could compare the prophecies about Jesus' coming to their fulfillment. Some count as many as 324 prophecies in the Old Testament that Jesus 100% fulfilled. I'm quite sure they often talked about those verses.

But what did they talk about that would leave them breathless, sliding to the edge of their seats? We know there were several of the "historian" types among them who had been carefully taking notes every time Jesus spoke. Luke, the doctor's Gospel 33 years later, and Matthew, the tax collector's Gospel 37 years later would have come from scouring over all the notes and comparing one set of notes against another for perfect accuracy. Scribes would have undoubtedly made copies of the available notes and sent them out to all the house churches.

- But what did the mom with two kids sitting there on Sunday morning want to know more than anything else? What did the man whose father had died that very week want to know more than anything else?

- What subject did the Church leadership come back to over and over – and everybody would go dead silent, waiting to see if anybody had even the slightest bit of new information to offer? What were they longing to know?

- Families would leave their house-churches on Sunday not knowing if they would even be alive when the next Lord's Day rolled around. Imagine going to church one week, and the next week the man who hosted the service the week before had been martyred, and the house you met in last week had been confiscated by the Roman government!

- So if they really were studying notes of everything Jesus said *(and they were)*, which parts of those notes would have left them in the most breathless anticipation? It would have been *(IMO)* <u>anything that had to do with Jesus' Second Advent</u>, and what would happen after!

Seriously, if all of us walked out of our churches on Sunday morning, and we really didn't know if we would be chased down by "the Empire authorities" and herded with our families into the center of the "circus" to fight against wild animals for the entertainment of the pagan towns we lived in – it would probably be pretty easy to come up with a list of things we wouldn't care anything about by 3 o'clock this afternoon! So what would really matter most to us?

The new early Church had serious questions. They were desperate to know what was coming next. "God, we know there is a Heaven because the Old Testament is jam-packed full of verses about it!" I am confident that they scoured those inspired Scriptures for answers far more than we tend to today.

- They must have returned to the two quotes we read earlier, thousands of times. Jesus said that he was going back to Heaven to prepare a place for us, and when he was ready, he would be coming back to get us.

- When Jesus ascended, the angels promised that he would be coming back exactly as we saw him go. "Oh Jesus, why can't it be today?"

- "We are caught up in the horrors of our families being persecuted for our faith. Oh Jesus – how we want you to come and take us to be with you where you are!"

But they knew their deliverance was not going to be that quick or that easy. How can you say that Sam? Jesus told them he would be back. Weren't they hoping it would be before they woke the next morning? No! They actually knew it wouldn't be, and here's why:

- The disciples had quizzed Jesus, *(probably incessantly)* on this very topic before he was crucified. I'm telling you this was in the forefront of every new Believer's mind for good reason.

- Just before Jesus' crucifixion – in fact, the very last sermon he ever preaches before going to his trial and death – was him answering their incessant questions on this very subject. His answers to them are the entire chapter of Matthew 24, and half of chapter 25.

Matthew 24:2-8: "He responded, 'Do you see all these buildings? I tell you the truth, they will be completely demolished. Not one stone will be left on top of another!' *(Jerusalem was going to be destroyed – and that wasn't going to happen for 40 more years!)* **Later, Jesus sat on the Mount of Olives. His disciples came to him privately and said, 'Tell us, when will all this happen? <u>What sign will signal your return and the end of the age</u>?'**

"Jesus told them, 'Don't let anyone mislead you, for many will come in my name, claiming, "I am the Messiah." They will deceive many. And you will hear of wars and threats of wars, but don't panic. Yes, these things must take place, but the end won't follow immediately. Nation will go to war against nation, and kingdom against kingdom. There will be famines and earthquakes in many parts of the world. But all

this is <u>only the first of the birth pains, with more to come</u>.'"

The birth pains are just the first part with more to come. "No, Jesus no! If you are going to leave, we need you to come back right away. We don't need to wait for the destruction of our beloved city Jerusalem at some unknown time in the future! Are you serious Jesus?"

Jesus' sermon goes on and on – We're not trying to cover all that in this book, *(It's all in my <u>Unmasking Revelation</u> book.)* but Jesus reaches a crescendo partway through his sermon, with this:

Matthew 24:29-31: "Immediately after the anguish of those days, the sun will be darkened, the moon will give no light, the stars will fall from the sky, and the powers in the heavens will be shaken.

"And then at last, the sign that the Son of Man is coming will appear in the heavens, and there will be deep mourning among all the peoples of the earth. And they will see the Son of Man coming on the clouds of heaven with power and great glory. And he will send out his angels with the mighty blast of a trumpet, and they will gather his chosen ones from all over the world—from the farthest ends of the earth and heaven."

That's not the end of Jesus' final end times sermon. It goes on for another half a chapter and right on into chapter 25 of Matthew. Clearly, this was what Jesus wanted lodged in his followers' minds as he went to the cross to die for their/our sins! But here is one of the reasons I brought up Jesus' final sermon in this chapter: This is what the Early Church was wrestling with! They had no written New Testament yet – but they did have the notes about this sermon.

- Can you imagine them, in their services, discussing the wars and famines and earthquakes part? Those things were already happening.

- But when Jesus had started talking about the sun being darkened, the moon giving no light, and the stars falling from the sky – that would certainly be a major hard-to-miss spectacle! *(It is interesting to me, how many modern people make no connection between this described event and Jesus' following "rapture of the Saints" even though the four sentences describing this sequence of events came right from Jesus' mouth in Matthew 24:29-31!)*

- And somehow those things immediately precede the return of Jesus – who with a mighty blast of a heavenly trumpet will gather his chosen ones from the furthest ends of the planet. That's mind boggling to us. Imagine how much it was to them!

The New Testament uses the Greek word "parousia" for the return of Jesus, the Second Coming of Jesus, the Second Advent.

But oddly; #1) the word **parousia** is used to describe an event in Scripture where Jesus comes in the sky with his angels, and with a mighty trumpet blast. He gathers Believers *(both living and dead)* from across the earth to meet him in the air and go back to Heaven with him.

#2) The same exact word **parousia** is used to describe

another event where Jesus comes down from Heaven with all the Saints already with him – they together come back to earth, where Jesus mops up sin and satan and the curse and begins his eternal reign.

Important question: Are those two different "parousia" events or are they both two parts of the same event? Can you imagine that conversation in an Early Church service? Remember, the earliest Church was trying to put this all together in their minds without any of the rest of the New Testament to compare it to. *(See Appendix D in the back of the book entitled, A Theology of the Rapture of Jesus Christ.)*

Here's what they did next. *(in my opinion)* Once they found out that Saul, turned the Apostle Paul, was no longer a scumbag Christian murderer, but was actually called by God to teach Jesus' Gospel to the Gentiles – they wrote him a letter. I say that, because the very first Epistles of Paul that show up in your Bible *(to the Thessalonians)* are clearly written as if they are answers to already asked questions! Someday we need to thank the people of Thessalonica because they turned on the flow of inspired letters that makes up half of the books in our New Testament!

20 years had gone by. Everybody was meeting every Sunday, and probably a whole lot more than that, trying to seek out more truth from the notes they had.

And finally the Thessalonians must have said, "Hey we need to know more! We're dying for information here." I mean <u>we are actually dying</u>! Many people in our church have been planted in the ground and we need to know what is coming next for them and for us! Please tell us, Paul, if you know!

And Paul, now writing under the inspiration of the Holy Spirit has some new, fresh answers – right from God for them. I've never noticed before that every single chapter in Paul's first letter to them includes some reference to Jesus' Second Coming!

> **1 Thessalonians 1:10: "And they speak of how you are looking forward to the coming of God's Son from heaven—Jesus, whom God raised from the dead. He is the one who has rescued us from the terrors of the coming judgment."**

> **1 Thessalonians 2:19: "After all, what gives us hope and joy, and what will be our proud reward and crown as we stand before our Lord Jesus when he returns? It is you!"**

> **1 Thessalonians 3:13: "May he, as a result, make your hearts strong, blameless, and holy as you stand before God our Father when our Lord Jesus comes again** (παρουσία- parousia) **with all his holy people."** (ἅγιος)

Stop right there! The only other "passages" these people had were notes of Jesus' sermons, including his final sermon – where he talked about him coming with his angels to gather the Saints up from the earth. This is clearly saying he is going to be coming down from Heaven to earth "with the Saints!"

- Can you imagine the neurons double-firing in the Thessalonians brain – trying to get a handle on this clearly new information?

- Wait a minute, we are here on earth. Jesus is there in Heaven. Jesus spoke of "coming to get us and take us to be where he is." Paul now speaks of Jesus coming back to earth "with all his saints." What is going to get us from here to there – so we can come back from there to here?

1 Thessalonians 4 is one of the most profound passages on Jesus' "parousia" in all of the Bible. It sure looks like Paul is writing it to answer previously asked questions, and the Early Church sure must have had questions.

1) What is coming next for us?

2) What is going to happen to all of our friends and family who have already died?

Remember, these people had friends and family members dying all the time, often not from old age or disease, but from violence at the hands of satan's evil followers. But the only definitive words they have on their future are Jesus words in Matthew 24, that he and his angels will gather "the living!"

Their question is a good one – what about all the Jesus-loving people who have already died? Are they going to miss out on the parousia? What will happen to the "already dead"? And here comes, from Paul, a massive helping of brand new inspired Scripture!

> **1 Thessalonians 4:13-14: "And now, dear brothers and sisters, we want you to know what will happen to the Believers who have died so you will not grieve like people who have no hope. For since we believe that Jesus died and was raised to life again, we also believe that when Jesus returns, <u>God will bring back with him the Believers who have died</u>."** Do we realize what big news this was to the Thessalonians? *(And we also do need to know – that the moment they got these letters, they would have scribed multiple copies, and sent runners to every other church in Macedonia, Asia, Greece and Israel.)*

Huge new news! Not only were the Believers who had died going to make it to Heaven – they were already there!

To understand why this was such a new exciting revelation, we need to understand a bit more of their thinking. The entire Old Testament taught the concept of <u>SHEOL – the holding place for the dead</u>. It wasn't just a hole in the ground. 65 times in the Old Testament the word is used. It's always taught as an active state of consciousness. But in some instances the people were in a place of punishment – and in some instances they were in a place of reward.

- The idea that dead people were in a holding place, some headed toward reward, and some headed toward punishment carried right on into the New Testament with the Greek word "Hades." And there is no doubt that the Thessalonians had this concept whirling around in their minds.

- Paul's letter to the Ephesians is eventually going to teach that when Jesus died and rose again, he emptied the reward side of Hades, directly into the presence of God in Heaven – and that from Jesus' resurrection on, every Believer who dies goes straight to Heaven. *(We'll look at that.)*

- But the Thessalonians didn't have the letter to the Ephesians yet. It wouldn't be written for 10 more years! But even without that letter, they now know from Paul's letter to them that "already passed" family members are already in the presence of Jesus!

But Paul has more to tell them: **1 Thessalonians 4:15: "We tell you this directly from the Lord: We** (ἐγώ – *ego*) **who are still living when the Lord returns will not meet him ahead of those who have died."**

Did Paul not believe what Jesus said in Matthew 24 – that there were still a whole line of prophesied and unfulfilled things needing to happen before his return? Yes, yes he did. **Matthew 24:14: "And the Good News about the Kingdom will be preached throughout the whole world, <u>so that all nations will hear it; and then the end will come</u>."** Paul was running his legs off trying to get Jesus' message to the world, but there wasn't a chance on God's green earth that it would be done in his lifetime.

263 years later Christianity became the official religion of the Roman Empire, but that still affected only a small part of the globe! 2000 years later we are just now, finally, only a handful of years from having the Bible in readable print for every person on the planet!

But Paul is not done unfolding brand-new inspired word pictures to the ancient Thessalonians:

1 Thessalonians 4:16-17: "For the Lord himself will come down from heaven with a commanding shout, with the voice of the archangel, and with the trumpet call of God."

Does that sound familiar? That's almost exactly what Jesus had said 20 years earlier. But now Paul is going to add to what they were so hungry to know.

"First, the Believers who have died will rise from their graves. Then, together with them, we who are still alive and remain on the earth will be caught up in the clouds to meet the Lord in the air. Then we will be with the Lord forever."

That creates the whole new question of – if our bodies stay in a grave here, or are cremated, or are blown to smithereens in an explosion and our redeemed soul moves on to Heaven at death to be in the presence of God – What do we do for a body while we are waiting for ours to be resurrected? Apparently, we are going to have a "borrowed" one because we are seemingly all "recognizable." When are we going to get our "new body" in "glorified" form, in perfect physical shape?

There's so much more to talk about! There is another classic passage in 2 Thessalonians that is a game changer. It's almost like the truth-hungry people got their first letter and then immediately sent some follow-up questions. Paul's second letter to the Thessalonians brings brand new truth to everyone who reads it. Once we find out **how** you are going to arrive in Heaven, we can start to talk about **what you will experience** once you get there, starting in the very next chapter.

Chapter 10

I'd rather be in hell with my friends!

Not everybody is excited about getting into Heaven: We've all heard directly or indirectly from those who have said, I'd rather be in hell with my friends than in Heaven with all those boring church people.

1) First off, that mindless attitude greatly underestimates the horrors of a Godless eternity. Put aside, for a moment, the Biblical concept of physical torment *(that Jesus himself mentioned 11 times)* and just try to grasp the idea of an eternity completely devoid of the presence of God in us or around us.

It is inconceivable what our world here would be like if all the blessing and grace, and presence of God were suddenly sucked out of it. *It's completely inconceivable!* But that will be the shocking reality of those in a godless eternity!

2) Secondly, that mindless attitude completely under-estimates the blessedness of living in Heaven in the non-stop, unclouded, unfiltered presence of God.

We started this book smacking down the absurd thought that Heaven means forever sitting on a cloud playing a harp. And as for Isaac Asimov's famous quote: "For whatever the tortures of hell, I think the boredom of Heaven would be even worse." What block-headed uninformed nonsense! "Whatever the tortures of hell" – are you kidding? The deep suspicion that Heaven might be eternally boring comes out of the sinful thinking of our fallen minds. It has been built into our subconscious mind – that sinning is where real fun and joy is found.

- It's so hard for us to imagine a place that is completely free of sin – but filled with the pure and endless pleasures of living in and among pure righteousness.

- Our fallen minds tend to overestimate the joys of living in a fallen sin-cursed world and grossly underestimate the pure pleasure of a sinless Heaven! *(Not to mention all that we will be busy doing – we'll get to that!)*

Where we are in our study right now is going to start to get very exciting to each of us personally. It's going to begin to open up like a flower, and we are going to get an increasingly clear picture of what is right around the corner in each of our own lives if we are a Believer.

As we've already studied, the Early Church didn't ignore this topic: It was like a banquet to a starving person. Every time they got a new piece of inspired information from the pen of Paul or John or Peter they would consume it, share it, and add it to the growing library of what they knew about Heaven!

Our central text for this study has been the powerful words of Jesus himself; **John 14:1-3 NIV: "Do not let your hearts be troubled. You believe in God; believe**

also in me. My Father's house (home) has many rooms; if that were not so, would I have told you that I am going there to prepare a place for you? And if I go and prepare a place for you, I will come back and take you to be with me that you also may be where I am." *(God's home becomes your home!)*

But after saying that, Jesus died! But He didn't stay dead. He rose victoriously, conquering sin, and satan, and death, and hell! Absolutely everybody in first century Jerusalem knew someone who had personally seen him alive after he had provably died! There was great excitement among his followers. They are surely all headed to a glorious grand finale! But then he takes them all out to the edge of town and ascends off the planet, back to Heaven, leaving them all there! All they have left are angels saying: "Don't worry he's coming back in the same way you saw him go."

- So they all go back to their homes and wait. One week, one month, one year – 20 years, 22 years! Our minds tell us that they had the Gospels, and the book of Acts to feed on because that is the way it shows up in the Bible, but that is simply not the case! Those books aren't written until well after several of Paul's Epistles.

- It is 22 years later before they get a single inspired word from anybody on the subject of where Jesus is, what he is doing, and when they can expect him to come back and get them.

- Persecution against the Christians has set in with a vengeance! Many have died. Now what? They all wonder. If Believers are dead and Jesus comes back, what in the world is going to happen to the "already dead" Believers?

We started into this in the last chapter – but let's brush back up against those verses, and then add in some more – to try to get us inside the minds of those new Christians. What they first get from the Apostle Paul in the next five years explodes their thinking wide open. And what explodes their thinking open – should explode our thinking open too!

Some of the most potent truths on what is getting ready to happen to all of us – show up in Paul's letters to the Early Church in that very decade. As we studied in the last chapter, the first two letters came to the church in Thessalonica, (*in response to, I'm convinced, a letter from them to Paul.*)

Paul's first two *letters (that we now call 1 and 2 Thessalonians)* arrive. The Thessalonian Christians are poring over every single word. But they are also copying *(by hand)* furiously what Paul had written to them and sending the copies off to surrounding churches. (*Look at the map above. Note the city of Corinth 350 miles southwest.*)

They excitedly share their brand-new prophetic truths with the growing multi-national church in Corinth, and that was probably a smart thing for them to do – because that is exactly to whom Paul writes his next two letters! And those two Corinthian Letters are also filled with amazing truths about Heaven and how we are all going to arrive there! The Corinthians, of course, scramble to send copies of their new inspired letters back to the Thessalonians. *That's how the early distribution of Holy Scripture happened!*

But those *(now)* four books in your New Testament have enough powerful facts in them about what is coming as we move toward our Heavenly Home to lift the hearts of the most persecuted people on earth – or to lift your heart through whatever circumstances you find yourself in today!

Try to put yourself in the place of the early Thessalonians and Corinthians. Imagine their utter excitement when they get Paul's first letters with several early references to Jesus' return, and then the letters explode open with three huge End of Time passages!

I'm telling you those dear persecuted people who didn't know from one morning to the next if they would be alive the following day were electrified by what Paul wrote! Imagine them hearing these now famous words for the very first time.

> **1 Thessalonians 4:13: "And now, dear brothers and sisters, we want you to know what will happen to the Believers who have died so you will not grieve like people who have no hope."**

Paul is getting ready to boost these people's "hope level" up by 10,000 gallons or so. He's going to draw a sharp line between the pagan people living with no hope in their eternal future – to these people living very brutal persecuted lives, but with an extreme hope for their future!

1 Thessalonians 4:14: "For since we believe that Jesus died and was raised to life again, *(and they all did, that was the centerpiece of their faith)* **we also believe that when Jesus returns, God will bring back with him the Believers who have died."** *(Remember, that's brand-new news! That was the answer to their nagging question.)* Somehow, their believing mother and father who had just died – were already with Jesus!

1 Thessalonians 4:15-18: "We tell you this directly from the Lord: We who are still living when the Lord returns will not meet him ahead of those who have died. For the Lord himself will come down from heaven with a commanding shout, with the voice of the archangel, and with the trumpet call of God. First, the believers who have died will rise from their graves. Then, together with them, we who are still alive and remain on the earth will be caught up in the clouds to meet the Lord in the air. Then we will be with the Lord forever. So encourage each other with these words."

- Ten thousand gallons of new future hope pouring into their rather empty soul-buckets! Now, if one of them faced death before the week was out, he/she knew exactly what was coming next!

- Instead of death being a source of horror – <u>death became a source of hope</u>! Stay with that! We will see that unfolding more and more, here!

Then Paul begins to add to the clues that Jesus had already given them in his final sermon *(Matthew 24)* about when he would finally return – and now we discover "the dead in Christ <u>would rise first</u>, and then those who are alive and remain will be caught up to meet him in the air." *(That's specific – we can log that truth into our minds – the Thessalonians sure did!)*

But Paul is a long way from being done. Remember this is a letter. There wasn't a chapter 4 and then chapter 5. When Paul finishes one paragraph he moves on to the next. Chapter 5 is just the next paragraph in Paul's letter to the Thessalonians.

> **1 Thessalonians 5:1: "Now concerning how and when all this will happen, dear brothers and sisters, we don't really need to write you…"**

With all due respect, Mr. Apostle Man, apparently you did! Whatever he may have told them when he made his first visit to them recorded in Acts 17, it obviously didn't sink in. That visit lasted at least three Sabbaths, with Paul seeing conversions among the Jews and the Gentiles – Acts 17 says so. But with many of these people just coming to Christ in that first visit, they may have been a little too preoccupied drinking milk, to take on a T-Bone steak of theology. Whatever Paul thought they had caught – they hadn't!

And then, there was the little incident of their host Jason being hauled into the theatre *(pictured here)* with the town's people screaming: Acts 17:6.

**"Paul and Silas have caused trouble all over the world
and now they are here disturbing our city too!"**

So whatever Paul had told them about Jesus' return, it had
gotten all washed out by Paul and Silas' sudden forced
departure – because the Thessalonians were still loaded
with questions.

> **1 Thessalonians 5:2-3: "For you know quite well that
> the day of the Lord's return will come unexpectedly,
> like a thief in the night. When people are saying,
> 'Everything is peaceful and secure,' then disaster will
> fall on them as suddenly as a pregnant woman's labor
> pains begin. And there will be no escape."**

I, like many people in evangelical circles in the last 100
years, kind of bought into the teaching that when Jesus
returns for us, coming down from Heaven with a
commanding shout, the echoing voice of the archangel, and
with the trumpet call of God – the Believer's graves will be
emptying out, and the living Jesus-followers will all be
rising to meet Jesus in the air!   All of that will, somehow,
take place with the rest of the world completely oblivious
that it is happening *(like a thief quietly sneaking in after dark).*
It never occurred to me to question how illogical that would
have to be!

I remember the almost shock when I realized just a few
years ago that after 1 Thessalonians 5:1-3, there follows
verses 4, 5, and 6! Who knew? Somehow we tend to stop at
verse 2.

It turns out the "thief in the night" phrase is talking about
<u>unbelievers</u> being unaware that they are on the verge of one

of the most world-changing events in all of history. But that is only <u>for the unbelievers</u>! The Believers are expected to know what we are supposed to be looking for! We are instructed to follow the Biblical clues. The Thessalonians were doing just that – 1900 years ago. Paul said so:

> **1 Thessalonians 5:4-6: "<u>But you aren't in the dark about these things, dear brothers and sisters, and you won't be surprised when the day of the Lord comes like a thief</u>. For you are all children of the light and of the day; we don't belong to darkness and night. So be on your guard, not asleep like the others. Stay alert and be clearheaded!"**

I was actually at home sick a few years ago, and this was all bugging me so much I spent the whole day cutting and pasting all the "clue" verses in the Bible about Jesus' Return. I finally arranged them into a crude chart and then our church's administrative secretary Penny Worley helped me color-code it and make it presentable.

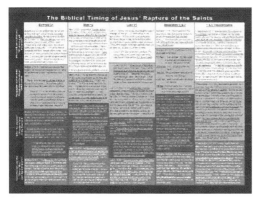 This is my color-coded take on how the verses in Jesus' sermon in Matthew 24 line up with First and Second Thessalonians, and with Mark 13 and Luke 21 and Revelation 6-7.

(You can <u>download this 11"x 17" color chart free</u> at <u>samchess.com</u>.)

(You may also want to refer to Appendix D in the back of the book entitled, <u>A Theology of the Rapture of Jesus Christ</u>.)

I'm purposely skipping one of the power-packed passages to the Thessalonians on the above chart. We'll come back to it. Remember, this new inspired truth is being feverishly copied and sent to the Corinthians and other churches. And about five years later the Corinthians get their first letter from Paul.

- I find it interesting that both churches that get two letters seem to get the second in the same year *(or so)*.

- It's like they are reading the first letter and writing back a list of questions. That's probably exactly what happened.

- I suspect the second letter is in part Paul's response to their list of new questions.

Let me jump forward to Paul's second letter to the Corinthians which would have been the same as the fourth letter to the Thessalonians. They were all excitedly sharing these truths.

> **2 Corinthians 5:1: "For we know that when this earthly tent we live in is taken down *(that is, when we die and leave this earthly body)*, <u>we will have a house in heaven</u>, an eternal body made for us by God himself and not by human hands."**

There is a reason Paul calls the body we are living in here a "tent" and says: "once this earthly tent is destroyed, we will have a building from God – a house not made with hands!"

- The redeemed Jews would have understood the ancient symbolism, of the tent/tabernacle in the wilderness their ancestors had worshipped in, being replaced by Solomon's amazing temple when they got established in the Promised Land.

- But the Corinthians and the Thessalonians were attaching this new truth directly to their present, and their future.

The "earthly tent they lived in" *(their bodies)* were in danger constantly. But the whole point of a tent is that it is temporary! We don't put up a tent to live in long term! We understand that a tent will deteriorate in the face of life's storms. When your tent starts to get too tattered to live in – it's getting time to move on!

 Paul defines our human bodies as a tent on purpose. Your earthly body is fine to camp out in *(for a while)*. It starts out strong and resistant but before long the tent will begin to sag, a stake or two will come out in the fierce storms, the seams will start to show tears. *(It's interesting that tears is spelled the same as tears.)*

- Some people act as if they are going to live in their tent forever, not realizing that it is about to collapse around them! Don't bother driving your stakes in too deep – you are going to be moving soon!

- Perhaps it is God's grace to us that as we age and look into the mirror – we're visibly reminded that our tent is sagging and we are rushing toward eternity! Paul, and the Corinthians, and then the Thessalonians, came to understand that their bodies were only a temporary dwelling:

2 Corinthians 5:2, 4: "We grow weary in our present bodies, and we long to put on our heavenly bodies like new clothing...While we live in these earthly bodies, we groan and sigh, but it's not that we want to die and get rid of these bodies that clothe us. Rather, we want to put on our new bodies so that these dying bodies will be swallowed up by life!"

2 Corinthians 5:6-7: "So we are always confident, even though we know that <u>as long as we live in these bodies we are not at home with the Lord</u>. For we live by believing and not by seeing."

2 Corinthians 5:8-9 ESV: "Yes, we are of good courage, and we <u>would rather be away from the body and at home with the Lord</u>. So whether we are at home or away, we make it our aim to please him."

Notice Paul's emphasis on "our home" being on the other side of this life! Remember Jesus saying that "he was going to prepare a place for us, and that he will come again and take us to be with him."

Most people don't view death as a good thing. We fear death. We see death as taking us <u>away from our home</u> rather than <u>to our home</u>! We become so attached to our "tent" that we don't want to ever move on!

Paul was comforted when he was told he would soon be dying. He kept referring to death as "far better" because it would be his final journey to his real home!

2 Corinthians 5:8 ESV: "Yes, we are of good courage, and we would rather be away from the body and at home with the Lord. So whether we are at home or away, we make it our aim to please him."

Paul clearly seems to be telling the Corinthians that they should prefer the "mansion" to the "tent"! Yes?

We still haven't yet gotten to one of the most astounding passages in the Bible on our pathway to Heaven. Let me give you a taste:

1 Corinthians 15:42, 51-55: "These dying bodies cannot inherit what will last forever.... But let me reveal to you a wonderful secret. We will not all die, but we will all be transformed!

"It will happen in a moment, in the blink of an eye, when the last trumpet is blown. For when the trumpet sounds, those who have died will be raised to live forever.

"And we who are living will also be transformed. For our dying bodies must be transformed into bodies that will never die; our mortal bodies must be transformed into immortal bodies. Then, when our dying bodies have been transformed into bodies that

will never die, this Scripture will be fulfilled: 'Death is swallowed up in victory. O death, where is your victory? O death, where is your sting?'"

If you realize the tent is tattered, and Heaven is really your eternal home – death loses its sting! Instead of death being a source of horror, death became a source of hope!

Death isn't going to take you from your home. It's going to take you <u>to your home</u>!

Chapter 11

_____

How can the "already dead" be rising from the grave if they are already in Heaven with Jesus?

It is not possible to overestimate how critical what Paul wrote to the Thessalonian and the Corinthian churches was! Other than in the book of Revelation, I don't know of any other group of verses in the whole Bible that is more descriptive about our journey from this life – on to our next life in Heaven. The Early Church desperately wanted information, and they got a truckload of it.

But there is a part of these verses that they would have all pondered over and over, week after week, trying to figure out what looks like a paradox. Let's read the now familiar five verses below again. There are two contrasting verses in there that should snap our brains into attention.

> **1 Thessalonians 4:13-17: "And now, dear brothers and sisters, we want you to know what will happen to the Believers who have died so you will not grieve like people who have no hope. For since we believe that Jesus died and was raised to life again, we also believe that when Jesus returns, God will bring back with him the Believers who have died.** *(I told you that would have excited them to the bottom of their toes!) (It turns out the already dead Believers were already with Jesus!)*

"We tell you this directly from the Lord: We who are still living when the Lord returns" *(watch that word* παρουσία *– parousia)*. Remember, that's a key word used in the New Testament by Jesus himself in Matthew 24 – and by Paul and Peter, John, and James – to describe Jesus' Second Coming.

"We who are still living when the Lord returns (παρουσία) will not meet him ahead of those who have died. For the Lord himself will come down from heaven with a commanding shout, with the voice of the archangel, and with the trumpet call of God. First, the Believers who have died will rise from their graves. Then, together with them, we who are still alive and remain on the earth will be caught up in the clouds to meet the Lord in the air. Then we will be with the Lord forever."

Right about there we should be snapping to attention and asking some hard questions.

#1) How can the "already dead" Believers be rising from their graves in verse 16 – if verse 14 says they are already with Jesus after they die?

#2) How can the Believers who have already died be coming back with Jesus, and the same Believers be rising from their graves to meet Jesus in the air?

There are answers, but we have to dig for them. And to be honest once we are done digging – we may arrive at a few different conclusions. That's OK.

When your loved one dies – do they go straight into the presence of God in Heaven? *You can find in Appendix B a study sheet entitled: Do we go* straight to Heaven when we die*?* The short answer seems to be a definite, YES!

When my friend, Jerry Katzmann, or your dear believing church member, or relative, or friend died recently – was he/she instantly in the presence of God? Yes! As Paul wrote: "To be absent from the body is to be present with the Lord!" (*2 Corinthians 5:8 KJV*)

> **Philippians 1:21, 23-24: "For to me, living means living for Christ, and dying is even better. I'm torn between two desires: I long to go and be with Christ, which would be far better for me. But for your sakes, it is better that I continue to live."** *(Paul wasn't planning on some kind of soul sleep for the next several years, was he?)*

So if Jerry went right to Heaven – is his body still here on earth waiting to join whatever part of him is already in Heaven? If only our soul goes to Heaven when we die – does our body then join with it after Jesus' return? Yes!

How is it then that "already dead" people reappear in the New Testament, like Elijah and Moses at the transfiguration of Jesus? How is it that they seem to have bodies, and how is it that Peter immediately recognized both Moses and Elijah – even though they had been dead hundreds of years before he was born?

I don't have answers to all of those questions. Some answers will always be speculative – but can't you imagine the Thessalonians and the Corinthians asking these questions?

Remember they didn't have any of the rest of the New Testament yet to even search for more answers. But I seriously doubt they just said: That's too hard to understand so they just walked away and forgot it. This is what modern Christians tend to do, even with all the rest of revealed, inspired Scriptures that we have on our laptop, and even on our phone.

I expressed my frustration with some of the great brilliant theologians who have devoted their lives to writing huge theological works, but only including a page or two about Heaven. Note: Louis Berkholf's wonderful theological works comprise 737 pages but only one page on Heaven.

Or Millard Erickson's "*Christian Theology,*" 1321 pages has only six pages about Heaven! I don't mean this disrespectfully, but I really do want to say "Please Mr. Erickson – if you would just take 40 measly pages or so and explain these mind blowing truths that Paul unfolded to the Thessalonians and Corinthians – that would be very much appreciated Mr. Erickson, Sir!" *(There is a reason he didn't. I'll explain it soon.)*

What does seem to be clear to me is that Paul includes six distinct steps:

1) Jesus is coming down from Heaven with a commanding shout accompanied by the "already dead" Believers.

2) The voice of the archangel and the trumpet call of God blasts out.

3) Believers who have already died (*their bodies*) will rise from their graves.

4) Those who are still alive will rise to meet Jesus in the air.

5) Both groups will then be with Jesus (*wherever Jesus is*) forever.

6) Jesus does not seem to first come to earth. The Believers meet him in the "air" and he seems to take the Believers back to Heaven with him. Yes?

παρουσία

parousia / coming; advent; presence

We've already seen that the Bible describes this first of two distinct events as the "parousia." We often tend to call the first one "the rapture." But, that brings up another issue:

We are going to read about the coming "man of lawlessness" in 2 Thessalonians 2:3 who brings destruction. He will "do the work of satan with counterfeit power and signs and miracles." (2:9) This is foretelling (*IMO*) to the Thessalonians (*and to the whole Early Church*) none other than the antichrist, the counterfeit-Christ satan sends in the end of times to try one last time to defeat Jesus and his Church. *(He had been prophesied back in the book of Daniel 650 years before – so they already knew something about him.)*

> **2 Thessalonians 2:4-5, 7-8: "He will exalt himself and defy every-thing that people call god and every object of worship. He will even sit in the temple of God, claiming that he himself is God.** *(That is exactly how Revelation 13 will describe the antichrist.)* **Don't you remember that I told you about all this when I was with you? For this lawlessness is already at work secretly, and it will remain secret until the one who is holding it back steps out of the way.**

> **"Then the man of lawlessness will be revealed, but the Lord Jesus will slay him with the breath of his mouth and destroy him by the splendor of his coming."** (παρουσίας)

That exact same event is also described in Revelation 19:20 when Jesus returns in his Glorious Second Coming, wipes out the antichrist once and for all, puts him into the lake of fire, and begins to set up his "forever" reign.

Here's the thorny issue again: The word "parousia" is used to describe both events! Imagine the Thessalonians trying to wrestle with that contrast. In one event, living Believers are here on a rather unsuspecting earth. Jesus comes down from Heaven, and they/we rise to meet him in the air.

In the other event *(recorded in high-definition in Revelation 19-20)* Jesus leaves Heaven, the white-robed saints *(all of us)* are already with him. Jesus doesn't stop part-way down – He comes down to the earth, wipes out the antichrist, sin and satan, and moves this planet from "this present age" to "the age to come." Revelation 20 moves us from <u>time</u> as we know it on into <u>eternity</u>! So what is going on here? Why is the same word used to describe two distinctly different occasions – with decidedly different events happening?

Some very smart "dead people" *(and some living ones),* solve the problem by making it all happen at the same time. It all unfolds together, they say, at the very end of time when Jesus comes down from Heaven.

We all, the dead and the living, rise to meet Jesus in the air. Then we all just come back down to earth with him – where he wipes out sin and satan and we all set up his earthly reign together!

But there are some massive holes in that explanation. *(IMO)* I'll mention two:

> #1) When Jesus comes in the air *(as Paul writes in 1 Thessalonians 4 and on into chapter 5),* the rest of the earth is living life completely oblivious to the massive event getting ready to happen. Jesus, in the famous Matthew 24 passage, says: "As the days of Noah were, so the coming of the Son of Man will be." Anybody want to take a wild guess at what word Matthew used there both times as he talks about the Son of Man's return? παρουσία!

> #2) But in <u>Jesus' Glorious Second Coming</u> in Revelation 19, this earth has just gone through the horrifying "trumpet and bowl judgments" that God's poured-out wrath sends on sin and satan. And the earth *(as described*

in the middle parts of Revelation) is like a nuclear bombed-out wasteland. It will be a bit hard (1) to have ¼ of the world's population killed by pestilence, *(Since the Covid-19 pandemic, we now get that part.)* (2) the sun going dark, (3) stars falling from the sky, and have John Q. Public still be nonchalantly enjoying life, *(as they were in the days of Noah)* – and those three events happen even before God's Trumpet and Bowl judgments on sin and satan are poured out. *(God's Wrath!)*

So Sam, are we expecting the "parousia of Jesus" to be one event – or two? My answer; Jesus' "parousia" <u>is one event</u>! But hang on! Remember Jesus' First Coming was far more than him being born and laying in a manger! Jesus' entire First Coming lasted 33 years! It started with the Annunciation of his birth and ended with his Ascension into Heaven.

So Jesus' Second Coming is one event – but with multiple parts. Imagine the Thessalonians trying to get their heads around that without all the rest of the New Testament that we now have.

I do believe the "beginning act" of Jesus' Second Coming will be the "lifting off – rapture" of the Saints, both living and dead to meet Jesus in the air as described by Paul in 1 Thessalonians 4. I do believe the unbelievers who are living in oblivious sin will be shocked. Remember the "thief in the night" line is said about unbelievers not Believers. Believers are not supposed to be surprised:

> **1 Thessalonians 5:3-4: "When people are saying, 'Everything is peaceful and secure,' then disaster will fall on them as suddenly as a pregnant woman's labor pains begin. And there will be no escape. <u>But you aren't in the dark</u> about these things, dear brothers and sisters, and <u>you won't be surprised when the day of the Lord comes like a thief</u>."**

> It's the people who aren't expecting Jesus' return who will be shocked out of their mind when **"the Lord himself comes down from heaven with a commanding shout, with the voice of the archangel, and with the trumpet call of God!"**

Imagine when people they know, work with, are married to, suddenly rise to meet Jesus in the air – and the graves of millions of people are opening up and bodies are rising. In this day of 24 hour cable news, arriving on every conceivable device we can imagine, do we honestly believe the whole world will just go on watching reruns?

I know many of us have been told all our lives that when Jesus returns and lifts us off the planet, the rest of the world will go on blindly unaware that much of anything has happened. I finally forced myself to ask the logical *(theological)* question: Really? A billion or so people leave the planet all at once, and nobody is asking: "Hey, where is old what's-his-name?" I'm not sure how we got this so twisted up, but Jesus himself, tells us that a "secret return" is not the way things are going to unfold in his Matthew 24 sermon:

> **Matthew 24:30-31: "And then at last, the sign that the Son of Man is coming will appear in the heavens, and <u>there will be deep mourning</u>** (Κόπτομαι – *koptomai – wailing, grief-stricken)* a**<u>mong ALL the peoples of the earth</u>. And <u>they</u>** *(They who? All the peoples!)* **will see the Son of Man coming on the clouds of heaven with power and great glory. And he will send out his angels with the mighty blast of a trumpet, and they will gather his chosen ones from all over the world — from the farthest ends of the earth and heaven."**

Is this not describing, right from the mouth of Jesus, the exact same event that we just discussed in I Thessalonians 4? Approximately how many people does Jesus say will notice what is going on and be grief stricken? And how many people does Jesus say will see the Son of Man coming on the clouds of Heaven with power and great glory? All of them!

Please don't try to make this apply to Jesus' Glorious Second Coming. In that one, he does not return in the air and send his angels out to gather his chosen ones from all over the world. In the Second Coming, <u>Jesus returns with his Saints and angels</u> – to a defiant antichrist and what is left of the God-hating armies of the world who have gathered for the Battle of Armageddon. (*Which Jesus supernaturally finishes as fast as it starts – we're getting to that!*)

The Thessalonians and Corinthians don't know about that part yet because they don't yet have the book of Revelation, but we do! Paul's advice to them is "the world around you will be sleeping at the wheel when Jesus returns, but not you!" And as people who have far more of God's revealed Word than those Early Christians did – it better not be us sleeping at the wheel either!

> **1 Thessalonians 5:4-6: "But you aren't in the dark about these things, dear brothers and sisters, and you won't be surprised when the day of the Lord comes like a thief. For you are all children of the light and of the day; we don't belong to darkness and night. So be on your guard, not asleep like the others. Stay alert and be clearheaded."**

We should know exactly what the Bible says
is getting ready to happen!

You are not the ones who are going to be "wailing in great mourning," You are the ones who are going to be shouting praises as you are gathered up, and you find yourself rising to meet your Savior in the air!

I told you these were power-packed passages that the Early Church was receiving for the first time. And Paul's not even done here yet. Clearly the Thessalonians had more questions and Paul sets out to answer them. But, why in the world is Paul writing answers to them concerning the antichrist? If they are being lifted off the earth in the "Rapture," why do they need to know anything about the counterfeit-Christ showing up at the end of time?

Well, let's just read the text, and let Paul's inspired pen do the teaching. It starts out like this:

2 Thessalonians 2:1-5: "Now, dear brothers and sisters, let us clarify some things about the coming of our Lord Jesus Christ and how we will be gathered to meet him. Is there any question about which part of the "parousia" we are talking about here with phrases like: 1) The Coming of our Lord Jesus Christ; 2) How we will be gathered up to meet him?

"Don't be so easily shaken or alarmed by those who say that the day of the Lord has already begun. Don't believe them, even if they claim to have had a spiritual vision, a revelation, or a letter supposedly from us. Don't be fooled by what they say.

"For that day will not come *(What day? – The day when Jesus comes and gathers us up to meet him!),* **that day will not come until there is…**

> **#1) a <u>great rebellion against God</u> (ἀποστασία – apostasia, falling away)** *(An apostasy, not in the world, they are already apostatized – it has to be talking about a "falling away" in the Church!)*

> **#2) and <u>the man of lawlessness is revealed</u>—the one who brings destruction. He will exalt himself and defy everything that people call god and every object of worship. He will even sit in the temple of God, claiming that he himself is God. Don't you remember that I told you about all this when I was with you?"**

Sam, are you saying that before Jesus will come back, send his angels out to gather his chosen ones from the end of the earth, and we all meet him in the air – are you saying that before that can happen there will be #1) a massive falling away from truth in the church, and #2) that the antichrist will have to be revealed – are you saying that Sam?

I'm not "saying" anything! I'm just reading from the pages of the inspired Holy Bible! ☺ If you have a problem with anything we've just read, please direct your comments to: *theapostlepaul@gmail.com*!

You might also want to read my book: *Unmasking Revelation!*

CHAPTER 11

Chapter 12

Do we go straight to Heaven when we die?

So we're now deep into the discussion of when and how each of us will move from the end of this life on earth on into our eternal Heavenly home. If Jesus doesn't return during your lifetime, most of us will get to Heaven – by first dying here on earth, and then being raised to new life in Heaven.

So is that all just some great unknown or is the Bible rather specific, *(perhaps even very specific)* on what that journey will be like? Most of our churches answer the question almost weekly, what does it take, *spiritually,* to get you to Heaven? We know the answer to that. Repentance for our many sins, embracing Jesus' death as our sin payment, accepting his gift of salvation, his soul-cleansing, his sin washing, transforming us from the old us – into a brand new us!

But let's assume that you have all taken that step, and then  this week you get hit by "the ice wagon." Our church administrator Mark Worley, says his former boss at a utility company used to say, "In case one of you gets hit by the "ice wagon" this weekend and don't make it back to work next week…"

Let's use that on ourselves. If one of us "gets hit by the ice wagon" before next Sunday, do we go straight to Heaven when we die? The short answer we have come up with, if you are a Believer *(and only if you are a Believer)* **is yes!** We didn't come up with that answer off the top of our hat. I dug out a number of Scriptures that strongly support that truth. *(If you want to see those references see Appendix B in the back of this book entitled, Do Believers go straight to Heaven when they die?)*

But a longer answer is a little more complicated. When Stephen was being stoned in Acts 7, he yells out at the very end in verse 59 – "Lord Jesus, receive my spirit!"

- Was his spirit or soul in the presence of Jesus before the day was over? Yes, according to Scripture. Paul said, "to be absent from the body is to be present with the Lord."

- But what about Mr. Martyr Stephen's body? What happened to that? It was probably buried under a pile of rocks to keep the jackals away until it dissolved back into dust. *"He didn't need it anymore. It was just a shell to house his soul while on this earth."* I've said that to many grieving family members over the years, but I was wrong! I will never say that again in that way.

- The Bible is very specific in saying that our body, this body, will one day be resurrected to reunite with our soul. But Sam, given enough time, it turns back to dust! What if the cremation urn gets knocked off the mantel by Rufus the dog, and accidentally gets sucked up in the ole Hoover vacuum?

- God formed Adam's body out of dust to start with and he's not going to get confused! But what if I'm eaten by a shark and digested as food? Same answer! What if I'm in a nuclear explosion? Same answer!

Let's get some Biblical context here. This subject is far bigger and deeper than one might imagine at first reading. In fact it is so big, we will not get it all covered in one chapter. What I'm going to say here, literally, is in the direct future of every single Believer who ever lived on this planet!

We are going to define some more what the Bible says is going to be happening to your redeemed soul in the near future. But we are also going to be defining exactly what the Bible says is going to happen to your existing body in the distant future.

Paul is very specific on that subject in his letters to the Corinthians, and elsewhere. And the final outcome will have nothing to do with whether we ended our final days here on this earth as food for a lion in Caesar Nero's *circus (as some of the Early Church were)*, or if we get run over by the "ice wagon."

Paul, in his 2nd letter to the Thessalonians jumps straight into the topic of their ongoing intense persecutions, and then makes a stunning new promise to them about Jesus' return:

2 Thessalonians 1:3-6: "Dear brothers and sisters, we can't help but thank God for you, because your faith is flourishing and your love for one another is growing. We proudly tell God's other churches about your endurance and faithfulness in all the persecutions and hardships you are suffering. And God will use this persecution to show his justice and to make you worthy of his Kingdom, for which you are suffering. In his justice he will pay back those who persecute you."

That may have been some comfort – although paying back an entire Empire for the godless pagan things they were doing probably seemed like a pipe dream. They couldn't even imagine our day – when the mighty Roman Empire is reduced to a memory and a few ruins. But here is what they almost certainly hung on to:

2 Thessalonians 1:7: "<u>God will provide rest for you</u> who are being persecuted and <u>also for us when the Lord Jesus appears from heaven</u>." *(ἀποκαλύψει – apocalypsis –revelation –unveiling)* The rest is on the way – even if you have died!

They probably thought the Roman Empire was so strong that it would last right up until Jesus' return – but if it did, this was when their relief would arrive! God promises them through Paul:

2 Thessalonians 1:7-9: "When the Lord Jesus appears from Heaven He will come with his mighty angels, in flaming fire, bringing judgment on those who don't know God and on those who refuse to obey the Good

News of our Lord Jesus. They will be punished with eternal destruction, forever separated from the Lord and from his glorious power." *(Bam, boom! The end of time – "the end of the age," as Jesus called it!)*

Remember Jesus' Great Commission: "Go into all the world and be my witnesses – and <u>I will be with you 'until the end of the age</u>!' This is it, right here! The end of time! But it hasn't happened yet! Jesus is going to be with us after the end of time too, but by then, time will have ended, and timeless eternity will have begun!

This gave the Thessalonians and the Corinthians new information about Jesus' Glorious Second Coming. As they dug the truths apart, they came to understand that this wasn't describing the same event as Jesus' coming part way to earth with the living and the "already-dead" bodies meeting him in the air!

The Corinthians are the ones who famously took this to the next level. And for the Corinthian – moving from the old pagan life into new life in Christ and then on to an undeserved reward in Heaven was quite the journey!

I've been there in the ruins of ancient Corinth *(perhaps you*  *have too.)* I've walked down that main street, stood in the Agora, the Roman Forum just south of the Temple of Apollo. I thought about all the 1st Corinthian Scriptures where Paul is trying to correct the Church's seriously yet-to-be-transformed sinful behavior.

In their defense, Corinth *(unlike Thessalonica)* was a seaport. In fact, they had an isthmus, a spit of land between two major oceans, so hundreds of ships docked on one side and had their cargo moved to a waiting ship on the other side. Consequently, every kind of idol worshipping heathen from all over the world was constantly invading their town and even their new churches.

But as much as Paul is using his letter to instruct the Corinthians on their less-than-righteous behavior – He's also using both 1st and 2nd Corinthians to unfold more of the most powerful teaching on Jesus' return, and about our being "gathered up to meet him in the air."

Can't you see the Corinthians pouring over their own copies of the Thessalonian letters, and then Corinthian Fred saying something like: "There is something here I don't get at all." And then all of them are discussing those strange points in their Bible studies. Finally, the Secretary of the Corinthian Church sits down and writes a "Dear Paul" Letter. "Dear Paul, we read everything you wrote to the Thessalonians about Jesus' return and we are very excited but it has left us with some serious questions. Please email your response to: thesinfulcorinthians@werereallysorry.com!

Pretty soon, in rolls Paul's third letter in your Bible, and it's to the Corinthians – and after dealing with the "we're really sorry to be so sinful" part, then comes the famous and informative chapter 15!

> 1) There is a notable chunk of 1 Corinthians 15 that is on the reality of Jesus' resurrection from the dead. Notice, the leaders in the Corinthian church didn't need to be convinced of that. That was the very foundational truth for them existing as a church at all!
>
> 2) There is a strong emphasis on the fact that Jesus' resurrection makes our own resurrection from the dead possible.
>
> *Paul:* **1 Corinthians 15:20-22: "But in fact, Christ has been raised from the dead. He is the first of a great harvest of all who have died. So you see, just as death came into the world through a man, now the resurrection from the dead has begun through another man. Just as everyone dies because we all belong to Adam, everyone who belongs to Christ will be given new life."**

I often use the story of Jesus raising Lazarus from the dead in funerals. Of course Lazarus didn't stay alive forever – he eventually died again.

But I often say, because Jesus died, and then rose from the dead, that's the guarantee that Lazarus will rise from the dead <u>again</u> to live forever.

- And that's the guarantee that your loved one will rise from the dead – and that's the guarantee that you will one day rise from the dead too!

But it seems Corinthian Fred and Sally and their church friends must have had yet another unanswered question – because Paul takes an unusual amount of his return letter to answer it.

And here was a real issue. If our soul goes directly into the presence of God when we die, but our *body (often our "broken down body")* goes into the ground to rot into dust, or is torn apart by wild animals or burned for light at Nero's garden party, or even if we go into a shark's belly to create its needed "protein and fat caloric intake" for the day. "How, Jesus how do you plan to reconnect our broken sinful human bodies with our redeemed soul, and come up with something that will be used by us for all of eternity?"

> **1 Corinthians 15:22: "Just as everyone dies because we all belong to Adam, everyone who <u>belongs to Christ will be given new life</u>."** What if that is talking about more than just the soul?

- *(They must have thought as they read through this for the first time.)* What if that "new life" isn't just the redeemed heart where, even though we are fallen products of the sin nature, we receive "New Life" because of, and only because of, our faith in Jesus as our Savior? The forgiveness and soul cleansing we talked about earlier is the reason – the only reason that our eternal soul ends up in Heaven when we die.

- The people who are up in Heaven now **are not there because they were so faithful to Jesus – they are there because Jesus was so faithful to them!**

- We know Heaven is a sinless place. If I get hit by the ice wagon this afternoon, and my soul is in Jesus' presence before the sun goes down here – I'm not going to be carrying my sinful nature up there with me!

Do we see the issue with what I am saying? Many of us have been radically transformed by the washing of regeneration and the infilling power of the Holy Spirit until we are nothing like we used to be! But that said, if I have a run-in with an ice-wagon on the way home – isn't there going to be some more "new-life transformation" before I stand in the presence of God in a sinless Heaven? No, Sam, because Jesus took all your sins on himself and paid the sin penalty for them all!

- Ok, so when Jesus returns in the Rapture amid a commanding shout, and the trumpet call, and a bellow from the archangel, we will all lift off this planet to meet him in the air. 1 Thessalonians 4 says this old sin-cursed body is going to come bounding up out of the ground or be gathered from the far reaches of the oceans or be sucked back together where it has been ionized by some explosion.

- My body is going to join my Jesus-redeemed soul in the sky. So am I then going to stumble on into eternity with this old worn-out misshapen body which my own granddaughter says sports an unusually large nose on the front of my egg-shaped head? Will this old worn out misshapen body wrap itself again around my eternal soul and go on merrily living forever? Yes? No?

Well, yes and no! First; <u>you will still be you</u>! One God-issued body for every person for all of time! You are not going to mistakenly get another person's body! There are grammatical reasons why the Bible is clearly saying – in Heaven, you will be you! You will apparently be recognizable as you! If you changed your whole appearance with plastic surgery – you are going to end up still being the original you after all!

But at the same time, the idea that these broken-down bodies, especially as we get older, or experience disease or sickness or deformity wrapping around our redeemed souls – are how we are going to spend all of eternity is Biblically incorrect.

> **1 Corinthians 15:50: "What I am saying, dear brothers and sisters, is that <u>our physical bodies cannot inherit the Kingdom of God</u>. These <u>dying bodies</u> cannot inherit what will last forever."**

In order for God to one day soon turn you from a "temporal earthly being" into an "eternal heavenly being," he's going to have to <u>do something with that "dying body" of yours</u>! Remember, your dying body is the result of the curse of sin! That curse of sin is not going anywhere near Heaven!

Again, God wiped out the effects of sin's curse in your soul by personally paying your sin penalty – but he's going to have to do something about the sin curse in your body if you are going to go on living forever – as you!

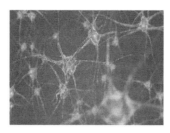 1) We start life with around 100 billion neurons in our brain. By age 40 we are losing up to 10,000 neurons a day – affecting memory, coordination and brain function.

2) Muscles start aging about age 30. Muscles are constantly being built up and broken down, but after age 30, the breakdown exceeds the buildup. Once adults reach age 40, they lose between .5 and 2 % of their muscle mass every year. *(That's why we go to the gym!)*

3) Bones start aging at age 35. Children's bone growth is rapid and all our skeletal system replaces itself every two years. Until our mid-20's, bone density is increasing. By age 35 our bones start shrinking in size and density. We loose two inches by age 80. *(I've already lost 2 ¼ inches of my original 6' 5" and I'm a long way from 80!)*

4) Hearts starts aging at age 40. Blood vessels become less elastic, and fat deposits form in the arteries.

5) Lungs start aging at age 20 and our lung capacity starts to decrease. At age 30, the average man can inhale 2 pints of air. By age 40 he's down to one pint.

Understand that the "aging process" is the result of the curse of sin! We weren't created to age! We were created to live forever in the presence of God! <u>Sin caused this mess</u>! Satan is our <u>physical</u> enemy along with being our <u>spiritual</u> enemy! Not only is sin in the human heart a big deal, but sin's corruption of the human body is also a big deal! But there is coming a day when sin's corruption of the body comes to a crashing halt!

> **1 Corinthians 15:42-44: "Our earthly bodies are planted in the ground when we die, but they will be raised to live forever. Our bodies are buried in brokenness, but they will be raised in glory. They are buried in weakness, but they will be raised in strength. They are buried as natural human bodies, but they will be raised as spiritual bodies."** Every one of those points are very important, we'll come back to them in the next chapter.

 <u>Joni Eareckson Tada</u> *(now 74)* was injured when she dove into shallow water in the Chesapeake Bay and severed her spine at age 17. She's had a broader ministry around the world than most could ever imagine.

She writes: I can still hardly believe it. I with shriveled fingers, bent fingers, atrophied muscles, gnarled knees, and no feeling from the shoulders down will one day have a new body! It's easy for me to be "joyful in hope," as it says in Romans 12:12 and that is exactly what I have been doing. My assurance of Heaven is so alive that I've been making dates with friends to do all sorts of fun things once we get our new bodies. And I don't take these appointments lightly. I'm convinced these things will really happen! [12]

Paul unfolds to the Corinthians brand new news, a "mystery" he calls it! *("the mysterion"* – *that which was hidden and is now being revealed.)* It's significant that Paul reveals this new truth to people that he has been blasting for their stumbling spiritual growth a few chapters earlier.

> **1 Corinthians 15:51-52: "But let me reveal to you a wonderful secret.** *(I'm telling you a mystery,)* **We will not all die, but <u>we will all be transformed</u>! It will happen in a moment, in the blink** *(ἀτόμος)* **of an eye, when the last trumpet is blown. For when the trumpet sounds, those who have died will be raised to live forever. And we** *(Believers)* **who are living will also be transformed."**

There is so much we need to peel back about this stunning passage. But let's end this chapter with these points. Here's the wonderful secret that was for the first time being revealed. When that trumpet sounds, almost certainly the same one that announces Jesus' return to meet his Saints in the air: *(1 Thessalonians 4)*

1) Those who have died *(their bodies)* will be raised to live forever!

2) But the dead and the living won't meet Jesus in the air the way they leave the grave.

3) Even the "living Believers" will have the same transformation as the "already dead."

4) On the way up to meet Jesus the dust of already-dead Joe and the worn-out sick body of still-alive Jack will change. They will be transformed into brand new bodies!

Approximately how long will it take for millions of people's bodies to be made completely new?

- It's the Greek word, "*atomos*" from which we get the world "atom." The smallest particle of time.

- Not the "blink" of an eye. Some of our versions call it the "twinkling" of an eye. That's closer.

- One scientist suggested that the twinkling of an eye is the time light moving at 186,000 miles per second takes to move from your iris to your retina.

- In approximately that length of time, we will all be changed – in the twinkling of an eye! We will all be transformed.

What is that going to be like?

Chapter 13

Let me focus us back very quickly on your transfer from earth to Heaven.

1) When are you going to get there?

2) How are you going to get there?

3) What will be the circumstances surrounding your arrival?

4) What will you look like when you arrive?

5) What will you do there for all of eternity?

We're not going to cover all that in this chapter! But I do want to dig deep into <u>When and How</u> you are going to get to Heaven, and what the circumstances around your arrival

 will be. But in the following chapter, I do plan to dig into the question: What will you look like when you arrive in Heaven, both inside and out?

I specifically dug out and printed every passage I could find in the New Testament on these subjects and spread them out on a conference table to look for clues on how they all fit together. I promise there are some exciting truths here that

I've never ever seen before this study! Some of you may be saying right about now: These truths are really starting to get my eyes less and less focused on the things in this chaotic world around me – and more and more focused on what is coming when this life is over. That makes sense, considering we are only here on this planet for 85 years – or 65 years – or 45 years – and then we, as Believers, are in Heaven for all of eternity!

- Bob Saget, the comedian died while I was writing this material, at 65 years of age. Betty White died one week earlier at age 99.

- Saget, not knowing he was going to die a week later, said about Betty. "She always said the love of her life was her husband Allen Ludden. If things work out by Betty's design in the after-life, they will be reunited."

- "I don't know," *Saget said*, "what happens after we die, but if Betty says you get to be with the love of your life, then I happily defer to Betty on this."

- Truth is: what happens in Heaven will not be by Betty's design – but by God's design. We probably should ask a more precise theological question like: If you outlive three spouses, and they were all "the love of your life," and all four of you arrive in Heaven – then what? We are often asking the wrong questions without any real knowledge of what God has clearly already stated.

But the more concerning part of that illustration is Saget's statement, "I don't know what happens after we die!"

- From a purely logic standpoint, it is inconceivable that we would talk about an after-life as if we believe in one, but make our way through 65 years of life and not find out everything we can about what is coming in that after-life.

- I'm not tossing around blame here. I had some people tell me, "I have been in churches all my life and no one has brought up this subject in a sermon." *God help us!*

- I told you I've been preaching for 44 years and never preached a sermon series on this subject – *Shame on me!*

So much of humanity tends to spend year after year focusing on things with no eternal value! Sometimes it takes something big to make us realize the temporal things aren't really all that important.

There are several places in the New Testament Epistles where you can see Paul, or Peter, or John trying to wrestle the Early Church people's mind away from their awful "here and now" and lift their eyes up to the realities of a waiting Heaven. Paul's letter, in **Colossians 3:2**, I often quote: **"Set your sights on the realities of Heaven not on the things of this earth."** Here's another one, from Paul, to the Philippian church:

> **Philippians 1:27: "Above all, you must <u>live as citizens of heaven</u>, conducting your-selves in a manner worthy of the Good News about Christ."** *(Yes, you are citizens of this earth for now, with all the sin-soaked horror that is going on around you.)*

217

Philippians 3:20: "But, <u>we are citizens of heaven</u>, where the Lord Jesus Christ lives. And we are eagerly waiting for him to return as our Savior." *(He's writing to terribly persecuted first-century Believers.)* Lift your eyes off of your circumstances and onto your Savior – and what he has prepared for you!

v.21: "He will take our weak mortal bodies and change them into glorious bodies like his own, using the same power with which he will bring everything under his control." *(It's an amazing explosion of new truth!)*
   a) "take our weak mortal bodies"
   b) "change them into glorious bodies"
   c) "like his own!" *(So many clues!)*

 "We are not going to be stuck in these old dying bodies for the rest of eternity!" The young and vibrant do become the wrinkled and worn out – but that's just the effects of the curse of sin, and it's only for the few decades of our journey here on this earth!

Paul says: **"lift your eyes up past your citizenship on this earth and begin to see yourself as <u>already a citizen of Heaven!"</u>** And, not only has Jesus promised to forgive and wash your sin-cursed soul and to cleanse your heart that you can be forever welcomed into a sinless Heaven – He's also going to do something amazing to your sin-cursed body <u>to make it gloriously useable by you for all the rest of eternity</u>!

Jesus is going to take our weak mortal bodies and change them – *change them into what*? Change them into glorious bodies! What's a glorious body? The same kind of body Jesus had after he defeated death and rose victorious to live and reign forever!   What must that even mean – that our eternal body will be "like his own"? *We'll come back there!*

The Early Church people are really struggling with this truth. The Philippians letter we just read from doesn't show up until 33 years after Jesus' ascension! As we have already studied – the very first communication to arrive on this subject is 22 years after Jesus' resurrection. *(1st and 2nd Thessalonians)*

When we get to Paul's second flurry of letters, the 1st and 2nd letters to the Corinthians *(five years after the Thessalonians letters)* he asked them straight out:

Why are you not believing what I already wrote the Thessalonians? Why are so many of you not believing that you, yourself, are going to bodily resurrect from the dead? You do believe that Jesus did resurrect right?   Yes, but, but...?

We need to be charitable to these people. They were all living in horrible times of persecution. Jesus is by no means the only person in the first century to be crucified on a cross!   Thousands of Christians were executed in that same way including Peter.

Imagine a family trying to get to the store to get supplies, and there was their family member hanging alongside the road.

- And the Romans had a way of quickly tidying up. They would put more wood at the base of the crosses and burn the whole lineup to ashes.

- That's the kind of things these people were experiencing everyday – and they are trying to fit the horror of what they are going through into the template of the new information Paul was giving them about what is coming next.

And Paul does that thing he does a lot of, verbally grabbing their sagging hearts and lifting them up to see that this life is not really about this life! They hadn't caught on to what the old North Carolina revival preacher of the last century, Vance Havner, used to say: **"The hope of dying is the only thing that is keeping me alive!"** Paul was trying to get their eyes up to that point. Maybe some of us need that today to remember what we said a couple chapters ago:

If this world is our home, then death is taking us AWAY FROM our home! If Heaven is actually our home, then death is taking us away from here TO our eternal home!

The Corinthians had not caught on to that, and Paul over and over tries to press that truth home to their minds and hearts! This isn't your final destination! Remember Jesus' words? "My Father's home has many rooms. I've gone to prepare a place for you!"

So, to you dear Corinthians: **2 Corinthians 4:8, 9, 14 NIV: "We are hard pressed on every side, but not crushed; perplexed, but not in despair; persecuted, but not abandoned; struck down, but not destroyed."** *Why? Why are we not crushed, not driven to despair, not forsaken by our gracious God and not destroyed?* **"because we know that the one who raised the Lord Jesus from the dead will also raise us up with Jesus!"**

"But will he?" That's what they were thinking. Everywhere they turned, evil seemed to be winning. And they weren't quick to draw the conclusion that God had a divine, and eternal, answer to it all.

They were seriously discouraged. "Why? Jesus, why? If you won the battle over satan by dying for humanity's sins on the cross. If you defeated sin and death by rising victoriously from the grave – why Jesus don't you just come back tomorrow, and put an end to all of this chaos?"

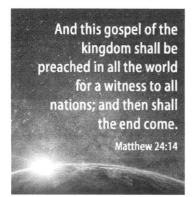

And this gospel of the kingdom shall be preached in all the world for a witness to all nations; and then shall the end come.

Matthew 24:14

But as we said previously, as much as they wanted that to happen, they knew it wasn't going to happen! Jesus himself had said he was going to "build his Church" *(on this earth)* and that the gates of hell would not prevail against it. That he would empower the church to bind and loose on earth what had already been bound and loosed in Heaven. (Matthew 16:18-19) They knew that Jesus had said in his last great prophetic sermon in **Matthew 24:14: "This** gospel of the kingdom shall be preached in all the earth," and then, *(and only then)* "the end would come!"

Some of them may have indeed still believed that the earth was flat – but they had enough geographic knowledge to know that the few churches that had so far been planted weren't even close to "preaching the Gospel to the whole world for a witness to all nations!"

So here is Paul purposely grabbing their 57 AD spiritual chin, and lifting it way up:

> **2 Corinthians 4:16-18 NIV: "Therefore we do not lose heart. Though outwardly we are wasting away, yet inwardly we are being renewed day by day. For our light and momentary troubles are achieving for us an eternal glory that far outweighs them all. <u>So we fix our eyes not on what is seen, but on what is unseen, since what is seen is temporary, but what is unseen is eternal</u>."**

There's truth here for all of us in our 21st century setting today. Even as you are dealing with things on the outside that are wrecking your earthly existence – your body, your mind, your will, and your emotions. As those things are being hammered with the wrecking ball of life in this sin-cursed world, the inner you can be built up into an inner spiritual giant that will end up reigning with Jesus for all of eternity. **"You're training for reigning!"** *(You say "I don't feel like that Sam" – me neither! But that's exactly what Paul is saying!)*

- Right while your body is sagging and shrinking, your eternal soul is supposed to be expanding!

- Your "light and momentary troubles" *(which often feel like monstrous and never-ending troubles)* are building into you – "An eternal glory."

Understand something here. Their "light and momentary troubles" may have lasted right up to them taking their last earthly breath, but <u>in God's much bigger picture</u> –they had <u>only used a finger-snap</u> of the time he had graciously given them when they were born onto this planet.*(That's us too!)* We only use a "finger-snap" of time on this planet – the rest is reserved for us in eternity!

2 Corinthians 4:18 NIV: "So we fix our eyes not on what is seen, but on what is unseen, since what is seen is temporary, but what is unseen is eternal."

I found several online stats on the "what is seen" part. I'm not sure how accurate these figures are, but they are probably not too far off. About the information that passes though our brains each day – we lose: [13]

> 40% of it in 20 minutes
> 55% of it in one hour
> 70% of it in two days
> 90% in one month

Here's another: People forget 50-80% of what happens after one day and 97-98% in one month. [14]

If you happen to be a little older than most, and you are reading this today, you might be thinking "What did I just read? Who are you, again, Mr. Author Man? What day is it?" Don't sweat it – we are all in this boat together!

But that's why I often preach *(from personal experience)* the things that are eating us up today, controlling our mind and emotions – a large majority of them we won't even remember in two weeks! That's why **"we fix our eyes not on what is seen, but on what is unseen, since what is seen is temporary, but what is unseen is eternal."**

Spend as much time as possible on the eternal because that's what you will still be remembering 1,000 years from now!

> **Romans 8:18: "What we suffer now is nothing compared to the glory that will be revealed in us later!"**

Paul writes in the next chapter – which was just the next paragraph of the same letter in 2nd Corinthians.

> **2 Corinthians 5:1-4: "For we know that when this earthly tent we live in is taken down** *(that is, when we die and leave this earthly body)*, **we will have a house in heaven, an eternal body made for us by God himself! We grow weary in our present bodies, and we long to put on our heavenly bodies like new clothing. for <u>we will put on Heavenly bodies; we will not be spirits without bodies</u>.** *(Another clue!)* **"While we live in these earthly bodies, we groan and sigh, but it's not that we want to die and get rid of these bodies that clothe us.** *(Everybody wants to go to Heaven but nobody wants to die!)* **Rather, <u>we want to put on our new bodies so that these dying bodies will be</u>**

swallowed up by life!'" What first seems to trap us – actually frees us!

"We are not in the land of the living moving toward the land of the dying – we are in the land of the dying moving toward the land of the living!"

It turns out the Corinthians were having a bit of a brain-freeze about this whole thing. They didn't want to die, because they were still not sure what was going to happen to them after death. Don't forget this was all very new to them. *Here's part of their problem:*

James - 49 A.D.	Philemon - 62-63 A.D.	Hebrews - 67.
First Thess. - 52-53.	Ephesians - 62-63.	First Peter - 67-68.
Second Thess. - 52-53.	Luke - 63.	Second Peter - 68.
Galatians - 55.	Acts - 64.	Jude - 68.
First Corinthians - 57.	First Timothy - 65.	
Second Corinthians- 57.	Titus - 65.	John - 85
Romans - 57-58.	Second Timothy – 66	Epistles of John 90-94
Philippians - 62-63.	Mark - 66.	Revelation 95 A.D.
Colossians - 62-63.	Matthew - 67.	*(approximations)*

- Notice: All of the Epistles *(from James to Jude)* comes crashing in on the Early Church within 19 years! It was a lot to grasp – and we know from Paul's later letters that there was confusion and disagreement that needed to be addressed.

As stated: not everybody in 57 AD Corinth was buying what Paul had written to the Thessalonians. Oddly, <u>they did believe that Jesus had risen from the dead</u>! That was the whole reason they established a church to start with! If they hadn't believed in Jesus' resurrection, they would have had no purpose to start a church, surely not just to worship some dead Jewish guy. Anybody who even went to a Christian church was putting a huge target on their back. Gentiles living 1900 miles from Jerusalem weren't going to do that for some dead Jewish Rabbi! <u>They definitely believed in a crucified and risen Savior!</u>

But people who read the first 11 verses of 1 Corinthian 15 often think its point is trying to prove that Jesus has indeed risen from the dead. I've often used it myself as an Easter Sunday morning text, and may do it again sometime – because it does clearly state that "now Christ Jesus is

BUT NOW IS CHRIST

RISEN

**FROM THE DEAD,
AND BECOME THE**

FIRST FRUITS

OF THEM THAT SLEPT.

1 CORINTHIANS 15:20

risen from the dead" and gives an amazing argument of how many people saw him after he was risen. *(Everybody knew somebody who knew somebody who had personally met him after his resurrection!)*

- But Paul's point is not to prove that Jesus rose - but to prove that <u>he rose as the first-fruit</u> of everybody else who has died!

- The "first-fruits" indicate the whole rest of the crop is on the way! They all knew exactly what Paul meant because they lived in an agricultural society.

- Paul paints Jesus rising from the dead as the prime high-definition example of why we can expect to rise from the dead too!

1 Corinthians 15:22-23: "Just as everyone dies because we all belong to Adam, everyone who belongs to Christ will be given new life. But there is an order to this resurrection: <u>Christ was raised as the first of the harvest</u>; *(the first-fruits!)* then all who belong to Christ will be raised when he comes back."

- I honestly don't know why these Corinthians would believe so strongly in Jesus dying. Then by the testimony of so many, believe Jesus rose victoriously from the grave – but not believe that they were going to rise after they died as well!

Paul writes: "Guys, do you not remember me telling you that Jesus himself said in **John 5:24-26, 28-29: "I tell you the truth, those who listen to my message and believe in God who sent me have eternal life. They will never be condemned for their sins, but they have already passed from death into life. And I assure you that the time is coming, indeed it's here now, when <u>the dead will hear my voice</u>—<u>the voice of the Son of God</u>. And those who listen will live.** *(again)* **The Father has life in himself, and he has granted that same life-giving power to his Son... Don't be so surprised! Indeed, the time is coming when all the dead in their graves will hear the voice of God's Son, and they will rise again. Those who have done good will rise to experience eternal life, and those who have continued in evil will rise to experience judgment."**

Do you not remember this – the One you say you believe in with all your heart? *(They did!)* Paul starts 1 Corinthians 15:1 with the words, **"Let me now remind you, of the Good**

227

News I preached to you before. You welcomed it then, and you still stand firm in it." And then the whole chapter is about – *Jesus' resurrection and our resurrection!*

So finally Paul just pins the Corinthians to the wall about their unbelief. He presents it all like a lawyer unfolding his case and using a backwards argument to form a forward point – then he just states the obvious:

> **1 Corinthians 15:12-13: "But tell me this, since we preach that Christ rose from the dead, why are some of you saying there will be no resurrection of the dead? For if there is no resurrection of the dead, then Christ has not been raised either."**

So what are you guys saying? You firmly believe that Jesus died and rose from the dead, but you then believe that when you die, you will just rot in your graves?

- Do you really believe that Jesus, the Son of God, God incarnate in human flesh – went to all that trouble to come to this earth to save you from your sins –just so you could live with the guilt and power of sin gone from your life for, say, the next 20 years, or up until the heavy hand of the Roman Empire dislodges your head from off your neck?

- Does it make sense to you that pagans would come to Christ as their Lord and Savior immediately putting a huge target on their back? The Romans pick them up two weeks later, hoist them up on a cross until the life drains out of them and then burn their bodies to ashes.

- Do you believe that what Jesus did was to last for a whole month in those new Believer's lives – or was it, in fact, supposed to last for all of eternity?

1 Corinthians 15:19: "And <u>if our hope in Christ is only for this life</u>, we are more to be pitied than anyone in the world."

You guys are "just plum pitiful"! Ok, Mr. Apostle Paul, but we're not trying to be rebellious. We really do love Jesus with all our hearts. But we are just struggling with this whole idea of living on after we die. Look at these bodies, look at the deterioration – look at your own body Paul! Most of us will probably die violently and our bodies will be cut to pieces or burned to ashes.

We know what you wrote to the Thessalonians about our soul going to Heaven, and at the last trumpet our graves here emptying out and our bodies rising to meet Jesus in the air. But we are struggling to understand! How can we make sense out of living forever with Jesus with these broken-down husks we call human bodies? Paul crafts an illustration just for them: "Listen up guys. You all understand agriculture. God has given you a perfect illustration to help you understand what is getting ready to happen to you!"

You take a shriveled-up kernel of corn and you bury it in the ground. It decomposes, but a couple of weeks later up pops a green little shoot, which then become a corn stalk, which then begins to yield lots and lots of new kernels of corn!

Likewise, you take a petrified, shriveled-up human corpse, or a bunch of ashes from the foot of a cross, and you plant them in the ground. And one day, by the power of Jesus' own resurrection, you will have sown a "perishable" body. But, lo and behold – out of the ground will come, an "imperishable" body!

1 Corinthians 15:42-44, 50: "It is the same way with the resurrection of the dead. Our earthly bodies are planted in the ground when we die, but they will be raised to live forever. Our bodies are buried in brokenness, but they will be raised in glory. They are buried in weakness, but they will be raised in strength. They are buried as natural human bodies, but they will be raised as spiritual bodies.

"What I am saying, dear brothers and sisters, is that our (present) physical bodies cannot inherit the Kingdom of God. These dying bodies cannot inherit what will last forever." But they don't have to – because <u>what you plant into the ground on this side, isn't at all what is coming out of the ground on the other side</u>! Paul unfolds to the Corinthians brand new news. *("Mysterion," that which was hidden and is now being revealed.)*

1 Corinthians 15:51-52: "But let me reveal to you a wonderful secret. (mysterion) We will not all die, but we will all be transformed! It will happen in a moment, in the blink (ἀτόμος) of an eye, when the last trumpet is blown. For when the trumpet sounds, those

who have died will be raised to live forever. And we
(Believers) who are living will also be transformed."

But Sam, What will my new body be like? We already mentioned it once, but I have found it in Scripture six different times.

1) Our new body will be *(become)* like Jesus' resurrected, glorified body. *What does that even mean?*

2) Our new body will be the <u>same</u> body, but <u>different</u>! Transformed!

> a) An old dying body → Becomes a new living-forever body!
>
> b) A body with physical properties → but re-made like Jesus!
>
> c) The same body, but different → brokenness to glory, weakness to strength, natural body to a spiritual body.
>
> *d)* Not just our soul, but also our body → becomes free of/from the curse of sin!

CHAPTER 13

Chapter 14

Jesus is the first-fruits of resurrection!

Let's keep ourselves locked inside the Corinthian heads and the huge hiccup in their theology in 1 Corinthians 15. They weren't struggling with whether or not Jesus had risen from the dead. But they were, for some reason, having a serious problem believing that they were going to rise too!

> **1 Corinthians 15:12-13: "But tell me this, since we preach that Christ rose from the dead, <u>why are some of you saying there will be no resurrection of the dead</u>?** (*for you?*) **For if there is no resurrection of the dead** (*for you*)**, then Christ has not been raised either!"**

Some of the earliest Christians had literally seen Jesus die. They saw his lifeless mangled body dragged from the cross and wrapped for burial. They then saw that same body, three or more days later, all seemingly back to normal, in fact more than normal, with only a residual scarring from the nails and spear. Clearly something very miraculous had happened to Jesus! So why, why couldn't they believe that something just as miraculous was going to happen to them?

That really was the sticking point of what was, or was not happening in their heads. Watch what Paul then asked them; **1 Corinthians 15:35-36: "But someone may ask, 'How will the dead be raised? <u>What kind of bodies will they</u>**

have?' What a foolish question!" (ἄφρων – *aphron: Fool!* – *You fools!*)

I'm not sure Paul is the kind of guy we would have all enjoyed having a cup of coffee with! I would sure hate to ask him a question and have him say – fool! I might mention to him that Jesus himself warned against calling somebody a "raca," which was the Aramaic version of "fool." But we are reading inspired Scripture here from the pen of the Apostle Paul *(or his scribe?)* so I guess we just thank God for outspoken people! ☺

But my mind more links with the Corinthians and their "need to know" on this subject. And Paul must have caught that, because he then goes on to answer their question with some amazing new "inspired by the Holy Spirit" truths.

 Here's ancient Corinth where Paul lived and walked for at least 1 ½ years of his life. I walked down that main street and stood in what they said were the ancient churches and pondered the "why" inside my egg-shaped head.

These people died off fast. The average lifespan in the first century was only 35 years of age. That's skewed a lot by the high rate of infant mortality, and the fact that the pagan Romans could legally kill a child in the womb, or even long after coming out of the womb. They could kill their own child that they didn't want, or offer them as a sacrifice to an idol up until age 8 and not be breaking any Roman law.

But the average "old" person was about 55 years old, not anything like our life-span today. But in a society where there were no hospitals, except for the rich, the Roman hierarchy, and the military – people's bodies just wasted away from disease in five or six decades. The disciple John lived perhaps into his mid 80's, when he wrote the book of Revelation, which was very unusual.

So the "eyewitness people", listed in the first part of 1 Corinthians 15 who saw Jesus' resurrected body, were probably all already dead or "barely living" 1900 miles away in Israel. Peter was still alive and traveling around the Empire. But the Corinthians did have second generation accounts, not least of which was Paul's. "I talked directly to the disciples – they told me…"

When you are used to seeing 45 year olds in your society with bodies riddled with disease, and the Christians even younger than that who are regularly being decapitated, fed to wild animals, and burned into a pile of ashes – and you put what you are seeing with your own eyes every day, alongside of the 1 Thessalonians 4 passage that "the dead are going to rise to meet Jesus in the air." – There is an obvious disconnect there, an obvious missing piece of the puzzle.

We are still having discussions on this subject 1900 years later, and we aren't all agreeing. If you die at 85 years of age now, and you're hobbling along with an obviously deteriorating body and only one good eye – what will your body be like when you get to Heaven? I happen to think that the Corinthian's question was a very good one and deserved something more than – Fool!

1 Corinthians 15:35: "How will the dead be raised? What kind of bodies will they have?"

That is actually a wonderful question, Mr. Apostle Man, one we are still wanting an answer to today. And thankfully Paul does back off and under the inspiration of the Holy Spirit, goes on to fill in more details. Before we go there:

They had some clues and you have the same clues, and more, too! All of them had the details of Jesus' own resurrection. While the Corinthians didn't have any of the Gospels in written form yet, they did have copies of the notes. And they had the second-hand witness of people coming to Corinth who had spoken with the first-hand witnesses. Here are some details that Luke would eventually put into print:

> **Luke 24:36-37: "And just as they were telling about it, Jesus himself was suddenly standing there among them. 'Peace be with you,' he said. But the whole group was startled and frightened, <u>thinking they were seeing a ghost</u>!"** Obviously, seeing somebody that they had watched all the blood drain out of standing in front of them alive – was somewhat "attention-grabbing"!

His body had been mangled beyond recognition (*which is what Isaiah 53 had prophesied*). And now, just three days later, he's standing there with an almost perfect body except for his hands, feet, and his spear-driven side. Eight days later he has doubting Thomas putting his fingers into the wounds. There are instructive clues here:

Luke 24:38-42: "'Why are you frightened?" he asked. 'Why are your hearts filled with doubt? Look at my hands. Look at my feet. You can see that it's really me. <u>Touch me and make sure that I am not a ghost, because ghosts don't have bodies, as you see that I do.</u>' *(That's a really important statement for us!)* **As he spoke, he showed them his hands and his feet. Still they stood there in disbelief, filled with joy and wonder. Then he asked them, 'Do you have anything here to eat?' They gave him a piece of broiled fish."**

We have Paul in 1 Corinthians 15 on hold for a moment. I'm going to insert some Scriptures in here that are really important. We won't dissect them, but they need to be put in right about now because they give strong clues about what we are going to be like after we die and resurrect.

Paul is going to say in **1 Corinthians 15:49 NASB: "As we have born the image of the earthly (Adam), so <u>will we bear the image of the Heavenly</u> (Jesus)!"**

John would later write **1 John 3:2 NIV: "We know that when Jesus appears** *(phaneroo – made manifest),* **<u>we shall be like him,</u> for we shall see him as he is."** *Before this thing is over you are going to be "like Jesus" – what must that mean?)*

Paul will write to the Philippian church **Philippians 3:20-21: "We are eagerly waiting for him to return as our Savior. He will take our weak mortal bodies and change them into glorious bodies like his own."** *Wow!*

So your weak mortal body is going to one day be a glorified body like Jesus' own? He's not just a spirit floating in the clouds –he has a body! *And it*'s not just any body, it's his body! He's recognizable! After three days Jesus' spirit *(wherever it went)* came back to the tomb and entered into the same body! Jesus didn't appear in some new "eyes like flames of fire, face shining like the sun," *(Revelation 1)* while his original earthly body continued to rot in the grave! You say: Sam, that's not a big deal to us that Jesus reentered his original body. Are you sure?

> Part of our "salvation" in this present life, is the Holy Spirit transforming us from the inside out by remaking the old inner us into "new creations in Christ Jesus,"*(That's in our soul.)* But then **Romans 8:11 NIV:** also says "**And if the Spirit of him who raised Jesus from the dead is living in you, he who raised Christ from the dead will also give life to your mortal bodies because of his Spirit who lives in you.**"

- Doesn't it make sense that if "sanctification" in this life is about our heart/soul being cleansed from sin and freed from the bondage of the curse of sin, that process will be completed when we finally meet Jesus?

- Doesn't it make sense that some future glorification process applies to the cleansing of the bondage of the curse of sin in our bodies, finalized as we rise to meet Jesus in the air?

- So much so that if your glorified soul got into Heaven without your glorified body, the fullness of God's process in you would not be complete!

1 Corinthians 15:35, 49: "How will the dead be raised? What kind of bodies will they have? As we have born the image of the earthly Adam, so <u>will we bear the image of the Heavenly</u> – Jesus!"

Q: T or F: So the same number of bodies that die will be raised back to life?

Q: T or F: The same bodies that go into the ground will come back out?

Q: T or F: But the "same" body will be "the same but different" – "glorified."

Q: T or F: The glorified, risen Jesus still had his same basic physical, recognizable form.

However, when we see Jesus in Revelation 1:13-16, he doesn't look the same at all. *(eyes like flames of fire, feet like polished bronze, voice thundering like mighty ocean waves, face shining like the sun, a sharp two-edged sword coming out of his mouth.)*

I'm not sure how you can figure all that into what your own resurrected, glorified body will be like one day. But you could also add in the fact that Jesus seemed to retain his personality, seemed to stay friends with people he already knew, and seemed to be able to enjoy eating – that excites some of us deeply! *(All those old jokes about all donuts, cake, and fried chicken in Heaven having no calories!)*

But my bigger point here is: Everything I just said *(except the reference from Revelation 1),* everything else we just looked at from the mouth of Jesus was available to the Corinthians! Even the letter to the Romans was written the same year as the two Corinthian letters. *(In fact many think Paul wrote it from Corinth, so it's likely he taught them those principles.)* Somebody there had to be wrestling with these Scriptures and the notes of Jesus' sermons. Somebody had to be saying, "Guys, look exactly at how Jesus came back from the dead; shouldn't that be saying something to us?" And that is what Paul dives into *(after calling them air-heads).*

> **1 Corinthians 15:42-43: "It is the same way with the resurrection of the dead. Our earthly bodies are planted in the ground when we die, but they will be raised to live forever. Our bodies are buried in brokenness, but they will be raised in glory."**

There is no way to sugar coat death if you have been present when people have died. I have been there on many occasions when a person breathes their last breath, and the final bit of life drains from their body, and it is not a good experience, ever! Remember the Early Church was regularly watching those dearest to them die, "buried in brokenness/dishonor." Maybe they, like us, put on the

person's best clothes – but there is no good way to camouflage death!

But for most of us *(except for the few who will be alive when Jesus returns)*, we will be "planted in brokenness." These bodies were not designed by God to ever die – they were never intended to be under the ground covered with dirt.

I came across this picture of my Grandma's funeral *(not too many years ago. She died at age 102!)* But I was struck by the fact that many of the other people in the picture are gone from this life too, including my mother, and dad, and my young cousin on the front row. That's the curse of sin! But remember God's salvation is the complete antidote for the curse of sin, soul and body forever! What will for most of us being **"planted in brokenness" – will be "raised in glory"**! Glory is a "God" word. That word "glory" is almost always used to describe God, and here it now is being used to describe us after our death and our resurrection! *(raised in glory – glorified!)*

> **1 Corinthians 15: 43-44, 50: "They are buried in weakness, but they will be raised in strength. They are buried as natural human bodies, but they will be raised as spiritual bodies.**
>
> **"What I am saying, dear brothers and sisters, is *that our physical bodies cannot inherit the Kingdom of God.* These dying bodies cannot inherit what will last forever!"**

Why? Because the stain of sin is written into every cell! Because the bondage of the curse of sin is pulling at every molecule every moment of every day. Even something as important as gravity is tugging us downward all day, everyday – and the curse turns even gravity from a blessing into a curse.

So one day satan and the curse of sin commits its final deed in our life. It brings every molecule in our body shuddering to a stop. "Yes," yells satan! "I killed another one. I took the body God made in his own image and I brought death where God had infused life!"

That "dead shriveled seed" is planted into the ground. Then one day, Bam! Out of the deadness comes life, but this time it's eternal life!

> **1 Corinthians 15:51-52: "But let me reveal to you a wonderful secret. We will not all die, but we will all be transformed! It will happen in a moment** *(atomos)*, **in the blink** *(twinkle)* **of an eye, when the last trumpet is blown. For when the trumpet sounds,** *(that's the same 1 Thessalonians 4 trumpet)* **those who have died will be raised to live forever. And we who are living will also be transformed."**

So the ones who are still living are going to be fast-tracked through the sin-dying – eternal life emerging process, because by the time we meet Jesus in the air we will all have been transformed!

> **1 Corinthians 15:53-54: "For our dying bodies** *(that's the sin-cursed ones)* **must be transformed into bodies that will never die;** *(that's the ones released from the curse of sin!)* **our mortal bodies must be transformed into immortal bodies. Then, when our dying bodies have been transformed into bodies that will never die, this Scripture will be fulfilled: 'Death is swallowed up in victory.'"**

The Corinthians should have been getting pretty excited by this time. Remember their concern was for all those who were already dead. And they apparently had serious questions about *"rising to meet Jesus in the air" with their old beat up sin-cursed bodies.*

Paul pushes all that out of their minds. His language is unusually expressive here, and these Early Church people *(who spoke and read Greek)* would have no trouble understanding how "over the top" Paul is in his declaration! <u>Death is swallowed up in victory</u>!

What Paul is saying, and what the Corinthians undoubtedly understood him to be saying, was that Jesus was finally going to destroy sin's effects in the lives of the Believers (<u>both in their souls and in their bodies</u>) so that sin couldn't do any further harm!

 It's kind of like a roaring forest fire that is raging, burning up everything in sight – and then the heroic first-responders come and put the fire out so that it can "not do any more harm." The problem, of course, is that it has already destroyed everything behind it – which is what a life-time of sin has done in each of our lives! And it's not even always just our own sins. It's often the vicious sins of others against us. The raging forest fire of sin's curse has left a lot of blackened tree stubs in our rear view mirrors. The ultimate example of what God is actually up to is supposed to be exploding open in our minds.

1) What looks, on the surface, like a victory for sin and satan in our dying bodies and in our final breath and the decay of our living tissue is utterly reversed!

2) Death ends up dying in defeat – and our bodies end up living on in eternal victory!

3) Death is not just defeated in that it can't do any more harm! Everything that has been done is now undone. All sin's effects have been totally reversed! Death is literally "swallowed up in victory"!

4) Death, sin, satan, and the curse, who thought they had us beaten, are swallowed into its abyss and digested! Death not only completely loses its stranglehold, but it is completely swallowed up itself instead!

Paul literally begins to taunt death, and indirectly satan, who is the author of death!

> *"Death is swallowed up in victory.*
> *O death, where is your victory?*
> *O death, where is your sting?"*

Sting - κέντρον – like the stinger of a bee. In fact, in reality *(just like the stinging honey bee loses its stinger)* when death plunged it's stinger into Jesus on the cross, <u>it left its stinger there</u>! Jesus actually bore the sting of death for us – so that death for us has no actual stinger!

- The dying process is still a hated enemy. We don't embrace it. Nobody wants to die! It buzzes around us and makes us dodge a lot!

- But death left its stinger in Jesus on the cross, and its been flopping around in the throes of its own death ever since. Satan just hasn't quite figured that all out yet!

Hebrews 2:14-15: "Because God's children are human beings—made of flesh and blood—the Son also became flesh and blood. For only as a human being could he die, and only by dying could he break the power of the devil, who had the power of death. Only in this way could he set free all who have lived their lives as slaves to the fear of dying." The actual "stinger of death" stayed lodged in our crucified and risen Savior! He <u>set free</u> all of us who lived our lives as slaves to the fear of dying!

1 Corinthians 15:56-57: "For sin is the sting that results in death, and the law gives sin its power. But thank God,

He gives us victory over sin and death through our Lord Jesus Christ!"

CHAPTER 14

HEAVEN: Part IV

CHAPTER 14

Chapter 15

What we do on this earth is just the introduction to our eternal lives!

I am going to move us *(biblically)* right up to the edge of the Throne Room of Heaven itself in this chapter. I have pulled everything in the Bible that actually describes inside of Heaven, and I'm going to try to unfold it to you.

 The week I was writing this material, my wife, Sue, and I had a pastor friend, L.C. Campbell, and a cousin, Pat Chess, graduate to Heaven. We got the news of their deaths ten minutes apart.

I sat in a board meeting that week. L.C. Campbell had been part of the board made up of pastors from several different traditions. I prayed aloud during the meeting about God calling L.C. home to Heaven, and how this life was just preparation for the next life, how he had obviously reached the end of what God wanted for him on this earth, and, how he had moved on to the "real eternal reason" that God had birthed him onto this planet.

Afterward, the pastors got into a spirited, *(friendly)* discussion with one pastor saying, "No, God really wanted to heal L.C. and keep him serving here on earth."

I, with months of studying this material etched into my brain, was making the argument, "No, what we do on this earth is just the introduction to our eternal lives!" The main part of our eternal existence is what we will be doing once we enter the "next-life part" of our future! This life *(however long or short)* is just preparation for the next life! *Many people are credited with the following quote:*

We tend to think we are in the land of the living, moving toward the land of the dying. But we are actually in the land of the dying moving toward the land of the living – eternally!

What a vivid illustration those two deaths were for me, for exactly where I was in writing this Heaven material. Both Pat Chess and L.C. were right then *(as I was first typing the above words)* freshly in the presence of God! Not everybody agrees with that view. Some think they will hang out in some holding place for a future resurrection, but the Apostle Paul seems rather clear in 1 Thessalonians 4. *(This should be sounding familiar.)*

> **1 Thessalonians 4:13-14: "Now, dear brothers and sisters, we want you to know what will happen <u>to the Believers</u> who have died so you will not grieve like people who have no hope. For since we believe that Jesus died and was raised to life again, <u>we also believe that when Jesus returns, God will bring back with him the Believers who have died.</u>"** *(There it is!)*

Let me hammer that home with another piece of inspired Scripture to the Corinthians. We've seriously focused on what Paul told the Corinthians about their future resurrection in the most famous passage on the subject in the whole Bible. *(1 Corinthians 15)* But let me show you something else in Paul's second letter to those same Believers in Corinth.

> **2 Corinthians 5:4-5: "While we live in these earthly bodies, we groan and sigh, but it's not that we want to die and get rid of these bodies that clothe us. Rather, we want to put on our new bodies so that these dying bodies will be swallowed up by life. God himself has prepared us for this, and <u>as a guarantee he has given us his Holy Spirit</u>."**

That is something we should lock on to! The infilling Holy Spirit, who is indwelling us Believers now, is supposed to be viewed as a tiny sliver of what is eventually coming for us! In fact, that has already exploded into reality in Pat Chess, who really struggled in her earthly body the last few years of her life. <u>The "deposit, the down payment," of the Holy Spirit will then become the explosive fullness of the presence of the Holy Spirit!</u> That has to be really important!

> **2 Corinthians 5:6, 8: "So we are always confident, even though we know that as long as we live in these bodies we are not at home with the Lord, Yes, we are fully confident, and we <u>would rather be away from these earthly bodies, for then we will be at home with the Lord</u>."** *(See that?)*

- So those two Saints, who died just as I was writing this material, and the others who died in our church *(and yours)* this last year, and all your departed

Believing loved ones <u>are right now in the presence of Jesus</u>!

I've personalized here what Paul wrote to the Corinthians. Let's just assume for the sake of personalizing this passage that Jesus is not going to return in your lifetime, and we are all going to die. *I'm not sure that is true at all!* But it's too hard to personalize this to include both possibilities. So even if you are sure Jesus' coming is right around the corner of the calendar, and you are still going to be living, please read along for the next few seconds.

1 Corinthians 15:42-44, 50: "My earthly body will be planted in the ground when I die, but <u>I WILL be raised to live forever</u>! My body will be buried in brokenness, but my old earthly body will be <u>raised in GLORY</u>. It will be buried in weakness, but it will be raised in strength. It will be buried as a natural human body, but it will be raised as a spiritual body! My <u>physical body cannot inherit the Kingdom of God</u>! This dying body cannot inherit what will last forever!"

1 Corinthians 15:51-55: "God is revealing to me a wonderful secret. It will happen in a moment, in the twinkling of an eye, when the last trumpet is blown. For when that trumpet sounds, we who have died WILL be raised to live forever. And those who are still living will also be transformed. But my dying body MUST be transformed into a body that will NEVER die; my mortal body MUST be transformed into an immortal body! WHEN my dying body has been transformed into a body that will never die, THEN this Scripture will be fulfilled: 'Death is swallowed

up in victory. O death, where is your victory? O death, where is your sting?'"

Jesus wasn't considered to be "resurrected" until his "still-living-inner-being" rejoined his formerly dead body and he walked out of the tomb!

We say we know Jesus is alive because his tomb is empty! Jesus holds the keys of death and hell and offers each of us eternal life because there was/is not a decomposing corpse left lying in the tomb! And somehow that same truth also applies to you and me!

God says that your decomposing dust is going to rise to meet Jesus in the air, and as it rises, your body will be transformed "from dying to forever alive," from mortal to immortal, from weakness to ultimate strength, from natural to spiritual, from brokenness to GLORY *(glorified)* whatever that means? – *we're getting there!*

So there are two points here that have been burying their  way into my egg-shaped head for the first time in my life. The first has to do with why is it so important to God that this body, this earthly shell that houses my soul, why does this body need to end up in Heaven? Why aren't we all issued little cookie cutter triangle-headed alien bodies?

Why is it so important that when you get to Heaven you ultimately end up there with that same body, but glorified, transformed, immortal, spiritual? Here's the Biblical answer: When Adam and Eve ate the fruit, God had told them that if they ate, they would surely die! *(Genesis 3:3)* They did eat, and they did die – and everyone following them!

> **Romans 5:12: "When Adam sinned, sin entered the world. Adam's sin brought death, so death spread to everyone, for everyone sinned."**

> **Romans 6:23: "For the wages of sin is death, but the free gift of God is eternal life in Christ Jesus our Lord!"** *This is Paul's huge theme in Romans 5,6,7,and 8.* We can make the case *(and do)* that Paul is talking about spiritual death, but few of us doubt he is talking about physical death too. Unless Jesus returns first – we are going to bear the physical wages of sin*! But – here's something huge:*

> **Romans 5:15, 17: "But there is a great difference between Adam's sin and God's gracious gift. <u>For the sin of this one man, Adam, brought death to many</u>. But even greater is God's wonderful grace and <u>his gift of forgiveness to many</u> through this other man, Jesus Christ.** (This is so important – what Adam's sin destroyed – God's grace is going to make whole!) **For the sin of this one man, Adam, caused death to rule over many.** *(All! Except Enoch and Elijah – I read somebody who said that the only three people in Heaven who will still have their earthly bodies are Enoch, Elijah, and Jesus! 'Dude, have you not read all these Scriptures we are reading?'* **But**

even greater is God's wonderful grace and his gift of righteousness, for all who receive it will live in triumph over SIN and DEATH through this one man, Jesus Christ."

Jesus' atoning death on the cross was designed to fix more than the effects of sin on our soul. It was also designed to fix the effects of sin on our body!

We can even make the case, when we get to the last two chapters of the Bible *(in this study on Heaven – and we most definitely will)* that Jesus' sin atonement will even reach as far as correcting the effects of the curse of sin on this planet and the whole universe – with a new Heavens and New Earth! But let's stay, for now, with what God is promising to do with our sin-cursed, sin-soaked, sin-destroyed bodies as this life winds down and as our eternal future unfolds.

#1) A key element of "the wages of sin" is the "dying" of the physical human body. Therefore, salvation from sin has to involve reversing the effects of sin and the curse on our human body! *(If you haven't tended to think of it that way, I'm suggesting to you – that's how God thinks! IMO)*

#2) If there is no physical resurrection of your body, then the death brought on by our sin *(the wages of sin that we earned)* has not been completely defeated!

#3) If your spirit goes to Heaven but your body stays in the grave – you are, in effect, still not "resurrected"! That was true of Jesus, until his spirit joined his body, and he came out of the grave alive leaving us with the evidence of an empty tomb!!

The next important part that is bouncing around in my head is this:

What if we don't really have the faintest concept of how massive of a deal what is going to happen to us is – as we rise to meet Jesus in the air? **1 Thessalonians 4:16-17: "For the Lord himself will come down from heaven with a commanding shout, with the voice of the archangel, and with the trumpet call of God. First, the believers who have died will rise from their graves. Then, together with them, we who are still alive and remain on the earth will be caught up in the clouds to meet the Lord in the air. Then we will be with the Lord forever."**

Try to let your imagination do something here with the soul of the Saints descending, our remains rising from our graves, along with the still alive. Remember, all the rising saints *(you included)* will be transformed in an *atomos*, the smallest particle of time. The explosive nature of that meeting will shock the world. I know that is not the way it has been often presented – as a quiet event everybody is unaware of. But remember, Jesus himself described this moment in time before he went to the cross.

> **Matthew 24:30-31: "And then at last, the sign that the Son of Man is coming will appear in the heavens, and there will be deep mourning among <u>all the peoples of the earth</u>. And <u>they will see the Son of Man coming</u> on the clouds of heaven WITH POWER AND GREAT GLORY. And he will send out his angels with the mighty blast of a trumpet, and they will gather his chosen ones from all over the world."**

Imagine yourself being part of this world-gripping event! You will be there one day! If you try to interpret the Bible literally, *(which I do)* the most basic rule of Bible interpretation is: "Interpret the Bible literally unless the author openly indicates they are being symbolic." *(If the plain sense makes sense, seek no other sense!)* The Bible, for the most part, is not a "secret code book." In most cases we are shooting straight to the plain sense of the text – digging deep into the inspired author's intent. And in my mind – it is most often literal.

#1) When Jesus says he will be returning with "power and great glory," he means just that!

#2) When he says he will send out his angels amid a trumpet blast to gather his Saints, he means just that!

#3) And when he says **"there will be great mourning among all the people of the earth,"** he means "all the people of the earth." His return will not be a "secret" in these days of cameras everywhere, posting every occurrence all over the world within 10 seconds.

So somewhere you one day will be rising out of the grave *(or off the ground)* in what I believe *(the Bible says)* is going to be a world shocking, "explosive event."

By the way, I find this same exact image in the last part of Revelation 6 and the first part of 7. I was going to leave this more controversial passage out, but it actually takes us from "meeting Jesus in the air" up into the Throne Room of Heaven. *(Where we are going to take our first look in a few pages.)*

Revelation 6:15-16: "Then everyone—the kings of the earth, the rulers, the generals, the wealthy, the powerful, and every slave and free person—all hid themselves in the caves and among the rocks of the mountains. And they cried to the mountains and the rocks, 'Fall on us and hide us from the face of the one who sits on the Throne and from the wrath of the Lamb.'"

Revelation 7:9: "After this, *(Kai eidon – a chronological time stamp)* **I saw a vast crowd, too great to count, from every nation and tribe and people and language, standing in front of the Throne and before the Lamb. They were clothed in white robes and held palm branches in their hands."**

- So you are rising to meet Jesus in the air along with every other Believer who is still living, and all the bodies of every other redeemed person who had ever lived.

- You and all of them/us, and Jesus, and the angels next stop will, according to Revelation 7:9, <u>be in the Throne Room of Heaven</u>!

But on the way up, besides your soul reuniting with your body completing the "process of resurrection" in you something else will happen "in a moment, in the twinkling of an eye"! Before you come into the direct presence of Jesus in the air, certainly before you set one foot through the "Pearly Gates" and make your way with millions, perhaps billions, of other Redeemed Saints and millions perhaps billions of angels, *(Angels that unknown to you have been protecting and guiding you toward that very moment in time.)* this has to happen! We'll look and then we'll talk about why!

> **1 Corinthians 15:51: "But let me reveal to you a wonderful secret. (μυστήριον) We will all be transformed!"** (ἀλλαγησόμεθα-Allaggo – transformed) (soma–body) **allagēsometha** | *ἀλλαγησόμεθα – the transformation of your body – into what? (1 Corinthians 15:50)* "Our physical body cannot inherit the Kingdom of God! This dying body cannot inherit what will last forever!"

- Hear this: your present body, as it exists right now, could not handle one second in the Throne Room of God!

- The fact is our present body could not handle one second in the direct presence of God, period! Moses thought he would pull that one off. "I want to see your glory, God," he asked. And God said you can't handle it, Moses my friend! When God allowed him to hide in a cave and see just a tiny sliver, his face shown so brightly for weeks that he had to wear a mask because the reflected glory terrified the three million Israelites.

That was just a sliver of God's presence! That's why Paul says the presence of the Holy Spirit in us is just a deposit, a down- payment on what is coming for us in Heaven.

Hear me when I say, in those times in your life when the power and presence of God has been the most real, the most intense, the most enveloping, I trust you have had those times. If you haven't, you need them, because those times are actually preparing you for Heaven! Those times, no matter how intense are like looking through a tiny crack in the curtain of God's presence. <u>If the curtain were suddenly pulled aside, you wouldn't last a millisecond</u>! *Our physical body cannot inherit the Kingdom of God! This dying body cannot inherit what will last forever!*

You hear people arrogantly talk about when they get to Heaven, how they are going to walk through those Pearly Gates, and they are going to walk straight up to the Throne, and they are going to ask God some tough questions that he is going to struggle to answer. No, they are not!

In the handful of times when people in Scripture had visions of Heaven – *(they weren't really there, they were just seeing in through a vision, through a crack in the curtain.)* When they stood at a long distance and saw into the Throne Room of God, they all had exactly the same reactions:

> 1) **Revelation 1:17 AMP: "When I saw him** *(Jesus)* **I fell at his feet as though dead."**

> 2) **Ezekiel 1:28 ESV: "When I saw it, I fell on my face."**

> 3) **Daniel 10:5-6: "I looked up and saw a man dressed in linen clothing, with a belt of pure gold around his waist. His body looked like a precious gem. His face flashed like lightning, and his eyes flamed like torches. His arms and feet shone like polished bronze, and his voice roared like a vast multitude of people."** *(Is this an angel? No! It's the pre-incarnate Jesus!)* This view of Jesus is almost word-for-word identical to what John writes in Revelation.

- So when we rise to meet Jesus in the air are we going to be seeing his earthly body with the nail scars in his hands or are we going to be seeing an awe-filled view of the King of Kings and Lord of Lords? (*John 20:25-27*)

- I'm not sure, but I can tell you what we are not going to do. We are not going to walk up to Jesus, slapping him on the back and saying, "Good to see you old buddy"!

- When we finally end up in the very presence of Jesus, we will have no strength even in our newly glorified legs. We will be falling before him in worship! Daniel was completely overwhelmed, and he was only seeing Jesus in a vision.

Daniel 10:7-11: "Only I, Daniel, saw this vision. The men with me saw nothing, but they were suddenly terrified and ran away to hide. So I was left there all alone to see this amazing vision. <u>My strength left me, my face grew deathly pale, and I felt very weak</u>. Then I heard the man speak, and when I heard the sound of his voice, <u>I fainted and lay there with my face to the ground</u>. Just then a hand touched me and lifted me, still trembling, to my hands and knees. And the man said to me, 'Daniel, you are very precious to God, so listen carefully to what I have to say to you.'"

I didn't really have much of a grasp on what L.C. and Pat Chess were experiencing as I was writing this material. But I think I am starting to get a tiny glimpse behind the curtain.

- They were in the direct presence of God, but they had not yet received their glorified, resurrected bodies.

- To get those they are going to have to return with Jesus when he comes back to rapture the Saints.

- If they are going to "come back with him," they are certainly "going to have met him ahead of time."

Have they already stepped into the Throne Room of God?

They are definitely not looking at their watches wondering  when you will arrive. There is no "time" in Heaven. To them next "year" is only a snap of a finger. If we don't arrive for 50 more earth years, that will still be a finger-snap to them.

A few people in our church have shared with me visions they have had of Heaven. I listened to and respect them. I have listened very carefully over the years to what one lady, Joyce Hietala, has vividly related to me.

- But there are a number of people out there in this world, who claim to have actually *(physically)* visited Heaven and come back.

- There are over 300 books that claim people, *(particularly children)* have been to Heaven and come back.

I will caution us as we dig even deeper. If a person's story about Heaven focuses on themselves instead of God, you should probably not put great weight in it. Because when we get to Heaven we are not going to be self-absorbed. I can tell you what Pat and L.C. are not doing right now – they are not focused on themselves.

Whatever is filling their Heavenly thoughts right now – it is a complete deep dive into the love of their Savior. They are absorbed in the worship of the God who loved them so much that he gave all so that they could spend eternity with Him.

CHAPTER 15

Chapter 16

So what are L.C., Pat, and Mike doing now?

So, another one of the dear Saints in our church, Mike Richards, went to be with Jesus the week I wrote this chapter. One Sunday, Mike was watching the sermon on YouTube. His wife Suzanne said he was excited at the thought of one day soon being in Heaven. Monday morning Mike had a massive stroke. By Tuesday morning he had left this world and entered the next.

So let's talk Biblical reality. What exactly happened to Mike? Where exactly is he now?

1) Purgatory? A lot of people in our church come from Roman Catholic roots. They were taught about a coming, future purgatory. What do you think? Did Mike go into extended future punishment to finish paying off the debt for his earthly sins? No, he did not! Jesus paid his/our sin debt in full. When you embrace Jesus' forgiveness your remaining sin debt is ZERO! Purgatory is not found anywhere in the 66 inspired books of Scripture.

2) Is he in some sort of "soul sleep"? Many people, even some evangelical Christians, believe that! Jesus told Mary and Martha that Lazarus was "sleeping." But then he raised him from the dead! *(It's a Greek "idiomatic" phrase – they understood then better than we understand it now.)* There's no such thing, biblically, as soul sleep!

3) Is he in a "holding place" called <u>sheol/OT; hades/NT</u>? No! That concept <u>is</u> in the OT and the early NT, but once Jesus defeats death, and rises from the grave – Jesus "sets the captives free" as Isaiah 61 had prophesied. He released the "righteous dead" and took them to Heaven with him. *(Ephesians 4:8-9: "When he ascended to the heights, he led a crowd of captives.") (Psalm 68:18)*

So where does the Bible say Mike is right now?!

2 Corinthians 5:6, 8: "So we are always confident, even though we know that as long as we live in these bodies we are not at home with the Lord. Yes, we are fully confident, and we would rather be away from these earthly bodies, for then we will be at home with the Lord." (ἐνδημέω – endemeo: *to be at home, to have gone home, to have reached your home.*) This is one of the proof texts we have already used to show that since Jesus' resurrection, when we Believers die, we are instantly in the presence of our Lord!

- But also there is the idea of where our real "HOME" actually is. **Hebrews 13:14: "For this world is not our permanent home; we are looking forward to a home (πόλιν/city) yet to come."**

- The idea that someday living in the New Jerusalem in a New Heavens and New Earth, *(talked about in the last two chapters of the Bible – we haven't gotten there yet, but we will.)* will be highly preferable to living here –

is not quite on most of our mental radars yet! We're very earthbound!

- I stood beside the body of my friend, Pastor L.C. Campbell at his memorial. *(I talked about him in the last chapter.)* I reached into his casket and touched his cold arm. I can assure you the thoughts going through my mind were not "Oh wow, I hope I get to stay on this planet for another 40 years." *(That kind of time tends to jolt our shallow earthbound thinking!)*

Philippians 3:20-21: "But we are *(right now)* citizens of Heaven, where the Lord Jesus Christ lives. And <u>we are eagerly waiting for him to return as our Savior</u>. He will take our weak mortal bodies and change them into glorious bodies like his own."

Colossians 3:1-2: "Since you have been raised to new life with Christ, <u>set your sights on the realities of Heaven</u>, where Christ sits in the place of honor at God's right hand. Think about the things of heaven, not the things of earth."

Please, don't get too attached to this world as your home! Your <u>real home</u> is already being prepared by Jesus on the other side of this life. Notice, Colossians 3:1-2 is in the form of a command. "Set your sights on the realities of Heaven! Think about the things of heaven, not the things of this earth!"

You say, "Sam, I can't help but think about the things of this earth. This is where my daily life is. This is where my job is, this is where the people I love are." This, right now, is my home! *I know – me too!*

So we "white knuckle" staying on this earth because something deep in our mind is telling us that we will be cheated out of a few days, or months, or years of enjoyment if we leave this earth too soon, and move on to Heaven.

Question: What have you done in the last three years that was so fantastic that it eclipses what is waiting for you in Heaven?

The problem is, Sam, I don't know what is waiting for me in Heaven. I'm still a little concerned about that "sitting on a cloud strumming a harp thing." We dealt with that 15 chapters ago. *(Whoever started that absurd idea was a nitwit!)*

But the part that really does make us all white-knuckle staying on this earth are <u>the relationships with the people we love</u>! *(That's very true.)* And perhaps that's a calling we sense God has given us on this planet that we don't yet feel we've completed. That's valid! *(The Apostle Paul expressed that too!)*

- It shouldn't be about the house we live in here, the nicest of which is going to seem like a matchbox, compared to your "mansion" in the New Jerusalem!

- We shouldn't be glued here because we'd like to take more exotic vacations – when in Heaven we will almost certainly be able to explore the most extreme parts of the universe – perhaps with just a thought from our glorified mind.

- If our glorified bodies are going to be like Jesus' own, when Jesus got ready to ascend to Heaven he just lifted off the planet! One would assume that option will also be available to you, too. You won't be needing the Starship Enterprise, to visit another galaxy!

And it needs to not be about your job. There are five places in the New Testament that say your future "occupation" will include "reigning with Jesus." Whatever that means, *(We'll look)* it's going to be a whole lot more fulfilling than your job is now!

- I promise you this: one earth hour after we arrive in Heaven, *(if we are thinking anything about earth at all)* we are going to say, "<u>Why in the world was I so intent on staying on the Earth</u>?"

Now the loved ones left behind, that is a big draw! L.C.'s son-in-law told Sue and I at the memorial that when the hospital finally allowed the family to visit him, family members were talking with him, praying with him, singing to him, and within minutes he just slipped away into Heaven. It's like something inside his brain said they are going to be OK until they join me on the other side – in our real home!

So back to Mike Richards arriving in Heaven, <u>What did he see</u>? <u>What did he do</u>? I'm not so much into a "he's probably standing in awe at the Heavenly gates made out of a single pearl or rubbing his feet on the streets of gold" kind of focus. I don't think those things are what will most draw our attention, even fractionally, when we first get to Heaven. *(Although we'll discuss their significance – soon.)*

There will be the immediate absence of the broken-down body caused by the curse of sin. I'm not sure how much of the pain we bore in this life we will remember. *(Probably not.)* But just from the standpoint of our redeemed souls at first being in Heaven. Try to imagine the effects of the sin that has torn you apart, on the inside, for years being washed out of your mind and soul. Imagine all the hurts and pain inflicted by others on you, and by you on yourself being washed from your memory with their corresponding inner chains of bondage inside of you being completely, totally gone.

- Imagine the insecurities and inadequacies that fill our mind constantly, and the "what if's" of fear *(often irrational fear)* brought on by the enemy of our soul, completely cleansed forever from our brain.

- Imagine that inner darkness that often invades our brains being divinely washed to a perfectly clear and unclouded mind.

- Imagine the weakness of mind that often leaves us not able to remember the most common things suddenly changed into the kind of un-fallen mind that Adam and Eve enjoyed in the Garden, filled with knowledge that was always just outside the edges of our brain.

- Imagine the tendency to sin, to pull away from the God you love, and who loves you so much, imagine that just being completely dissolved forever!

Now imagine the pervading presence of God that fills all of Heaven – the presence that in the most sacred times here on earth, we only experience like we were looking through a tiny crack in the curtain. Imagine that all-pervading presence filling every nook and cranny of your soul, breaking up all the scar tissue built in by the trauma of sin.

- Imagine the "Joy of the Lord" that every once in a while in this life breaks strongly through and lifts you to a place of worship that you would give anything to experience all the time. Imagine that becoming what continually lifts your soul <u>with no hindrances, no black corners, no hidden compartments</u> in ways you can not possibly now imagine while on this sin-drenched earth.

- We won't have our glorified body yet, but we don't need one for this kind of transformation to set in. You won't have yet walked down those streets of gold for all this sinless transformation to explode open inside of you.

ONE HOUR IN HEAVEN

Did I mention, One earth hour after we arrive in Heaven, we are going to say, "<u>Why in the world was I so intent on staying on the Earth</u>?"

You won't have traveled, by a thought in your mind, to the ends of the universe yet. You may not have yet seen the "mansion/room" Jesus went to prepare for you in the "New Jerusalem." You may not even have met Jesus face to face, or spent one minute in the Throne room worshipping God yet – but all the enticements of earth, after that first moment in Heaven, would not be able to pull you back to this sin-soaked planet. *(The people who say they have personally visited Heaven, yet <u>enjoyed</u> coming back to this earth, are in conflict with Scripture.)*

> **John 3:12-13:** Jesus *(to Nicodemus)* **"If you don't believe me when I tell you about earthly things, how can you possibly believe me if I tell you about heavenly things? <u>No one has ever gone to heaven and returned</u>. But the Son of Man has come down from heaven."** *(Jesus said that!)* (Some have had visions of what Heaven is like but, Jesus says they have not actually been there and returned!)

We need to insert some other important Biblical facts right about now. The Heaven you will arrive at one minute after you die is not the final Heaven you will reside in for all of eternity. Does that shock you? Wherever Heaven is right now, I suspect it is already a big place, I already showed you this shocking visual.

You may have figured out that I am intrigued by *the Bootes Void.* The empty place in space that is a billion light years across *(1,000 times bigger than our galaxy).* It is devoid of stars, gas and other normal matter, and it's also empty of the mysterious "dark matter" that permeates the universe.

I'm not saying that this massive void that we can't see into is where Heaven is right now, but wherever Heaven is, it is undoubtedly very large and impenetrable to our telescopes, because if we could look out into the universe and see Heaven right now we would see this:

> **1 Timothy 6:16: "Who (**God**) alone is immortal and lives in <u>unapproachable light</u> whom no one can see." The NLT says, "He alone can never die, <u>He lives in light so brilliant that no human can approach him</u>. No human eye has ever seen him."**

> **Revelation 21:23: "And the city (New Jerusalem) has no need of sun or moon, <u>for the glory of God illuminates the city, and the Lamb</u> (**Jesus**) <u>is its light</u>."**

If our most powerful, yet obviously inferior, telescopes were able to see inside Heaven, it would be by far the brightest image in the entire universe. That is where Mike, and L.C., and Pat Chess are right now! Just the change in lighting alone will be breathtaking – *and that is just the beginning of what we are going to be seeing in the pages ahead.*

That said, in whatever vastness and brightness Mike finds himself today which is far beyond earthly comprehension, that place where he is now is not where Mike will eventually be. *(What?)* We sometimes refer to it as the "<u>intermediate Heaven</u>," or the "<u>present Heaven</u>," because however large and glorious Heaven is right now – the end of the book of Revelation says it will one day expand to include the entire universe, in <u>a New Heavens and a New Earth</u>!

Heaven will eventually completely encompass this cleansed-from-the-curse earth! In fact the New Jerusalem, the "place Jesus went back to prepare a place/room/ mansion for you" – that "New Jerusalem" with your "mansion" in it is going to one day come down here!

> **Revelation 21:1-4: "Then I saw a New Heaven and a New Earth, for the old heaven and the old earth had disappeared. And I saw the Holy City, the New Jerusalem, coming down from God out of Heaven like a bride beautifully dressed for her husband.**
>
> **"I heard a loud shout from the Throne, saying, 'Look, God's home is now among his people! He will live with them, and they will be his people. God himself will be with them. He will wipe every tear from their eyes, and there will be no more death or sorrow or crying or pain. All these things are gone forever.'"**

- If it's a Biblical fact that the New Jerusalem where you are one day going to have your place/room/mansion is eventually "coming down from Heaven" – then where is this New Jerusalem right now? "<u>Up</u>" <u>in Heaven</u>!

- Where did Jesus go back to, to prepare a place for us? <u>Back to Heaven</u>!

- And where exactly is Mike right now? <u>In Heaven</u>!

- Where is Jesus coming back from, with the "already dead" Saints to rapture the rest of the Believers and resurrect the already dead Saints bodies? <u>From Heaven</u>.

But when we use the term "intermediate Heaven, "we have to be careful not to imagine ourselves sitting in a packed driver's license office waiting room waiting for our "New Heaven and New Earth event" to begin. Mike is right now sitting somewhere in holy awe as all the effects of the curse of sin have been washed from his redeemed soul. He is surrounded by a level of heavenly glory that his earthy mind could not have handled one week before he died. Just the concept of the unapproachable light of the glory of God that is pervading every nook and cranny of Heaven has Mike far more wide eyed that anything he ever imagined.

Mike's job in this life was a luxury jet pilot. He had some  great stories of flying famous people around the world. He had what some would imagine as a dream job with more wide eyed experiences than most of us ever have. But one minute in the unfiltered glories of Heaven and everything he ever did here would seem like a new-born baby shaking a plastic rattle. Mike is in Heaven, *(the intermediate Heaven yes)* but that is where Jesus is right now as well! So has Mike met Jesus face to face?

1 Corinthians 13:12: "For now we see only a reflection as in a mirror; <u>then we shall see face to face</u>. Now I know in part; then I shall know fully, even as I am fully known." *(Does that mean a face-to-face with Jesus? I think it does.)*

Colossians 3:1, 4: "Since, then, you have been raised with Christ, set your hearts on things above, where Christ is, seated at the right hand of God. When

Christon, who is your life, appears, <u>then you also will appear with him in glory</u>."

But, I'm telling you, it is not going to be *(like we said in the last chapter)* us walking up to Jesus, slapping him on the back, saying "How you doing old buddy. Thanks for dying for my sins." We get brief glimpses of Jesus inside Heaven, not from those who were there, but from those who were allowed to peak through the curtain in a vision.

- Stephen the Martyr, as the stones were thudding against his body snuffing out the last bit of life, peered through that "crack in the curtain" and saw what Mike is perhaps seeing right now:

- Perhaps Stephen had met Jesus personally, watched him die as the blood flowed from his body, saw him laid in a tomb. Stephen then saw personally *(or knew many who had seen)* Jesus alive again after three days. Stephen became a firm Jesus' follower right up to, not recanting his faith, being stoned to death! As he is dying he screams out:

Acts 7:55-57 NIV: "But Stephen, full of the Holy Spirit, looked up to heaven and <u>saw the glory of God</u>, and <u>Jesus standing at the right hand of God</u>. See that? He is allowed to peer through a crack in time and space, and he sees what he is going to be experiencing, in person, in just a few minutes. He sees what Mike and Pat are experiencing, right now!

"'Look,' he said, '<u>I see heaven open and the Son of Man standing at the right hand of God</u>.' At this they covered their ears and, yelling at the top of their

voices, they all rushed at him." *Notice the unbelievers couldn't stand the mental picture of what was expanding the Believer's soul!*

But, this is definitely not going to be a "How you doing Jesus, thanks for dying for my sins" moment. Remember Daniel's reaction: **Daniel 10:8-9: "My strength left me, my face grew deathly pale, and I felt very weak when I heard the sound of his voice, I fainted and lay there with my face to the ground."** I also showed you Moses' reaction to seeing God in Exodus 33.

Notice Isaiah's words in the famous Isaiah 6 "woe-is-me" passage. *(This is not symbolism- this was real)* **Isaiah 6:1-3: "It was in the year King Uzziah died <u>that I saw the Lord.</u> He** *(the Lord)* **was sitting on a lofty throne, and the train of his robe filled the Temple. Attending him were mighty seraphim, each having six wings. They were calling out to each other, <u>'Holy, holy, holy is the LORD of Heaven's Armies!</u> The whole earth is <u>filled with his glory!'"</u>**

That perked up my spiritual ears. Remember early in this book we studied many of the uses of the word "Heaven" in the Old Testament.

<u>**265 times**</u> the phrase is used in the Bible, <u>Lord of Hosts, Lord of Armies, Lord of Heaven's Armies.</u> Every single time *(IMO)* that seems to be referring to the pre-incarnate Jesus! Long before Jesus came to this earth as a baby in a manger, he was the Lord of Heaven's Armies, the commander of

millions of Heavenly Beings. The one in charge of blocking the forces of sin and satan!

We tend to always think of Jesus in sandals and a dusty white robe, but that was only for a 33 year sliver of time in all of eternity past, and all of eternity future.

> **Isaiah 6:5: "Then I said, 'Woe is me! I am doomed, for I am a sinful man. I have filthy lips, and live among a people with filthy lips. Yet I have seen the King, the LORD of Heaven's Armies.'"** מֶלֶךְ *(melek) - King of* יְהוָה *(Yah·weh)* צְבָאוֹת *(tsə·ḇā·'ō·wṯ - war, armies)*

This is 700 years before that King of Heaven's Armies would squeeze into the embryo of a Jewish virgin girl so that he could be born to die for the sins of all humanity. One high-definition view of Jesus, even before he came here as a baby and then died, has Isaiah saying, "I'm a dead man" because I looked through a crack in time and space and I saw the King of the Universe!

> **Isaiah 6:6-8: "Then one of the seraphim flew to me with a burning coal he had taken from the altar with a pair of tongs. He touched my lips with it and said, 'See, this coal has touched your lips. Now your guilt is removed, and your sins are forgiven.' Then I heard the Lord asking, 'Whom should I send as a messenger to this people? Who will go for us?' I said, 'Here I am. Send me.'"** I've heard this used in mission services for years *(and rightly so),* but when Isaiah is saying *it* – He is going from seeing this insane visual of the real Heavenly Jesus, to thinking he's a dead man, to offering

the rest of his life in service to this King, "the Lord of Heaven's Armies." *Watch these amazing facts:*

- Exactly one chapter later, Isaiah is announcing that a virgin will conceive and give birth to a son, and he will be called **Emmanuel – God with us!**

- Three chapters later, he is prophesying that a Son is going to be born who will be the **Wonderful Counselor, Mighty God, Everlasting Father, Prince of Peace!**

- Just 47 chapters later, he is prophesying that the Messiah will become a suffering Savior taking on himself the sins of the world in Isaiah 53.

- When he said, "Here am I, send me," to the Lord of Heaven's Armies – he apparently meant it!

We do understand that whatever Mike Richards or Pastor L.C. Campbell are experiencing as they meet Jesus for the first time, it's not a "Yo Jesus, old pal" moment. I realize that Jesus is our dearest friend, He's closer than a brother, and I don't want to mess that up in our minds.

But when we get just inside of Heaven and the self-sovereign, self-absorbed, self-centered part of our sinful character is stripped away in a moment of time. And we focus for the first time on the face of our risen Savior without the veil of sin between us – we will have entered the "GLORY" part of our eternal future. And nothing, I mean nothing, will be the same as it is now!

When John, Jesus' first cousin, in his old age, got his prophetic look inside of the Throne Room, right there was the same One who had been his close friend on earth – but how much had changed!

> **Revelation 1:13-18:** "**And standing in the middle of the lamp-stands was someone like <u>the Son of Man</u>. He was wearing a long robe with a gold sash across his chest. His head and his hair were white like wool, as white as snow. And his eyes were like flames of fire. His feet were like polished bronze refined in a furnace, and his voice thundered like mighty ocean waves. He held seven stars in his right hand, and a sharp two-edged sword came from his mouth. And his face was like the sun in all its brilliance. When I saw him, I fell at his feet as if I were dead. But he laid his right hand on me and said, <u>'Don't be afraid! I am the First and the Last. I am the living one. I died, but look—I am alive forever and ever! And I hold the keys of death and the grave.</u>'"**

Can you imagine the awe as Pat Chess met the Lord of Heaven's Armies for the first time? Mike also loved Jesus here on earth even though he had not seen him. They confessed their sins and received forgiveness purely by grace through faith. Now they are meeting the one who loved them so much that he gave his earthly life in exchange for their eternal life! It's stunning! And he did the same for you and me!

Chapter 17

Mike became a transformed man!

I showed you this picture in the last chapter of Mike Richards flying people who could afford such things anywhere they wanted to go. I bring it up again because of what I then witnessed in his memorial service. I've heard a lot of raw things at funerals. I've had family members meet me right up in front after a memorial service yelling out in anger. I was talking once about the life change we saw in a man just weeks before his death – and a person yelled out from the audience. "That's not true, he was a jerk!"

But what we heard in this memorial service, was Mike's children saying, "I didn't even know my own Dad for the first few years of my life, because he was married to flying airplanes, flying somebody else's kids around the planet. But one day something inside of my dad was so changed, so transformed – that he became a truly godly man! That's what I so loved and respected in my dad! That's the transformed man who breathed his last breath and entered into Heaven!"

I tried in the last chapter, for the first time in over four decades of preaching to imagine with you, and put into words – what those first few moments in Heaven will be like. We try so hard to hang on to these earthly bodies, *(what the Apostle Paul calls these "dying bodies," this "temporary tent.")* One day we will receive our new "glorified bodies." Some of you reading this are suffering severe physical issues with your "temporary tent."

For us to try to mentally grasp that one minute after arriving in Heaven, all that laying on a white sheet with uniformed people poking needles into every square inch of our earthly "tent," and doctors slicing through your hide and sawing off your bones, and pinning you back together with staples and glue – and diseases eating your body from within – all that is forever gone!

But as transformational and inviting as that part seems, it will actually be the smaller part, as we suddenly realize that the inner hurts and pains, and fears, and inadequacies, and brokenness, that infect and affect much of our thinking and actions, *(whether we admit it or not)* – in a split second will all be gone too!

Imagine yourself one earth minute after you realize that your mind is in complete harmony with **"the peace of God that passes all understanding guarding your hearts and minds in Christ Jesus."** I've prayed that **Philippians 4:7** promise with people, hundreds and hundreds of times, and often watched as a divine peace would seep into their minds even in the most grueling of life situations.

Unfortunately in these fallen bodies and minds, that peace tends to fade, or get swamped by the next crisis. Imagine that <u>divine peace</u> in all of its fullness consuming your entire being! Now imagine <u>worry</u> being drained out of your mind forever! You are never again going to be rationally, or irrationally, <u>fearful</u> about the next minute, or hour, or day, or year, for all the rest of eternity!

Then, if you will let me repeat again four sentences from the last chapter. This brought tears to my eyes as it sank in.

- Imagine the pervading presence of God that fills all of Heaven, the presence that in the most sacred times here on earth we only experience like we were looking through a tiny crack in the curtain. Imagine that all - pervading presence filling every nook and cranny of your soul, breaking up all the scar tissue built in by the trauma of sin.

- Imagine the complete "Joy of the Lord" that every once in a while in this life breaks through and lifts you to a place of worship that you would give anything to experience all the time – imagine that becoming what continually lifts your soul, with no hindrances, no black corners, no hidden compartments in ways you cannot possibly now grasp while on this sin-drenched planet.

One earth hour after we arrive in Heaven we are going to say, "Why in the world was I so intent on staying on the Earth?"

So let's just say that all we just discussed and more exploded open into Mike's soul in the first few moments and then the whole reality began to enlarge more and more. *Then what?*

I did somewhat downplay the "gates of pearl" and the "streets of gold" in the last chapter, saying that those would not be the big things Mike would be focused on. I don't want to under-emphasize things God took time to describe in Scripture but I still say that's not what Mike has been <u>most</u> fascinated with. *(IMO)*

I'm going to do what I have promised and that is, take you *(Scripturally)* right into the Throne Room of God. *(Perhaps Mike is there right now!)* And I will suggest to you, that a street made out of gold is something we can somewhat grasp because we know what a street looks like, and we have seen and touched gold right here on earth. But the Throne Room of God – that's something else entirely!

We need to take the time to read this again because it's going to affect what we see about God's Throne Room.

Isaiah 65:17: "Look! I am creating new heavens and a new earth, and no one will even think about the old ones anymore."

Revelation 21:1-3: "Then I saw a New Heaven and a New Earth, for the old heaven and the old earth had disappeared. And I saw the Holy City, the New Jerusalem, coming down from God out of Heaven like a bride beautifully dressed for her husband. I heard a

loud shout from the Throne, saying, 'Look, God's home is now among his people!'"

As we discussed, all of Heaven will eventually surround this completely renovated Earth in a "New Heavens and a New Earth." You say, Sam that sounds like something borrowed from science fiction! Note: this picture of Heaven and the Scriptures describing it existed long before there was such a thing as science fiction! If anything, science fiction borrowed from Scripture!

- 300 years before Jesus' birth and 400 years before the book of Revelation people still thought the earth was flat, the stars were just up beyond the clouds, and the sun was revolving around the earth! Imagine first century Christians trying to get their heads around John's description of a New Jerusalem, with the Throne Room of God in it, coming from wherever it is "up there" down to earth.

- Imagine how utterly confused they would have been when John describes the New Jerusalem in ways no city on earth even came close to – but then John goes so far as to give the dimensions of the Holy City, and that is more than any of their brains can possibly absorb.

Revelation 21:10-11, 15-16: "So he took me in the Spirit to a great, high mountain, and he showed me the Holy City, Jerusalem, descending out of Heaven from God. It shone with the glory of God and sparkled like a precious stone…. The angel who talked to me held in his hand a gold measuring stick to measure the

city. When he measured it, he found it was a square, as wide as it was long. In fact, its length and width and height were each 1,400 miles." *(2220 kilometers)* The whole country of Israel is only 290 miles long *(470km)*. The length of the Holy City is only 200 miles less than the distance from Jerusalem to Babylon *(in Iraq)*! And it is every bit as wide as it is long! And it is every bit as high as it is wide and long! The City's size would have been beyond comprehension to the ancient Jews.

This Holy City where Jesus is preparing our future home is 1,400 miles high! *(This illustration would mean nothing to the ancients, but it does help us get perspective. – "A picture is worth*  *a thousand words.")* I've already used this mental picture, but to me it is so helpful. The International Space Station is orbiting 205 miles up. If we were there and looked over the side, the earth would look like this picture. But the Holy City will actually <u>extend seven times higher than the space station orbit</u>. Imagine being on the top floor and looking out at the New Earth – you will, almost certainly, do that one day!

It sounds like something out of a Star Trek movie. This 1,400-mile cube, descending Holy City is going to be massive! If one corner of it lands near Jerusalem, the rest would cover most of the Middle East. If each level was one-mile high *(imagine that, if the ceiling in your "mansion" were one mile up)*, the total surface area inside the New Jerusalem would be 2,628,072,000 square miles – which is more than 13 times the land surface area of the entire Earth!

When we finally see this New Holy City descending from Heaven, slowing down as it approaches Earth, and finally settling into what appears to be its final resting place, we will be beyond stunned! Stay with that word, "stunned." Remember, this Holy City, the place that Jesus went to prepare for you, is right now housed inside the vastness of wherever Heaven is.

- And where is Mike Richards right now? Inside the vastness of wherever Heaven is! So has he seen this Holy City from the outside? Almost certainly! *(That exterior description is described vividly in the Bible, we'll look!)*

- But has Mike actually stepped through the Gates of Pearl and walked on the Streets of Gold? Because those Pearly Gates and those Golden Streets aren't said to be throughout all of Heaven – they are said to be specifically inside the New Jerusalem! Yes, he almost certainly has.

Very carefully now what else is located inside the already existing New Jerusalem?

This from the last chapter of the Bible: **Revelation 22:1, 3-4: "Then the angel showed me a river with the water of life, clear as crystal, <u>flowing from the Throne of God and of the Lamb.</u> No longer will there be a curse upon anything**. *(So finally the curse of sin will be completely removed from this planet!)* **<u>For the Throne of God and of the Lamb will be there, and his servants</u>**

will worship him. And they will see his face…" *(That last phrase is a very important.)*

Since Jesus left 2000 years ago to "prepare our room" in the Holy City, is it possible that <u>the New Jerusalem is being formed around the already existing Throne Room of God</u> – which has been there since infinite eternity? What kind of wild speculation is that Sam? *(It's not completely wild, and it's not completely speculation!)*

- The Psalmists are already writing extensively about God's throne 1000 years before Jesus was born.

- Psalms 9:7: "The Lord reigns forever, executing judgment from his **throne**."

- Psalm 33:14: "From his **throne** he observes all who live on the earth."

- Psalm 45:6: "Your **throne**, O God, endures forever and ever."

- Psalm 47:8: "You rule with a scepter of justice, God reigns above the nations, sitting on his holy **throne**."

- Psalm 89:7: "The highest angelic powers stand in awe of God. He is far more awesome than all who surround his **throne**." *(15+ times – The Psalmists are getting brief glimpses inside of Heaven – 1000 years before Jesus was born.)*

- **Psalm 93:2: "<u>Your throne, O Lord, has stood from time immemorial</u>. You yourself are from the everlasting past."** How long did this Psalmist say God's Throne had been in existence? *Forever!* Were there <u>already angels worshipping God around the Throne</u>? Yes?

Was the rest of the 1400 mile cube called the New Jerusalem already formed around God's Throne? We don't know, but Jesus did say, "I'm going back to Heaven to prepare a place for you!"

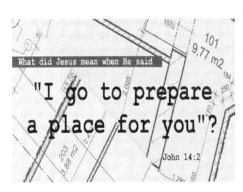

This is where the temperature in Scripture, begins to turn up a notch. Finally, God begins to allow a few select people to see through a crack in the curtain between time and eternity. They get to look not just into Heaven, but directly into the Throne Room of God.

I found six people who actually got to see inside of Heaven and recorded it in Scripture *(six people, 10 visions)*, if we don't include all of Revelation as just one heavenly vision. *(Revelation 4, 7, 11, 19)* There are four places in the Bible where we are given a slight to strong glance inside of the Throne Room, and two places where we are given a "high definition stare" right into the Throne Room of God.

Let me belly-ache a bit. I told you I bought every book I could find on Heaven written in the last 100 years. I had other people who got in on the search and brought me books or book titles. With all that help, I still only managed to accumulate 26 books. In contrast, there are more than 300 books now in print, from people who say they had a traumatic experience, died, visited with God, and came back to earth – even though Jesus stated clearly in **John 3:13: "No man has ever gone to Heaven and returned. But the Son of Man has come down from Heaven."**

But here's a brand new factoid. Out of those 26 books – how many do you think take a hard look, and write more than a passing sentence on these Biblical visions right into the Throne Room of God? The answer is: <u>Three</u>!

- It is just so utterly curious to me. If every single one of us Believers are going to spend all of eternity in Heaven. And if the centerpiece of Heaven present and certainly Heaven future is this New Jerusalem, the place we will all one day have our "home."

- And if the centerpiece of the New Jerusalem is the very Throne Room of God where every one of us is going to spend a substantial chunk of time in our eternal future.

- And if the Bible has 91 verses *(I counted)* describing the inside of God's Throne Room where we are all one day going to fall in worship – why would we all not be talking about it at least every other week for the rest of our lives?

For the last three years, parts of our family have rented villas in the mountains of the extreme north part of Georgia. Before we leave home, we look at pictures of the particular villa we are going to stay in. We look at maps of the surrounding area. We get brochures of what is available to do. We look online for any local activities. We ride horses, we visit water-falls, we zip-line, *(at least those do who are not bluntly told "you exceed the weight limit." Even the horses were groaning in despair!)*

But we are all just days, months, a few years – from entering a place that will make the mountains of Dillard, Georgia seem like an ant hill. *(Where there is no weight limit on zip-lining, and all the food is without calories.☺)* We are all professing our excitement at arriving in Heaven one of these days. Yet many Christians could not point out even two of the six passages *(91 verses)* where the inside of Heaven, especially the inside of God's Throne Room, is described in Scripture.

Let's fix that right now. The very first prophetic vision into Heaven we looked at in the last chapter was Isaiah's "Woe is Me" in Isaiah 6. We're not going to look hard at that one again but in a nutshell. What was so stunning to me was realizing this sequence:

Isaiah 6:1: "<u>I saw the Lord</u>." He *(the Lord)* was sitting on a lofty Throne.

> **6:2-3 "Attending him were mighty seraphim, calling out "<u>Holy, holy, holy.</u>"**

> **6:5 Isaiah's response: "<u>Woe is me! I am doomed</u>… I'm a sinful dead man!"**

> **6:5 "Because, I have seen the King, the LORD of Heaven's Armies." *Jesus!***

> **6:8 Lord "<u>Who will go for us?</u>" (Isaiah said, I will!) "<u>Here I am. Send me!</u>" (*One chapter later, Isaiah prophesies;)***

Isaiah 7:14: "A virgin will conceive a son and he will be called Emmanuel!" *(Two chapters later, Isaiah prophesies;)*

Isaiah 9:6: "A child is *(will be)* **born; He will be Wonderful Counselor, Mighty God, Everlasting Father."**

Something about Isaiah's view into Heaven changed his perspective forever! There isn't a doubt in my mind that when these Bible prophets saw into Heaven and got a brief glimpse right into the Throne Room, that their lives were never, ever the same again. And remember they were just seeing Heaven in a vision, just looking through a crack in the curtain. But for Isaiah – it ejected him into becoming the greatest Messianic prophet in the Old Testament!

But it didn't leave him, or any of the others beating their chest. All of them had the same reaction. 1) Isaiah screamed, "I'm a dead man." 2) Daniel fell on his knees trembling then fainted. 3) Ezekiel fell on his face on the ground. 4) John when he saw his risen Lord, in Heaven, fell at his feet as though he were dead!

Here's another amazing example. A more vivid view into the Throne Room from the prophet Daniel. **Daniel 7:1, 8: "Earlier, during the first year of King Belshazzar's reign in Babylon, Daniel had a dream and saw visions as he lay in his bed. He wrote down the dream, and this is what he saw. →** (four beasts + 10 horns + little horn) **This little horn had eyes like human eyes and a mouth that was boasting arrogantly."** *(antichrist?)*

Daniel 7:9-10: "I watched as Thrones were put in place and the Ancient One sat down to judge. *(This may be the first time anyone has seen God with an actual form.)* **His clothing was as white as snow, his hair like purest wool. He sat on a fiery Throne with wheels of blazing fire, and a river of fire was pouring out, flowing from his presence. Millions of angels ministered to**  **him; many millions more stood to attend him."** *(Ok, so Isaiah saw inside the Throne Room but he didn't tell us exactly what he saw. He just slobbered all over his shirt.)*

A Glimpse of the Throne Room

- Daniel is, for the first time in the Bible, giving us an actual visual of the Father, the Ancient of Days.

- He sits down! Does the Ancient of Days have legs, knees, and a lap? We don't know!

- His clothing was "white as snow." Is it actual clothing, like you buy at JC Penny's? Probably not! *(Light?)*

- God sits on a "blazing throne" with "wheels of blazing fire." There is fire coming from his chair, especially the wheels – or is it just brilliant light?

- There are attending angels, the "Seraphim" – the word actually comes from the Hebrew root word for "fire"!

- And there is also a "river of fire" flowing from his presence. We get all that from just two verses, and there are 80 more verses in Scripture describing the same scene even more vividly. It's important to understand that the Throne of God you are trying to grasp exists right now. Those who have gone before us have been in the same room with that Throne and have personally viewed the Ancient of Days. One of these days soon we will also be inside that Throne Room. This is your future reality!

- There are also millions of angels there, "ministering" *(whatever that means)* and then many millions more of "another group" there in front of the Throne too. John tells us that <u>those many millions</u> more are the "<u>already dead, redeemed Saints</u>." *(Revelation 7:9)* What if Mike, and our loved ones are standing there right now?

This fire-ejecting Throne starts to seem too weird, like special effects in a movie, except this was written long before there were movies, or electricity. The guy writing this has never seen the inside of a room anywhere ever that was lit with anything more than candlelight, or torches – always fire of some sort. But the brightest interior lighting he's ever seen was dim and flickering.

Daniel, living as a statesman in Babylon the most advanced city of his day, would have no "mental frame of reference" for a massive room, far bigger than their whole city, filled with blazing lights. Remember he had never seen an electric light bulb! He had never seen lights with color – other than flickering fire. He rode in chariots with wheels, I'm sure, but the wheels were wood or iron, and had they been blazing with fire, he would have been bailing out of that chariot "forthwith"!

We have to try to understand a person taking a quill pen in their hand and trying to describe something they have absolutely no framework in their brain to put into words. You say "yes," but the Holy Spirit was guiding them. Yes, indeed! That's how they did as well as they did!

Remember in Revelation when John is describing "huge locusts that were spitting fire?" I put a picture up on our screens at church, of an "Apache attack helicopter," which looks exactly like a huge locust spitting fire! How could John, a man who had never seen a combustion engine, who never saw a projectile shot from a barrel, who never saw anything but birds flying in the sky – how would he describe what to you now seems common and normal? That is *(IMO)* why more people don't write about these visions into Heaven. They come out sounding so weird because the people who wrote them are trying to describe the indescribable!

Ezekiel also has a high definition vision right into the Throne Room of God. Remember Daniel and Ezekiel are both living in Babylon at exactly the same time. They were almost certainly friends, fellow visionaries, fellow-prophets of God! You can be sure, they discussed together what they were both seeing in their visions! And what Ezekiel saw, as he was looking into the Throne Room, makes Daniel's vision seem almost tame. He writes:

Ezekiel 1:1, 13-16, 18, 24: "The heavens were opened and I saw visions of God. The living beings looked

like bright coals of fire or brilliant torches, and lightning seemed to flash back and forth among them. And the living beings darted to and fro like flashes of lightning. As I looked at these beings, I saw four wheels touching the ground beside them, one wheel belonging to each. The wheels sparkled as if made of beryl, each wheel had a second wheel turning crosswise within it. The rims of the four wheels were tall and frightening, and they were covered with eyes all around. As they flew, their wings sounded to me like waves crashing against the shore or like the voice of the Almighty or like the shouting of a mighty army."

You can imagine why authors don't want to write on Ezekiel's vision into Heaven. What am I going to say about the brilliant torch beings and the wheels covered with eyes? You are not going to say anything. That's the whole point! You've got an Ancient living 2600 years ago trying to describe the indescribable using images he has seen in his lifetime, in his society, or in his imagination.

The point being Mike Richards walked into the Throne Room for the first time, with far advanced knowledge over anything Ezekiel could have ever imagined. But even the most technical electronics, and the most far-out special effects Mike had experienced, still left him standing there dumfounded and speechless – because there is just no way this fallen life can prepare us for what is coming in Heaven!

And yet as fumbling as the Prophets seemed in their descriptions, what they did see under the inspiration of the

Holy Spirit was life changing truth to every human who would ever walk the face of the earth. Let's circle back and finish with the rest of Daniel's vision in Daniel 7:

> **Daniel 7:13-14: "As my vision continued that night, I saw someone like a son of man.** *(the Son of Man)* **He approached the Ancient One and was led into his presence. He was given authority, honor, and sovereignty over all the nations of the world, so that people of every race and nation and language would obey him. His rule is eternal—it will never end. His kingdom will never be destroyed."**

That became Jesus' favorite name for himself, the Son of Man, and every time he called himself that, the religious leaders, the disciples, the other people watching – knew full well he was equating himself with this Daniel 7 vision! Jesus doesn't use the phrase as a term of humanity. Every time he uses it, he is declaring his divinity! *Watch this explosive end to Daniel's vision:*

> **Daniel 9:25-26: "Now listen and understand! Seven sets of seven plus sixty-two <u>sets of seven (483 years) will pass from the time the command</u> is given to rebuild Jerusalem until a ruler—<u>the Anointed One (the Messiah-Prince)</u>—comes. Jerusalem will be rebuilt with streets and strong defenses, despite the perilous times. After this period of sixty-two sets of seven, <u>the Anointed One will be killed</u>, appearing to have accomplished nothing."**

Exactly 483 years after Daniel's vision, Jesus rides into Jerusalem on the back of a donkey. The people scream,

"Hosanna, Blessed is he who comes in the name of the Lord." They weren't entirely surprised – some of them had been watching their calendars. A handful of days later, some of the same voices are shouting, "Crucify him, crucify him!"

Chapter 18

_____

The pathway to an eternal Heaven is through the forgiveness of our sins!

We've been imagining in the last two chapters what Mike Richards experienced the first few moments in Heaven when his fallen, deteriorated body was suddenly gone. And his "sin nature" was gone, and all of the pains and hurts and heart-crushing traumas of life were washed away. One earth minute inside Heaven – and that was all gone, forever!

In the last chapter, and now again in this chapter, we are no longer talking about all the necessary parts leading up to us getting to Heaven. <u>We are now looking straight into Heaven</u> and asking what do we biblically see? What will you be experiencing in the first moments after you arrive?

- And I need to say this: The pathway to an eternal Heaven is through forgiveness and heart cleansing that only comes when we repent of our sins and embrace Jesus as our Lord and Savior!

- The common idea that everybody is on their way to Heaven, regardless of who or what they did or did not believe, is completely false according to Jesus!

John 3:14-15, 17-18: "As Moses lifted up the bronze snake on a pole in the wilderness, so the Son of Man must be lifted up _(on a cross)_**, so that everyone who**

believes in him will have eternal life. For God so loved the world that he gave his one and only Son, that whoever believes in him shall not perish but have eternal life. For God did not send his Son into the world to condemn the world, but to save the world through him. Whoever believes in him is not condemned, but whoever does not believe stands condemned already because they have not believed in the name of God's one and only Son." - JESUS

So we are going to take a second, even stronger, look into Heaven. We are going to look right into the Throne Room of God where you, as a Redeemed Son or Daughter of God, will one day be standing *(kneeling)* in worship.

As I was writing this, the Russian invasion of Ukraine was freshly underway. We were watching images of people scrambling for their lives. They had dropped any future plans and ambitions they might have had – because a narcissistic madman had decided to invade their sovereign country!

- I watched several young couples fleeing, saying "we don't have any idea what is coming in our lives in the next few hours/days/weeks – ever!"

- One young wife was asked what are your plans? "We don't have any, we don't know what comes next for our family." And then through tears she said: "How could one man be so evil?" Which is by the way satan's mode of operation. "He comes to steal, kill, and destroy." Jesus' counter-plan, is that we all might experience <u>abundant life</u>! *(John 10:10)*

But even closer to my heart, as I prayed for the Ukrainians, was a picture posted by my wife's relatives of a young family that are their church's missionaries.

Misha and Lena are Ukrainians with a driving passion to plant churches and bring people into a relationship with Jesus. In one week's time, their life dream in their home county of Ukraine had turned into a nightmare.

They, their parishioners, and millions of other Believers were praying their hearts out even as they watched evil seemingly triumph. Young Christian families were either fleeing or hiding. Or perhaps Misha was taking one of the rifles the government was handing out to defend his family and his country.

- I'm guessing that the Ukrainian Christians eternal focus was sharpened to a razor edge. The things of this earth instantly fell into the background – and the things of Heaven sprinted into their frontal view.

- If Misha was trying to protect his family, he had to know that he might not live to the end of the week. That would have a way of bringing Heaven into stark view – wouldn't it?

But that's exactly what God desires to bring to the forefront of our minds – even when our lives and futures aren't being threatened. When life is comfortable, we tend to focus almost all of our thoughts on what we imagine the next day/week/year is going to bring. We tend to give very little attention to what "one minute after our last breath" on this earth will bring!

> **Colossians 3:3-4: "For you died to this life, and YOUR REAL LIFE** *(the real reality – the real reason you were born)* **is hidden** (κρύπτω) **with Christ in God.**
>
> **"And when Jesus Christ, WHO IS YOUR LIFE, is revealed to the whole world (Jesus' return), you will share in all his glory!"** (δόξη)

Here's the big A-HA moment that I discovered as I was studying these passages. Every example that I could find in the Bible where somebody is allowed to look into Heaven in a vision and record it for us to read – every single one of them happened to people who were in similar circumstance to the people in Ukraine!

- King David talked often about Heaven and the Throne of God. But I could find no evidence in the Bible that he actually got a view inside!

- Solomon, when dedicating the Temple had lots to say about Heaven; but in his life full of comforts, he didn't seem to have any personal idea what was there.

- Nehemiah was a hero of the Old Testament, but he was laser focused on getting a destroyed Jerusalem ready for the coming Messiah to arrive.

On the other hand:

1) Moses and 73 of Israel's Elders go onto Sinai and get a vision of God's Throne after they have been driven

from Egypt across the Red Sea and are stuck in the Wilderness at Mt. Sinai.

Exodus 24:9-11: "Then Moses, Aaron, Nadab, Abihu, and the seventy elders of Israel climbed up the mountain. There <u>they saw the God of Israel</u>. Under his feet there seemed to be <u>a surface of brilliant blue lapis lazuli,</u> as clear as the sky itself. And though these nobles of Israel <u>gazed upon God</u>, he did not destroy them. In fact, they ate a covenant meal, eating and drinking in his presence!"

Did you know that happened just before Moses went up the mountain alone to receive the Ten Commandments? That descriptive sentence: **"under his feet there seemed to be a surface of brilliant blue lapis lazuli."** We know they are looking directly into the Throne Room, because that is also described in Ezekiel 1:26 as the color of the surface under the Throne. *Who knew?* If you don't like bright blue, you might need to brace yourself!

2) Isaiah, as we noted, sees inside Heaven as he is warning northern Israel in the year King Uzziah died *(Isaiah 6)* that if they didn't turn away from their idol worship, they were going to be invaded by their own "Russian" invasion, the Assyrians. They didn't and they were!

3) Daniel is in Babylon as part of the Captivity. The two southern tribes are invaded 100 years after the ten northern tribes, and Daniel is forcibly removed into

his own politically motivated "refugee camp." He writes from exile in Babylon.

4) Ezekiel is with him in exile in Babylon. He scratches out his prophesy sitting alongside the Babylonian Kebar River – a 712 word description of the inside of God's Throne Room that is utterly amazing! But he's trying to "describe the indescribable," and it is so hard for us to understand, that most people just ignore it!

5) John in Revelation. The Jews are being heavily persecuted, captured, killed, fed to wild animals, hung on crosses, burned to ashes. John has been arrested and put on the prison Island of Patmos where <u>he sees into Heaven</u>! *(We'll look into that!)*

Notice these five people get to not only see inside of Heaven but beyond that – they all got to see a vision of God the Father and Jesus the Son inside of the Throne Room. *(That's a big deal!!)*

- I need to remind you that a high-definition view is what every Believer reading this book will one day personally see! It will be the most significant visual you have ever seen in this lifetime or will ever see for all of eternity!

- Nothing of beauty that you have locked your eyes onto on this earth, will even fractionally be what you will see when you first walk into the Throne Room of God!

Someday *(many somedays!)* you will leave your Jesus-prepared home in the New Jerusalem. We'll pause our other activities, *(We'll talk about what those will be)* and we will all make our way *(often)* into the Throne Room of God where we will fall on our knees in awe and worship of our God! Let me show you John's vivid glimpse *(wide-eyed stare)* inside the Throne Room.

> **Revelation 4:1-6, 8: "Then as I looked, I saw a door standing open in heaven, and the same voice I had heard before spoke to me like a trumpet blast. The voice said, 'Come up here, and I will show you what must happen after this.' And instantly I was in the Spirit, and <u>I saw a throne in heaven and someone sitting on it</u>. The one sitting on the throne was as brilliant as gemstones—like jasper and carnelian. And the glow of an emerald circled his throne like a rainbow. Twenty-four thrones surrounded him, and twenty-four elders sat on them. They were all clothed in white and had gold crowns on their heads. From the throne came flashes of lightning and the rumble of thunder. And in front of the throne were seven torches with burning flames. This is the sevenfold Spirit of God. In front of the throne was a shiny sea of glass, sparkling like crystal, in the center and around the throne were four living beings, each covered with eyes, front and back. Each of these living beings had six wings, and their wings were covered all over with eyes, inside and out."**

That's almost certainly the same Seraphim that Isaiah 6 describes – But they sound so strange that we are tempted to shut them out of our minds. Don't! One earth minute inside the Throne Room, and it will all make sense! **"Day after day and night after night they keep on saying, 'Holy, holy, holy is the Lord God, the Almighty—** *(same picture we got in Isaiah 6)* **the One who always was, who is, and who is still to come.'"** *(Revelation 4:8)*

You need to hear me when I say this. One day you are going to be inside that Throne Room! It's a real place! Your Heavenly Father will be sitting on the Throne in front of you. And I promise you, the knocking sound in the engine of the old Buick isn't going to be important anymore! The dingbat driving 40 mph in the left lane of the turnpike is going to be long gone from your memory. And we are going to find ourselves entering into a level of worship like nothing we ever imagined on this earth!

> **Revelation 4:9-11: "Whenever the living beings give glory and honor and thanks to the one sitting on the Throne (the One who lives forever and ever), the twenty-four Elders fall down and worship the one sitting on the Throne (the One who lives forever and ever). And they lay their crowns before the throne and say, 'You are worthy, O Lord our God, to receive glory and honor and power. For you created all things, and they exist because you created what you pleased.'"**

Who is that? Who is going to be falling down and worshipping the One on the Throne? Who is going to be laying their undeserved crowns at his feet?

- I'm the guy who is always saying, "always interpret the Bible literally, unless the author indicates symbolism."

- But in this case. I believe there is a reason there were 12 tribes of Israel (OT) and there were 12 disciples (NT) out of whom came Jesus' whole church. Those "24" represent us all! Those 24 "Elders" are us! *(IMO)*

- Imagine yourself falling on your face before the Throne of God and from deep within your being the words begin to flow in unison with millions and millions of other Redeemed Saints. **"You are worthy, our Lord and God, to receive glory and honor and power, for you created all things, and by your will they were created and have their being."** *(Revelation 4:11 NIV)*

- And then watch this cosmic-sized event roll over into Chapter 5 and see it swell even bigger in magnitude:

Revelation 5:8-10: "The four living creatures and the twenty-four elders fell down before the Lamb. Each one had a harp and they were holding golden bowls full of incense, which are the prayers of God's people. And they sang a new song, saying: 'You are worthy to take the scroll and to open its seals, because you were slain, and with your blood you purchased for God persons from every tribe and language and people and nation. You have made them to be a kingdom and priests to serve our God, and they/<u>we will reign on the earth</u>.'"

Revelation 5:11-12 ESV: "Then I looked and heard the voice of many angels, numbering thousands upon thousands, and ten thousand times ten thousand. They encircled the throne and the living creatures and the Elders. In a loud voice they were saying: 'Worthy is the Lamb, who was slain, to receive power and wealth and wisdom and strength and honor and glory and praise!'" So you've got millions and millions of angels surrounding the Throne, surrounding the strange living creatures *(whatever they are)*. Around them are the 24 Elders – Us! And then surrounding us are wave after wave of angels and they all in unison sing out: **"Worthy is the Lamb, who was slain, to receive power and wealth and wisdom and strength and honor and glory and praise!"** *(Say it with me – "I'm going there!")*

What I am reading to you is an actual event that is going to happen in your future – possibly more than once. This may be something we experience over and over.

- Have you ever been in a worship service in a huge stadium with thousands – tens of thousands of Believers, singing praises in unison? I have! Now try to imagine that in a crowd of a billion or more redeemed Saints, surrounded by another billion+ angels!

- We're in a massive setting that is so immensely beautiful that we can't possibly imagine it now in our wildest dreams. Our Heavenly Father and our loving Savior will be sitting right in the middle!

- The 24 Elders, a billion Redeemed Saints sing their Heavenly song. A billion angels encircling them answer in song, "antiphonally." Then all those masses of angels and a billion+ of us Saints – all join together in perfect unison, with perfect pitch:

Revelation 5:13-14 ESV: "Then I heard every creature in heaven and on earth and under the earth and on the sea, and all that is in them, saying: 'To him who sits on the throne and to the Lamb be praise and honor and glory and power, for ever and ever!' The four living creatures said, "Amen," and the elders fell down and worshiped!" *(Beyond Amazing!)*

I used to go online and look at artist's digital pictures of the inside of the Throne Room and think, how factually wrong, how weird, how inaccurate! Then it occurred to me, these artists are trying to draw the un-drawable!

Remember, so many of these inspired descriptions of the inside of Heaven sound so weird too – because these are written by human authors, *(under the inspiration of the Holy Spirit,)* but they are trying to "describe the humanly indescribable."

We looked at Ezekiel in the last chapter writing about the blazing fire coming from the Throne of God and the River of Fire flowing from it, and the wheels, and the wheels inside of wheels and the wheels with eyes in them. That all sounds so ridiculously weird that we tend to ignore the passage altogether. But then, as we noted, we should remember that the author, Ezekiel, had never ever seen an electric light. He had never seen brilliant lights in mind-boggling color. The same is true even for our 21st century minds as we try to picture Heaven. When we see it ourselves one day, our minds *(with all we have seen that these ancients hadn't)* will be completely blown. All of Heaven, particularly the inside of the New Jerusalem – more particularly the inside of your future home that Jesus went to Heaven to prepare for you – most particularly, the inside of God's Throne Room – will be beyond anything all of our imaginations could ever come up with!

But there is something else here that has grabbed my brain and won't let go!

- We are not just given a look inside of Heaven by these five authors, in seven visions.

- We are not just given a look inside the Throne Room of God, we are also given a brief physical description of God the Father! And a very High definition physical description of Jesus the Son, as Isaiah, and Daniel, and John see him inside the Throne Room.

So what does God the Father look like?

Most of us would tend to say: God is a Spirit, so he would not have any actual form. We read before that God "dwells in unapproachable light." So perhaps a wispy Spirit refracting brilliant light? He definitely doesn't look like the traditional old white-haired man in a white robe on a gold throne, although that is the way most would picture God.

Moses in Exodus 24 says they "saw him," but there's no description. Isaiah 6 just says he "saw him," and he was sitting on a Throne. Daniel 7 gives us the best description so far:

> **Daniel 7:9 NIV: "As I looked, thrones were set in place, and the Ancient of Days took his seat. His clothing was as white as snow; the hair of his head was white like wool. His throne was flaming with fire, and its wheels were all ablaze."**

John in: **Revelation 4:2-4 NIV: "At once I was in the Spirit, and there before me was a Throne in Heaven with someone sitting on it. And the one who sat there had the appearance of jasper and ruby.** *(They're both red gems.)*

"A rainbow that shone like an emerald encircled the throne. *(Have you seen an emerald green Northern Lights display in the Arctic? It makes you slightly understand God's paintbrush.)* **Surrounding the throne were twenty-four other thrones, and seated on them were twenty-four Elders. They were dressed in <u>white</u>** *(Always describing the Redeemed!)* **and had crowns of gold on their heads."** *(Which they will lay down before the Throne.)*

One more view from Ezekiel. After this passage you know everything there is to know *(on this side of eternity)* about what God, the Father, looks like:

> **Ezekiel 1:26-28: "Above this surface was something that looked like <u>a Throne made of blue lapis lazuli.</u>**

And on this Throne high above was a figure whose appearance resembled a man. *(So – some sort of form?)*

"From what appeared to be his waist up, he looked like gleaming amber, flickering like a fire. And from his waist down, he looked like a burning flame, shining with splendor. All around him was a glowing halo, like a rainbow shining in the clouds on a rainy day. This is what the glory of the LORD looked like to me. When I saw it, I fell face down on the ground."

- So tell me please, Sam, what exactly does God, the Father, look like? I only have a shadowy picture in my mind. But now you know as much as I know!

- But I have a deep certainty that when Mike Richards walked into His presence his reaction was the same as Ezekiel's,

- "I fell, face down on the ground." And then coming from deep inside our Redeemed beings will be something like: **"You are worthy, O Lord our God, to receive glory and honor and power."**

There is one more visual in the book of Daniel that might be a bit shocking. Let's put the first visual back in our minds;

After Daniel sees the Ancient of Days sit down on the Throne in Heaven – he then sees a second part to that same vision. **Daniel 7:13-14: "As my vision continued that night, I saw someone like a son of man** *(the Son of Man- Jesus!)* **coming with the clouds of Heaven. He approached the Ancient One and was led into his presence. He was given authority, honor, and**

sovereignty over all the nations of the world, so that people of every race and nation and language would obey him. His rule is eternal—it will never end. His kingdom will never be destroyed."

We talked about why Jesus so often called himself "the Son of Man." In some Gospel passages, in every third sentence he is referring to himself as the "Son of Man." There was no doubt in any of his listeners mind, that he was equating himself with the One who would come before **"the Ancient of Days and be given all authority, honor, and sovereignty, whose kingdom would be eternal, and never end!"**

Daniel had to be wrestling in his own mind with exactly who this Eternal Ruler was going to be. Remember it's in Daniel 9:25-26, two chapters later, that <u>Daniel prophesies the coming of the "Messaic Nagad" – the Messiah Prince</u>. And he prophesies not only that the Messiah Prince is going to arrive, but exactly which year, he will arrive. *(v. 25)* And Daniel then says, for the first time ever, that *(v. 26)* **the Messiah will be killed**. The only indication of that up to this point was Isaiah 53.

But then Daniel has a second vision into the Throne Room and this time he gets a better look at exactly what this Messiah looks like. I'm assuming that he is sharp enough to connect the Eternal Ruler, who will be given all authority, honor, and sovereignty, with the Messiah he said was going to arrive in Jerusalem and then die – and then connect those clues with the figure he now sees in Heaven, in the Throne Room at the end of Times.

Clearly <u>the One he now sees is no longer dead</u>! I'm not sure what Daniel did with that in his mind, 600 years before Jesus was born. But here's what he saw when he looked inside the Throne Room a second time, one chapter later!

> **Daniel 10:5-6, 8-9: "I looked up and saw a man dressed in linen clothing, with a belt of pure gold around his waist. <u>His body looked like a precious gem. His face flashed like lightning, and his eyes flamed like torches. His arms and feet shone like polished bronze, and his voice roared like a vast multitude of people.</u> My strength left me, my face grew deathly pale, and I felt very weak. Then I heard the man speak, and when I heard the sound of his voice, I fainted and lay there with my face to the ground."**

Some have said that Daniel's second vision was not him looking into Heaven, but him simply being visited by a very impressive angel in his room. An angel that left him slobbering all over his shirt, and fainting. I was taught that, and I might buy it, if I hadn't lined all these Scriptures up.

- And notice when John the Revelator looked into Heaven <u>he also saw someone he called – the Son of Man</u>. His description matches almost exactly what Daniel wrote in Daniel 10!

Revelation 1:12-16: "I turned to see who was speaking to me. And standing in the middle of the lamp-stands was someone like the Son of Man. He was wearing a long robe with a gold sash across his chest. His head and his hair were white like wool, as white as snow. And his eyes were like flames of fire. His feet were like polished bronze refined in a furnace, and his voice thundered like mighty ocean waves. He held seven stars in his right hand, and a sharp two-edged sword came from his mouth. And his face was like the sun in all its brilliance."

There is no question who we are looking at here, because the Son of Man then introduces himself to John: **Revelation 1:17-18: "Don't be afraid! I am the First and the Last. I am the living one. I <u>died</u>, but look—I am <u>alive forever and ever</u>! And I hold the keys of death and the grave."**

If Mike Richards has been in the Throne Room, he has now seen the Father, and understands what we cannot now put into words. He's also seen the Son, the Messiah, Jesus our Savior. Our minds tell us that we are going to sidle up to the Jesus in his dusty white robe and sandals, and ask to touch the nail prints in his hands. Maybe at some point we will, but I'm getting fairly sure that the Jesus that we will see in the Throne Room of God is this Jesus with a face like the sun in all its brilliance, and a voice like mighty ocean waters!

And I am quite sure what we are going to be saying back to him is: **"Worthy is the Lamb, who was slain, to receive power and wealth and wisdom and strength and honor and glory and praise!"**

HEAVEN: Part V

CHAPTER 18

Chapter 19

"Salvation comes from our God who sits on the Throne and from the Lamb!"

We read in Revelation 4 and 5, the description of millions/billions of Saints on their knees and faces before the Throne, worshipping God, surrounded by millions/billions of angels praising with the Saints in antiphonal songs.

> **Revelation 4:1, 5:9-10: "Then as I looked, I saw a door standing open in heaven. 'You are worthy to take the scroll and break its seals and open it, for you were slain, and your blood has ransomed people for God from every tribe and language and people and nation. And you have caused them to become a Kingdom of priests for our God. And they will reign on the earth.'"**

<u>That will be us</u>! God's biblical word pictures are designed to let us look through a crack in the curtain and begin to see where we will one day be worshiping! Here is the moment, I believe, when all of us will arrive in the Throne Room at the same time.

> **Revelation 7:9-12: "After this** (*kai eidon - the very next chronological event*) **I saw a vast crowd, too great to count, from every nation and tribe and people and language, standing in front of the Throne and before the Lamb. They were clothed in white robes and held palm branches in their hands. And they were shouting**

with a great roar, 'Salvation comes from our God who sits on the Throne and from the Lamb!' And all the angels were standing around the Throne and around the Elders and the four living beings. And they fell before the Throne with their faces to the ground and worshiped God. They sang, 'Blessing and glory and wisdom and thanksgiving and honor and power and strength belong to our God forever and ever! Amen.'"

Picture yourself in that massive worship-filled place one day soon. What sensations, what thoughts will be filling your redeemed mind, and your now glorified body?

- We've discussed already what it will be like when the pull of sin and satan is gone, completely gone!

- The deep hurts and anguishes of this life – completely healed!

- And despair, the broken hearts, the doubt and worry – all replaced by pure unclouded joy!

- The Bible goes to some effort to say these things will be in your rear view mirror forever. There will be no more death!

Revelation 21:3-5: "He will live with them, and they will be his people. God himself will be with them. He will wipe every tear from their eyes, and there will be no more death or sorrow or crying or pain. All these things are gone forever! And the one sitting on the throne said, 'Look, I am making everything new!'"

- No more fatal accidents. No more incurable diseases! No more funeral services. No more final farewells!

- Never again will we ever think about sickness, pain, disease or dying a slow death!

- Or even lying, or contentious people *(including ourselves)*, envying, quarrels, slander, junk-yard-dog bad tempers – all the things God has offered to cleanse us Believers from in this life.

- No more lawsuits, no more infidelity, no more senseless wars, fighting, bloodshed, no more murders or rape, or kidnapping, or stealing, or home invasions. No more need for policemen, or attorneys, or doctors, or dentists.

Notice **Revelation 21:4:** doesn't say "tears" in general, it says, **"God will wipe every tear** (πᾶς δάκρυον – pas dakruon) **from our eyes."** Tears on the outside – and tears on the inside too!

"GO TO HEAVEN FOR THE CLIMATE, HELL FOR THE COMPANY." - MARK TWAIN

Revelation 21:3 tells us **"There will be no more curse!"** Imagine the curse of sin that infects every part of our lives falling away forever!

Let me inject here, on the subject of the glories of arriving in Heaven. Atheist Mark Twain is famous for joking – "Go to Heaven for the climate, go to hell for the company."

An awful lot of people have followed Mr. Twain's view that hell is going to be one huge party, and Heaven is going to be a boring eternity-long church service.

I might remind those who choose hell over Heaven that everything I just talked about that we inherit from God when the curse of sin falls away is <u>not going to be in the future of those who choose sin as their master.</u>

Remember atheist Isaac Asimov stating, "I don't believe in the afterlife, so I don't have to spend my life fearing hell, or fearing heaven even more. For whatever the tortures of hell, the boredom of Heaven would be even worse." Notice both of the above guys say they don't believe in God, then go on to talk about Heaven and hell as if they are real places! But both of them base their conclusion on a horribly flawed understanding about both God and satan.

Seriously, what has satan ever done for this universe? If you even slightly believe in the existence of evil and an adversary, a "satan," *(it's hard to imagine anyone looking at our world and not seeing that!)* who would want to be stuck with satan's brand of leadership for all of eternity? Where in the world did the idea come from that satan is the father of "good parties"? God is, by the way! We're going to study soon, about the famous Revelation 19 "<u>Marriage Supper of the Lamb</u>," *(about an 18 month long heavenly party by my calculations!)*

What did satan ever produce? What did he ever create? What enhanced the lives of us humans? This universe is what God created! Satan was *(perhaps)* an archangel in Heaven before his fall, but he was still very much serving the God who created him, just like that same God created us! And <u>what exactly has satan done for this earth since he rebelled against that God and fell</u>?

All of the things we just talked about, no longer being part of our lives in Heaven – <u>it was satan who brought that pain and suffering on humanity</u>. What foolish idiocy, Mr. Twain, to say that satan and hell are something desirable for the company we would find there.

In fact, the company you are going to find in Heaven in the form of other redeemed, glorified people is going to blow your mind. *(We're coming to that soon!)* Can you even imagine being perfectly compatible with everyone you meet? No suspicious false fronts, no underhanded motives, no jealous betrayals, no selfish promotions. I can assure you, "hell's company" is not going to be made up of people like that!

So, let's pop back inside the Throne Room and highlight a few more new exciting points, and then we'll soon *(I promise)* step outside the Throne Room, and begin discussing what else we will be doing in Heaven.

- Is Heaven going to be an eternally-long church service? No! Will we be "hymn-humming" forever? No. And not "ho-humming" either. *(because that is what a lot of people believe too.)* Not forever "ho-humming" and probably not always "hymn-humming" either!

- But do think about the differences in who you are, when you arrive in Heaven. Besides all the fear and doubt and sin and anger, etc., that we already discussed, falling away – what else about you will never, ever be the same again?

Let's pin down a couple of other changes in you, when you first find yourself with that "vast crowd, too great to count, from every nation and tribe and people and language, standing in front of the Throne and before the Lamb – shouting with a great roar":

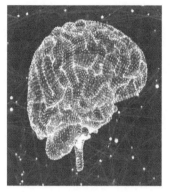

Observation #1: <u>Heavenly changes in your brain</u>: You've heard the statement that we only use 10% of our brain capacity, and if you look that up (*I did*) you will immediately find scientific articles saying, "that is just a myth and they can show us examples of brain scans that show almost everybody's neurons are firing all over their brain."

With all due respect Mr. Scientist, nobody is saying that we are only using a 10% segment of our brain, or 10% of our brains neurons. We non-scientists all understand that we have been putting information into our brains at a rapid clip for decades and when we reach for it, it just isn't there!

- Even you younger people who are reading this book, you study all kinds of information, then set down to take a test on it, and it's just outside the ends of your memory. Isn't it?

- And you "older" people *(God help us all!)*, I've gone into a gas station and paid for gas, gone outside, got into my truck, driven to the next town, looked at my gauge, and realized I never put the gas in. *(The information just slipped out of my brain – or did it?)*

Science Daily 11/22/08: "Whenever a special point of contact called a synapse forms at the end of an appendage, information can be transferred from one cell to the next, and new information is learned. Once the contact breaks down, we forget what we have learned." But the new synapse remains there.

Understand that Adam and Eve in their pre-fallen state had a head full of knowledge. And then they spent day after day in the presence of God absorbing even more and more. I've seen Ken Hamm show pictures of pre-flood etchings of what are obviously "flying machines" – pre-dating the flood!

We're conditioned to think of Adam and Eve as the original cavemen, they weren't. After their rebellion the world became totally evil, **"Everything they thought or imagined was consistently and totally evil."** *(Genesis 6:5)* A "caveman" is where "the fall into sin" led humanity!

It took humans centuries/millennium to try to resurrect the knowledge that God had first inserted into Adam's pre-fallen brain. We need to understand that what we will find at the end of the Bible takes humanity full circle to where God started out with Adam and Eve*! (created in God's unshattered image and likeness)*

- When we arrive in Heaven, we will start *(at least)* at the point God first made Adam and Eve, and then real learning will begin in earnest for all the rest of eternity. *(IMO)* Remember God is infinite in knowledge. There is going to be a lot available to learn!

- But imagine arriving in Heaven with all your glorified synapses now all firing in perfect sequence. Your ability to process what you are experiencing is going to explode, and your ability to learn new information will leap forward a million times over.

- So when you first arrive in the Throne Room, you are going to be stunned – but not like the earthly people who just saw visions into Heaven. You're going to be right there in God's unfiltered presence, and God is going to give you the divine capacity to understand what you are seeing and what you are experiencing – and that knowledge will expand more and more throughout all of eternity. *(IMO)*

Observation #2: Heavenly changes in your vision: I was intrigued to see the prophets *(in the previous pages)* falling all over their words as they tried to put into print what they were seeing in their visions. *(John's Revelation is the most familiar.)*

Revelation 4:-2-3, 5: "I saw a Throne in heaven and someone sitting on it. The one sitting on the Throne was as brilliant as gemstones—like jasper and carnelian. And the glow of an emerald circled his Throne like a rainbow. From the throne came flashes of lightning and the rumble of thunder. And in front of the throne were seven torches with burning flames."

This picture is "kaleidoscope jasper." We discussed how these Ancients were trying to explain what they were seeing by likening it to things on Earth they had already seen. John must have seen something like the kaleidoscope jasper we are looking at and he's describing what he is seeing in the Throne Room with the best word description he can find. Imagine John, after he died and actually walked into the Throne Room he had been trying to describe on earth. Imagine yourself when you get there!

Lets' test our own knowledge for when we approach our first moments in Heaven. How many primary colors are there? Three? Red, Green, Blue. If you are an artist and involved in painting you might respond red, green, and yellow, but in the refraction of light it's RGB. LED lights can be made into hundreds of different background colors, but the bulbs are all <u>red, green and blue</u>.

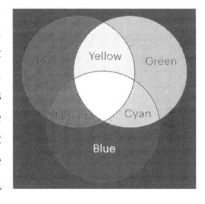

Now, out of those three colors, how many shades of color can your eyes pick up and your brain record right now here on this earth? We're told that number is <u>one million</u>!

"Researchers estimate that most humans can see around one million different colors. This is because a healthy human eye has three types of cone cells, each of which can register about 100 different color shades, amounting to around a million combinations." [15]

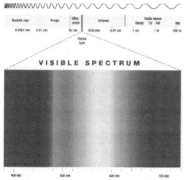

VISIBLE SPECTRUM

Do you see the tiny spectrum of light in this picture that our eyes can actually pick up? Do you see the vast number of light rays, bouncing all around us all the time that our eyes simply cannot see?

In our fallen state, we can see a million different colors. But there are, right now, on earth two to three million more shades of color that we know we cannot see at all. Is it possible that Adam and Eve in the Garden had a view of color like none of us have ever seen or imagined before? Of course!

What do you think our "seeing" is going to be like when we arrive in Heaven – when we see, in person, the colors John and Ezekiel tried so hard to describe? What if we are then seeing four million shades of color? What if there are actually far more than that, *(6 million, 10 million)* that our technology has not picked up on yet?

Observation # 3: Heavenly changes in all of our senses: What if the same principle applies to all of your senses? What if when your fallen, sin-cursed human brain is replaced by a glorified, sinless brain – your sense of smell, and hearing, and taste, and touch are all divinely affected as well? Your senses were all created by God to start with – and God said after creating humanity that we were "very good." My goodness, our dogs can smell, and hear, and see at night, far better than we can. Do we honestly think that is God's final plan?

- Do you think maybe, just maybe – that there are far more sensory experiences available in Heaven than anything we ever can experience on this fallen earth?

- Somebody asked me if we will have juicy steaks in Heaven. I don't know. But don't you imagine there are flavors by the millions that we can't even begin to imagine right now?

- Nobody will get Covid-19 and lose their taste. Nobody will have nose surgeries (*like I've had two of*) and lose their sense of smell and a lot of their sense of taste.

- What if we have only five senses on this earth – but in Heaven there are twelve or twenty?

1 Corinthians 13:12: "Now we see things imperfectly, like puzzling reflections in a *(cracked)* mirror, but then we will see everything with perfect clarity. All that I know now is partial and incomplete, but then I will know everything completely, just as God now knows me completely."

I keep coming back to these "glorifed bodies," "like Jesus," and "sharing his glory" verses that we have already highlighted. This is saying something very powerful about your future in Heaven.

1 John 3:2 NIV: "We know that when Jesus appears, we shall be like him, for we shall see him as he is."

What does it mean that you are going to be like Jesus when you get on the other side of your last breath here?

Philippians 3:20-21: "We are eagerly waiting for him to return as our Savior. He will take our weak mortal bodies and change them into glorious bodies like his own, using the same power with which he will bring everything under his control."

- I don't completely understand in what ways, and how much our newly glorified, sin-free bodies will be "like Jesus' own glorified body." But whatever that means, it can't be us limping into Heaven with a broken down frame, bad eyes, and poor taste.

- You say, "Sam, you can't take it that far," and I would respond: "How can I possibly not take it that far – and even farther?"

However much Jesus' earthly body was broken down as he paid the price for our many sins and died the death we should have died – that is not even remotely who the risen Lamb of God is now! And that is apparently not what we are going to be either!

Romans 8:17-18: "And since we are his children, we are his heirs. In fact, together with Christ we are heirs of God's glory. But if we are to share his glory, *(συνδοξασθῶμεν – sharing his glory – being glorified with him!)* **we must also share his suffering.** *(now!)* **Yet what we suffer now is nothing compared to the glory he will reveal to us later."**

1) We are <u>heirs of God's "glory"</u>!
2) We are to <u>share in his glory</u>!

3) That "glory" he will reveal to us "later"!

4) Not my words – God's words about you!

Since I've gone clear to the edge of the plank and stepped over it in the stretching of our thinking about what Heaven will be like – I might as well take one more step out into the void!

We all live our lives in what we call three dimensions.*(length, width, and depth)* Scientist have concluded that there is a fourth dimension, and that is time – all still within Einstein's theory of General Relativity and Quantum Mechanics.

 But back in 1926, scientists were adjusting Einstein's theory to a 5D universe based on the principles of light movement in space – and this eventually led to String theory, then Superstring theory, Loop Quantum Gravity, and Super-Gravity.

Few of us understand what that means, except they all work on the theory that there are at least 10 space-time dimensions on this earth although we humans only relate to four – because our normal measuring methods are set up for three dimensions plus time.

From a spiritual perspective, without a single mathematical equation – we already know there are more than three dimensions! If we believe in angels, *(which we do)* then we believe that, as Scripture indicates, angels are moving among us, as "ministering spirits sent to serve those who will inherit salvation." *(Hebrews 1:14)*

We, living here on Florida's Treasure Coast, are praying that God will send his angels and protect our spouse and children as they travel down our very own Daytona 500 – which we affectionately call US #1. If you've got protective angels on your car and a couple on the front and back bumpers – things are going to get a bit crowded and your vision of the guy going 20 mph in the left lane is going to be restricted, if all of you are operating in only our familiar three dimensions. *(Clearly angels are not usually operating in our three dimensions!)*

- In the pages of the Bible, as we've already noted, there is a very active "spirit world," and it does not operate inside our length, width, and depth dimensions.

- And we also have other clues in Scripture: After rising from the dead, Jesus was in the room with his disciples and then he wasn't! How did he get out of the room without using the door? There are more than three dimensions!

So what if the prophets are trying, *(even with the inspiration of the Holy Spirit)* to describe what they are seeing, but it all lies beyond their frame of reference – to adequately describe the indescribable GLORY OF GOD! What if they are trying to draw snapshots inside the Throne Room but are hampered because they are <u>trying to do it in three dimensions,</u> when, in fact, once we arrive in Heaven, we realize that there are really four, or five, or six, or my personal favorite seven!

This whole chapter has been me trying to define the indefinable and we haven't even touched yet:

- What it will mean to walk outside the Throne Room and still be encased with the constant filling, joyful presence of Jesus?

- What it will be like to travel to the ends of the universe and never leave Jesus' presence?

- "We will see him face to face." And that's not just staring nose to nose – it means something more than that!

What will it be like to revel in the concept of <u>rest</u>! How desperately most of us want rest! But if rest means sitting drinking lemonade for all eternity, that is going to get old real fast! Scripture clearly teaches the idea of "work" *(serving God)* in Heaven. How do we fuse the ideas of <u>work and rest</u> all at the same time using God's example? What would it be like to work at something we absolutely love – and never grow tired?

In what ways will your interests and gifts here carry on into Heaven? If you are a good cook here, will you be a divinely good cook there, in ways you can't now imagine? Will your spiritual gifts be expanded even more once you arrive there?

And what is this whole teaching about "ruling and reigning" with Jesus. Who are you going to be reigning over? Are the most faithful here on earth going to have the greater responsibility in Heaven?

Are we going to know everything on day one – or are we going to be learning more and more, and growing deeper and broader through the activities we are going to be doing throughout all of eternity?

Chapter 20

A Tour of Heaven.

Let me introduce a brand new color chart describing your journey into Heaven and what will happen there after you arrive. I'm going to give you a tour of Heaven, using these eight columns. *(You can download this 11"x 17" color chart free at samchess.com)*

As we move from the peach column on the left to the light purple column on the far right, you will find your future life unfolding in these columns. And you will literally be able to plot your journey into, and inside of, Heaven!

Column #1: We spent some time studying the "original" Heaven before Lucifer and a third of the angels tried to overthrow their Creator. That rebellion didn't end well for them, as Lucifer and his minions are forcefully expelled from Heaven. But it also didn't end well for us, because Adam and Eve fall for satan's temptation and lead us all down a sin-cursed path.

Column #2: God reaches out to humanity with love and forgiveness and many turn away from sin and satan and follow their Creator God. We read 65 times in the Old Testament of a place called "Sheol" in Hebrew, and on into the New Testament "Hades" in Greek – where the dead, both righteous and wicked, are held waiting for what the prophets say is coming next.

Meanwhile a battle rages on earth and in the heavens for the souls of humanity. 265 times we find the Old Testament term "the Lord of Heaven's armies" who was fighting against the evil one and his minions for the souls of humanity. That must have been the pre-incarnate Jesus with the "angel armies of Heaven" pushing back the forces of sin and satan!

Column #3: Sure enough, God loved humanity so much that he comes to this earth, takes on human form, and voluntarily dies the awful death we all should have died, to pay the penalty for our many sins! *But Jesus doesn't stay dead,* He defeats sin, and death, and satan, and hell, and rises victoriously from the dead bringing the promise of eternal life to all who believe!

At that moment Isaiah prophesied, *(Isaiah 61:1)* and Jesus declared in Luke 4:18 that he came to set the captives free! When Jesus rose from the dead he emptied the "righteous" half of Sheol/Hades and for the first time – "Saints" arrive in Heaven with God and the righteous angels. *(Ephesians 4:8-10)*

Column #4: (Death of the Redeemed) This is where all of humanity is still living right now. Before Jesus ascended to

Heaven, he said to all who will come to believe in **John 14:2-3:** "**I'm going back to Heaven to prepare a place for you. When everything is ready, I will come back and get you so, you will always be with me where I am!**"

Revelation 4 at the top of the 4th column gives us the first Biblical look at the Redeemed right now in Heaven. This includes your "already-dead" redeemed loved ones.

> **Revelation 4:3-4, 10: "The one sitting on the throne was as brilliant as gemstones—like jasper and carnelian. And the glow of an emerald circled his throne like a rainbow. Twenty-four thrones surrounded him, and twenty-four elders sat on them. They were all clothed in white and had gold crowns on their heads. The twenty-four elders fall down and worship the one sitting on the throne, and they lay their crowns before the throne."**

As I previously stated; I'm the guy always saying "interpret the Bible literally if possible," but in this case, I do believe, the number 24 – represents the 12 Tribes of Israel/ OT Saints and the 12 Apostles who formed the Church/NT Saints. Our additional clues – are the "white robes," the "gold crowns," and the "laying of the crowns before the Throne." You will see those phrases used often to describe us Believers, across this chart.

Column #5: is a huge upcoming event! Jesus will gather all the Redeemed Saints in Heaven and return in what we now commonly call "the Rapture." God will bring back with him the Believers who have died. **1 Thessalonians 4:16: "The Lord will come down from heaven with a commanding**

shout, the voice of the archangel, the trumpet call of God. Believers who have died will rise from their graves." *(Their bodies will rise!)* Those still living are also caught up to meet the Lord in the air. We will all *(from that moment on)* be with the Lord forever! **Revelation 7:9: "A vast crowd from every nation, tribe and people and language,"** suddenly shows up in Heaven before the Throne, "clothed in white robes." *(That's us!)*

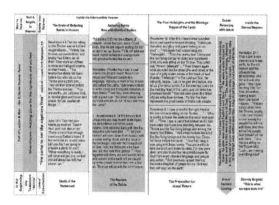

At the top of the fifth column arrow – every person who has embraced Jesus' gift up to this point is now in Heaven! You, me, your aunt Matilda – we are all there!

We explored what it will be like when we are falling before our loving God, laying down our "crowns" at the feet of our risen Savior – realizing how unworthy, yet how thankful, we are to have reached our reward!

We've talked about what it will be like when we realize that the sin-curse has fallen away, and the pain and the tears and the hurts and the traumas of this life have dissolved. And the fears and worries about tomorrow that are right now racking our world, and our personal lives fade from view.

We talked about what it will be like when the sin curse is suddenly gone from our feeble minds and our limited senses of sight and touch, and smell, and taste. What will it be like to be back where Adam and Eve started in the Garden before the fall, and then to progress upward from there?

Column #6: So now we have all arrived in Heaven. What comes next for us? Notice these "Four Hallelujahs," I call them. This vast crowd who arrives in Heaven in Revelation 7 *(all of us included)* are now involved in a huge worship celebration.

> **Revelation 19:1, 3-4, 6-8:** "After this, I heard what sounded like a vast crowd in heaven shouting, 'Hallelujah, Salvation and glory and power belong to our God.' And again their voices rang out: 'Hallelujah!' Then the twenty-four Elders and the four living beings fell down and worshiped God, who was sitting on the Throne. They cried out, 'Amen! Hallelujah!' Then I heard again what sounded like the shout of a vast crowd or the roar of mighty ocean waves or the crash of loud thunder: 'Hallelujah! For the Lord our God, the Almighty, reigns. Let us be glad and rejoice, and let us give honor to him. For the time has come for the wedding feast of the Lamb, and his bride has prepared herself. She has been given the finest of pure white linen to wear.' For the fine linen represents the good deeds of God's holy people."

This is, by the way, the only four times the word Hallelujah shows up in the New Testament! That's because Hallelujah is not a Greek/ New Testament word – it is a Hebrew/ Old Testament word. It's one that has been picked up now by virtually every language on the planet. The reason the Saints in Heaven are shouting "Hallelujah" is because they learned to shout it here first!

- That will be followed by this huge event *(in Revelation19:7)* called the Marriage Supper of the Lamb or the Wedding Feast.

Column #7: We are now the "Armies of Heaven dressed in the finest of pure white linen." So Jesus *(with the angels and us in attendance)* returns and brings an end to satan's reign on this earth! And he/we will set up the eternal reign of Jesus on this earth.

So committed Christian Fred wakes up this morning just fine, but on the way to work has a run in with the ice wagon and by evening time, he is in Heaven with Jesus. Again I ask the question, now what? I want you to put aside for a moment all that we've discussed about losing the sin-curse, losing the sickness, pain, sorrow, and tears, and being filled with unclouded joy – and at least some of the time being inside the very Throne Room of God praising him alongside of Moses and Peter, and the Afghan and Ukrainian Christians who just recently arrived in Heaven, and my dad, and Mike Richards, and your family member. *(Let's explore another practical side of this picture.)*

Let's just say that Fred was 32-years-old. He thought his whole life stretched out ahead of him. He had plans. He got educated to achieve them. He had talents he was just starting to get really good at using. As a Believer he had spiritual gifts that God had given him to invest in the lives of others. He was already using them at his church. And now he is dead! In Heaven! That's our ultimate destination, but is Fred, in fact, going to be forever involved in a never-ending sing-along? Are you? No!

Remember God created Fred here on this planet, in his image and likeness – and part of that image and likeness was for him to develop his God-given talents, and gifts, and dreams and ambitions. Fred was doing that and then along came the ice wagon! Now Fred gets to suddenly go to Heaven *(with all the heavenly benefits we discussed)*, but he loses all the purpose and passion God instilled into him in this life – right?

Fulfill your purpose! We tell people that all the time. We encourage our young people to maximize the gifts and talents God gave them and "fulfill the purpose for which God put you on this planet."

I say that to our church all the time in sermons and often in prayers, "maximize the purpose for which God put you on this planet"! But does the "purpose for your life" end when you breathe your last breath! What if it doesn't?

- What if all eternity isn't just about worshipping God in the Throne Room? *Understand how careful I'm trying to make that statement when I just spent two chapters describing how that event is going to be beyond anything you can possibly ever imagine in this life!*

- But now we have to step back and look at another side of this picture as well. The Bible presents multiple snapshots of what Heaven is really going to include!

First, here is a passage that is often quoted about what we will all be doing in Heaven. We especially like to quote this passage when we are completely exhausted from pouring out our limited energy day after day.

> **Revelation 14:13: "And I heard a voice from Heaven saying, 'Write this down: Blessed are those who die in the Lord. Yes, says the Spirit, they are blessed indeed, for <u>they will rest from their hard work</u>; for their good deeds follow them!'"**

If you are living in utter exhaustion, the idea that when you get to Heaven – you can put down the old towel, or trowel is pretty inviting. Heaven is like the ultimate retirement! Right? The ultimate retirement in this earthly life is to get up at noon, sip lemonade, play a round of golf, vegetate in front of the TV, and go to bed? Yes?

- No! <u>Life's real meaning is all about having purpose!</u> If you really do get up at noon and accomplish absolutely nothing of value all day, everyday, it isn't long before you feel absolutely useless, and many people will descend into deep depression.

- <u>We weren't created to do nothing</u>! We were created in God's image, to have purpose and passions, to create things and cultivate things.

- Does anybody actually think that becoming more like God in Heaven means sitting directionless and purposeless for all of eternity?

John 5:16-18: "So the Jewish leaders began harassing Jesus for breaking the Sabbath rules. But Jesus replied, '<u>My Father is always working, and so am I</u>.' So the Jewish leaders tried all the harder to find a way to kill him. For he not only broke the Sabbath, he called God his Father, thereby making himself equal with God."

- Remember God started this whole thing *(in the beginning)* by working six days to create all that is and then resting on the seventh day.

- In John 14, Jesus left this earth and went back to Heaven not to rest but "to prepare a place for us"!

- In Revelation 1, after we get that amazing view of what John says Jesus looks like now in the Throne Room, we're then told that Jesus is walking among "seven golden lamp-stands," and then in verse 20 we are told the lamp-stands are, in fact, the Churches.

- So besides preparing our future home, and interceding for us before the Father *(Romans 8:34)*, Jesus is also right now redeeming, and building, and encouraging and protecting his church to the very ends of the earth. <u>He's quite busy</u>!

- The Holy Spirit is working too, infilling, and guiding, and convicting and transforming every Believer on the planet, from the old sinful us into a brand new righteous us!

Your Savior is in Heaven right now accomplishing, and creating, and overseeing, and encouraging, and you are going to become "like him" in your glorified body. **1 Corinthians 15:49: "As we have born the image of the earthly Adam, so will we bear the image of the Heavenly Jesus!"** It seems, we may be creating, accomplishing, and overseeing too!

We've been trying to understand what it means that our glorified body will "be like Jesus' glorified body." Now we begin to run into verses that seem to suggest we are going to be, perhaps, like him in our actions as well. Exactly how Jesus-like are you going to become after you arrive at the "Pearly Gates"?

If Jesus is working overtime to get us all safely to Heaven – is his high level of activity going to stop once we all arrive? No!

And when we all return with him and he sets up his "forever rule" on this earth – we're told over and over that we will be "reigning with him." *(That's columns 7 and 8 on your chart)* Jesus is not going to spend his eternity sitting in an armchair sipping lemonade – and I suspect we are not either.

Let me show you a new *(to me)* principle here: When God created a perfect Adam and Eve and put them in a perfect Garden of Eden, that "picture of perfection" did not include them sitting under a tree all day, every day. They had two primary responsibilities: <u>Work and worship</u>!

> **Genesis 2:8-9, 15: "Then the LORD God planted a garden in Eden in the east, and there he placed the man he had made. The LORD God made all sorts of trees grow up from the ground—trees that were beautiful and that produced delicious fruit. The LORD God took the man and put him in the Garden of Eden to work it and take care of it."**

"Well, of course, somebody had to pull the weeds and pick up the rotted fruit." No! This is before the curse, there were no weeds, there was no rotted fruit!

- Remember the Garden was created perfect. Adam and Eve were created perfect! But the Garden was not self-sustaining. Adam and Eve had to cultivate it! Why?

- Because that is what we were made in God's image to do! *(Create things, cultivate things, sustain things, accomplish things, and develop things.)*

- Do we actually believe that God would build purpose and passion into us in this life to achieve and create and cultivate – and then on the day when our earthly heart refuses to take the next beat, all that "in-his-image" stuff in this life is going to disappear when we get to the next life? No!

WHAT WILL WE DO IN HEAVEN?

What if the things that so interest you in this life – what if the things you become so good at doing in this life – what if the things you are most passionate about in this life are simply precursors to what you will be focusing on in the life to come?

What if God built into Christian Fred's life passions for things he loved to do, was trained to do, wanted desperately to accomplish, and then his life was "cut short" at an early age?

- What if Fred shows up in Heaven with all the spiritual benefits we have discussed when leaving the curse of sin behind, but the things he hasn't left behind are his abilities, his spiritual gifts, and the things he struggled so hard in this life to learn and improve?

- What if he gets to Heaven, and through the providence of God, he simply picks up where he left off here? But now without any of the cursed-brain, cursed-senses hindrances that so often held him back in this life, or caused him to stop because he had hit a wall, and he just didn't have the knowledge of how to break through?

- What if all that held him back is now gone, and his "righteous, passionate pursuits" have absolutely no barriers to his eternal "success"?

- If God plants a will or desire or passion for some righteous pursuit in this life, and then gives you the talents, skills, and gifts to pursue it – why would that not be the best indicator of what you will be pursuing in the life to come?

If you are a musician in this life, why in the world, would you not be one in the life to come, but now without any restraints?

If you have a searching scientific mind in this life, why would you not be out in front of pursuing the vast infinite storehouses of God's limitless knowledge – that *(I believe)* we are going to be learning more and more about throughout all of eternity?

If you love to cook in this life why would you not be a "heavenly cook" in the life to come, with all the un-fallen sensory enhancements we talked about in the last chapter? If you love to organize things here, you are going to love every timeless "second" in Heaven. You are going to be "ruling" in Heaven, building on the beginnings of what you learned here. *(we'll come to that.)*

Here's the burr under the saddle. We tend to <u>tie the word "work" to the word "tired</u>," and we tend to tie the words "not-working" to the word "rest." But we do understand, don't we, that exhaustion from work is purely a result of the fall? God said it was going to be so! We know God didn't rest on the seventh day of creation because he was tired, right? He's God! He is infinite in strength! We're not.

Revelation 14:13: "And I heard a voice from Heaven saying, 'Write this down: Blessed are those who die in

the Lord. Yes, says the Spirit, they are blessed indeed, for they will rest from their hard work (κόπων- *kopos: laborious toil involving extreme weariness and deep fatigue*); **for their good deeds follow them!'"** (ἔργα – *ergon; good works from inner desire, intension, or purpose*)

- Is this verse saying you are not going to "work" in Heaven, or that your work in Heaven will be birthed out of your inner desires, intents and purposes? That even in the midst of eternal work – you will find "rest from your laborious toil involving extreme weariness and deep fatigue"?

- You know what it is like to work on a hobby that would be laborious for others, but to you it is restful, relaxing and fun. Now take away the entire effects of the curse and multiply the restful part by 10,000,000 – and you know what work will be like in Heaven!

I'm taking a while to establish that "the you" here on earth will become the enhanced, glorified "you" in Heaven. The things that make you tick now – will make you tick dramatically more loudly then.

Your personality is not going to become some completely new unrecognizable personality when you get to Heaven. Your body, after the Rapture, will be "glorified." The "corruptible will become incorruptible." The sin chains that plagued you on this earth will be gone. But <u>you will still be you</u>!

From what we can see in Scripture, we will be easily able to recognize each other in Heaven. We have not established what approximate age we will all be in Heaven, but it is doubtful that the elderly will show up in Heaven looking old and it is not possible *(IMO)* that a miscarried baby will show up in heaven as a fetus. We are all, perhaps, going to be at some level of a prime age. I put an illustration earlier in this book where we looked at when our human organs quit developing, and when they begin their long decline toward death, and the average ages that we looked at seemed to be about our mid-thirties. Some of us might theorize that because Jesus rose from the dead at 33 years of age – we will all appear about that age in Heaven? *Who knows?*

The more important point is, that if you miscarried a baby and they actually appear in Heaven full grown – you will instantly know who they are. You will instantly know your grandfather who died before you were born. You will instantly know the brother you were separated from at birth. I say that using the Transfiguration as our guide, and the fact that the three disciples, Peter, James and John instantly knew who Moses and Elijah were as they visited with Jesus, even though they had been dead 800-1600 years.

> **Matthew 17:1-4: "Six days later Jesus took Peter and the two brothers, James and John, and led them up a high mountain to be alone. As the men watched, Jesus' appearance was transformed so that his face shone like the sun, and his clothes became as white as light. Suddenly, Moses and Elijah appeared and began talking with Jesus. Peter exclaimed, 'Lord, it's wonderful for us to be here! If you want, I'll make three shelters as memorials—one for you, one for Moses, and one for Elijah.'"**

The truth is, when you get to Heaven and meet Moses outside the Throne Room, <u>you will instantly know him too</u> – and oddly <u>he will instantly know you</u>! And that will *(perhaps)* be true of every Believer you will ever meet in Heaven regardless of when they lived, what their nationality, or at what age they died.

> **1 Corinthians 13:12: "Now we see things imperfectly, like puzzling reflections in a *(cracked)* mirror, but then we will see everything with perfect clarity. All that I know now is partial and incomplete, but then I will know everything completely, just as God now knows me completely."**

Remember Atheist Mark Twain's famous insane comment, "Go to Heaven for the climate, Go to hell for the company!" Can you imagine being in hell with Osama Bin Laden, Attila the Hun and Joseph Stalin, and Chinese communist Chairman Mao who killed 100,000,000 of his people along with every other murderer, and rapist, and wife abuser and every other bound-up-in-sin person – and to somehow imagine that hell will be a wonderful place to enjoy great company?!

When, in fact, in Heaven, you will be able to meet in perfect instant harmony with David, and Isaiah, and Luke, and Mary. Even if you are an introvert, you will be comfortable sharing with William Wilberforce, or C.S. Lewis, or Fanny Crosby or Dwight L. Moody. You will enjoy instant fellowship with everyone you ever meet, and you will know exactly who they are, and they will know you too!

Chapter 21

Attending the Marriage Supper of the Lamb.

So we are all going to get into Heaven by death or the Rapture.

We are going to arrive there before God begins the final process of mopping up evil from this planet. Meanwhile, we are all going to be increasingly responding with the ever louder "Hallelujahs." We'll look at these Scriptures in just a moment. And then – we are all going to enjoy together the "Marriage Supper of the Lamb"!

- What's that? Is that an actual event? Of course! Why would anybody think it wasn't?

- The coming "Marriage Feast" is only mentioned twice in Revelation 19:7-8, but every Early Church Israelite reading what we are getting ready to read would have had an instant mental picture! We don't because most of us are not Jewish, and none of us live in the first century. Few of us celebrate weddings like they did.

- But when the people in the first century read this, and saw the words "Marriage Supper," they instantly had a whole mental movie of what was included playing in their brains.

Ancient Jewish weddings in Bible times were always structured around three elements. They really didn't vary, except perhaps in lengths of time. Let's look.

Part #1) The Betrothal, the engagement, "being espoused" *(from which we still get the word spouse).* This was a legally binding, signed contract between two sets of parents, and/or the groom and the bride's parents. Breaking the contract *(morally)* was considered infidelity.

- That's why when the virgin Mary got pregnant with Jesus, Joseph considered whether to divorce her publicly, or put her away privately. *(By this point in history, stoning for adultery was losing its popularity.)*

- The Groom would use the engagement period to get a house ready to bring his bride home. <u>Is this ringing any bells in your mind</u>?

Part #2) The Presentation: As the wedding day approached, the Groom would go where she lived to get his Bride and bring her to the "presentation" in his home town. The bride would be formally presented by the bridegroom, both to his Father *(and mother),* and to the guests who were gathering for the ceremony itself.

- This "presentation" would last a week or more while the bride was proudly being presented as the "forever spouse" of the bridegroom.

- If you think a modern wedding is expensive, imagine feeding and lodging the guests for a whole week. If the parents or groom were wealthy, the "preparation" part of the marriage could go on for months.

- That was probably the situation in the wedding in Cana, where the feast went on so long, that the guests drank all the wine – and Jesus had to create more out of water.

Part #3) The Last part of the Wedding - the Marriage Supper!

This Feast could also last for a long period of time. This part was where the final vows would be exchanged, and the Groom would promise his Bride his unending devotion forever.

This may seem like just a symbolic illustration to us in the 21st century, but I have a sense that in the mind of God, it is "far more real" than we might often imagine. God really takes this whole imagery far more seriously than we do. Ask yourself:

1) Within this imagery: What stage of a "marriage" is your present relationship with Jesus while living as a Believer on this earth?

2) Within this imagery: What is the significance of Jesus going to Heaven "to prepare a place for you"?

3) Within this imagery; At what point does the "Groom" go to collect his Bride and bring her to his home?

4) Within this imagery: When does the Groom present the Bride to his Father?

Let's just imagine that in God's way of looking at things, the whole "Hallelujah worship time" would be in the celebration preceding the wedding ceremony. So if God really is taking all the above as seriously as we think he probably is, do you think there is actually going to be a real Marriage Supper of the Lamb in Heaven that we will all be attending, before we mount up with Jesus to come back to Earth in his glorious Second Coming? Of course there is! And as a Redeemed Believer, you will be there! Can you imagine the intensity of the moment when Jesus promises each of us that we will never, ever again be outside his immediate presence again – that his devotion to us will be personal, and infinite, and eternal!

- That there is no possible chance that he will ever "divorce" us as his Bride, or even find us less than perfect in his eyes.

- The promise of "Emmanuel, God with us," will finally be completely fulfilled with all its divine intensity!

Let's dig into the Scriptures behind what we just read:

Here's the "Rapture" from The Living Bible paraphrase:

1 Thessalonians 4:16-17 TLB: "For the Lord himself will come down from Heaven with a mighty shout and with the soul-stirring cry of the archangel and the great trumpet-call of God. And the Believers who are already dead will be the first to rise to meet the Lord. Then we who are still alive on the earth will be caught up with them in the clouds to meet Jesus in the air and we will then remain with him forever." Every redeemed person, living or dead up to that point in time, is now in Heaven – *Now what?*

Do we all then make our way over to the "big cafeteria in the sky" and present our meal ticket for "the Marriage

Supper of the Lamb"? Isn't that what the Bible says? No, no it doesn't!

> **Revelation 19:1, 3 NIV:** *(Four chapters from the end of the Bible)* **"After this I heard what seemed to be the loud voice of a great multitude in Heaven, crying out, 'Hallelujah! Salvation and glory and power belong to our God.' Once more they cried out, 'Hallelujah!'"** *(Remember this is us shouting!)*

There is obviously an increasing intensity in a mass worship service in Heaven – of which you will be a part! We, the Redeemed, will keep responding with louder and louder "Hallelujahs!" to God's final destruction of the effects of sin and the curse here on this earth. The "judgments" *(Trumpets and Bowls)* listed in Revelation are pouring out on earth – we are apparently watching from Heaven! Here's the "four Hallelujah grand finale," and it ends where we need to stop and study!

> **Revelation 19:6-9 ESV: "Then I heard what seemed to be the voice of a great multitude, like the roar of many waters and like the sound of mighty peals of thunder, crying out, 'Hallelujah! For the Lord our God the Almighty reigns. Let us rejoice and exult and give him the glory, for the Marriage Feast** *(gamos)* **of the Lamb has come, and his Bride has made herself ready; it was granted her to clothe herself with fine linen, bright and pure'** *(always, always a description of the Redeemed in Heaven)* **for the fine linen is the righteous deeds of the saints. And the angel said to me, 'Write this: Blessed are those who are invited to the Marriage Supper of**

the Lamb.' And he said to me, 'These are the true words of God.'"

So after you join in the last Hallelujah, and the sound echoes out across the universe and bounces back for the last time – you then grab your meal ticket, head over to "the great cafeteria in the sky" and say: "I'm here for the Marriage Supper of the Lamb!" Yes?

- You say to the angelic attendant at the door: "I don't know what Marriage Supper of the Lamb means, and to be quite honest it has always sounded a little strange down on earth, even downright embarrassing to we who have been privileged to live our lives in the 21st century western world.

- When the men in our churches talked about "being part of the Bride of Christ," we would pass over it quickly and move on to other words like "the Church," or "the Body of Christ" because they sounded more socially acceptable.

Is this whole "Bride of Jesus" thing just a metaphor? Is the Marriage Supper of Christ just a metaphor? *(a figure of speech)* Or are you one day going to be sitting down with Jesus while God honors you, celebrates you, as the Bride of Christ? *(Whatever that means to God)* Are you going to actually be eating a meal in Heaven one day and the marquee outside will say: "Come on in to the Wedding Feast of the Lamb!" Let me show you some things *(a whole lot of things)* that I had never noticed before:

Revelation 19:9 ESV: "And the angel said to me, 'Write this: Blessed are those who are invited to the Marriage

Supper of the Lamb.' And he said to me, '<u>These are the true words of God</u>.'"

Why is that last phrase there? Isn't the whole book of Revelation the true words of God? Doesn't the book start out with the words *"This is a Revelation from Jesus Christ"?* John wrote a Gospel and three other Epistles that had already, by this time, joined 22 other letters to become the inspired Words of God. Why does this particular sentence need to be emphasized with "these are the true words of God"?

God himself is stating this! God seems to be saying: "If you gloss over anything else you have read, make sure you don't gloss over this! Blessed are those who are invited to the Marriage Supper of the Lamb"!

By the way: "Blessed are those who are invited to the Marriage Supper" is the 4th "blessed" in the book. We always talk about the Eight Beatitudes *(Blessed are's)* in Matthew 5 – without realizing there are four more in Revelation. But this is the only one that ends with the exclamation point: These are the true words of God! God wants us to give this serious attention.

- I might add here: I told you I found only 26 books written on Heaven in the last 100 years.

- But if we think books written about Heaven are scarce, try finding one about, *(or even a sermon about)* the Marriage Supper of the Lamb!

- It's the one entry God puts a huge exclamation point at the end of – and it's amazingly ignored in Christian literature! *(Trust me, I looked!)*

Here's another curious thing: Why are the words "the Lamb" tacked onto that phrase The Marriage Supper of the Lamb? The word "lamb" was a word used back on earth when Jesus was taking our sin debt on himself and paying our sin penalty. He was then the final sacrifice for sin, <u>but why carry that name on into Heaven</u>? The "dying part" for Jesus, was all on the earth side – then he rose from the dead, and now He lives forever! Why still refer to Jesus as "the Lamb" in Heaven? Why not call him the *Lion of the Tribe of Judah,* or the Old Testament name we studied, *The Lord of Heaven's Armies?*

Just seven verses later, in Revelation 19:16, Jesus is returning to earth with all the Saints *(us)* in his Glorious Second Coming to finalize the destruction of the Armageddon army and the antichrist, and to chain satan in the Abyss. His name is then said to be: <u>The King of all kings and Lord of all lords</u>!

So it must be true that whatever is going to be happening inside that massive room at the Marriage Supper of the Lamb – there must be some part of that dinner that is "a look back" by all the millions of redeemed peoples sitting there in Jesus' presence!

We are apparently going to start that celebration *(which I believe will last about 18 earth months)* by spending some time focusing on the plan of salvation that got us into that room! Otherwise, the meal should be called the Marriage Supper of the King of all Kings and Lord of all Lords!

It occurred to me that we need to put the mental images of the Last Supper and the Marriage Supper of the Lamb side by side in our minds. At the last Supper, Jesus is explaining to his disciples exactly what he is getting ready to do. In the Marriage Supper Jesus will explain, not to a small roomful of disciples, but to a massive room with millions of people in it who are now part of his Bride:

- Exactly what he did on the cross, and how what he did snapped the chains of sin, and then finally began to crush the power of satan in our lives! *(IMO)*

- The whole truth will finally come cascading into our glorified minds, in ways we cannot even imagine now – of exactly how Jesus' sin-sacrifice led to us sitting at the Lamb's table at his Marriage Feast!

I've spent 44 years preaching about what Jesus' sin sacrifice means to me and to those I am ministering to. But I have a strange feeling that when I am finally sitting at the Marriage Feast table, and Jesus stands up in front of us and begins to connect all the dots – I think I'm going to discover that I only understood the tiniest fraction of what there was to know! Some of you are probably going to come up to me and say: "Well, thanks a lot, Chess. It would have been nice if you had told us the other 99%!"

The only written sermon I could find, where a pastor actually used a whole sermon to try to describe what would be happening as we sit with Jesus at his Marriage Feast, was written by a chap named Charles Spurgeon. It was written in the flowery way an Englishman from the late 1800's wrote, and spoke!

So many others who've gone before us, just start from the viewpoint that the phrase "Marriage Supper of the Lamb" is just a metaphor for "You finally made it to Heaven! The Saints came marching in!"

As I read his sermon, it struck me what a brave man Charles Spurgeon was to even try to describe Jesus' Marriage Feast. Think about how a Pastor in Spurgeon's time (*late 1800's*) would have struggled with their thinking. They had read all the prophecies in Ezekiel and Jeremiah that Israel would one day rise again as a nation. They had read all the inclusions of Israel and Jerusalem in End Times Scriptures – and there are a lot!

But there <u>was no nation of Israel</u> and had not been for 1800 years! And there was no Jewish city of Jerusalem in any kind of a condition to house the events prophesied in the Book of Revelation! Many, many preachers and theologians adopted a symbolic view of all of the End Times because "how could any of it possibly be literally true, if the prophesied centerpiece of real-estate during the End Times was in the hands of the Ottoman Turks and Arabs"? And there seemed to be no possibility that it would revert to Jewish control. After the First World War that control went to England and then the United Nations, but:

Think about a pastor, even 60 years after Charles Spurgeon at the end of the Second World War, trying to make sense out of all the inclusions of Israel as a nation into End Time prophecy. Not only was there no Jewish control of Israel – Adolph Hitler had made it his business to kill every Jew on the planet! During WWII, Hitler annihilated 6 million Jews! That was ½ of all the Jews who were alive at that time on the earth! And he fully intended to take out the rest if he hadn't come to a sudden end, biting down on a cyanide capsule.

And we should understand clearly that the idea to kill all the Jews on the planet was not really Hitler's idea. Satan in his war against God was trying to stop the prophesied plan of the Almighty! He thought if he could take out all the Jews and assure that none of them could be anywhere near Jerusalem when the last seven prophesied years of human history arrived, he would win the war for human souls and Jesus would lose!

Satan underestimated Jesus, or greatly overestimated himself!

At midnight on May 14, 1948 the provisional government of Israel proclaimed a new State of Israel! The world was left with their mouths, literally, hanging open! Surrounding

361

nations tried to batter Israel back into submission. They failed!

Since 1948, Jews have been pouring into their new homeland just exactly as Ezekiel and Jeremiah had prophesied. Right now more than 1/2 of all the Jews on the planet are living in Israel gearing up *(whether they know it or not)* for the final events recorded in Bible prophecy to unfold.

Pastors, in ever growing numbers over the last 70 years, have been startled into the reality, that if God fulfilled that very important prophecy of Israel's return as a nation, right to the tiniest part – perhaps the rest of prophecy is not just symbolism either.

- Perhaps there is a real seven-year period coming that will be the end of the age and the Church will be "snatched away" just as Paul and Jesus himself said. My goodness, Revelation 11 and 12 literally divide that final seven years into two equal halves of exactly 1,260 days each. Does that sound like symbolism?

- The very first rule of Bible interpretation: "Always go with the plain meaning of the text, unless it is clear that the author meant it to be symbolic!"

- Perhaps there is a literal Marriage Supper of the Lamb coming in your future and you will be sitting at Jesus' celebration table – perhaps indeed!

Let's ask a few more curious questions and answers before we try to determine what we will be doing in that massive Heavenly Banquet hall for 18 earth months. Do we leave at night? *(There is no night!)* Do we take breaks when we get tired? *(We won't get tired!)* Do we go back to our room? Now that is a real biblical question. Remember in John 14:2-4 – "I'm going to prepare a place for you."

- You DO have a room/mansion waiting in Heaven! It is in the Holy City, the New Jerusalem. And as we've already studied – after Jesus' Second Coming, the New Jerusalem is coming down here! That's very specific in the last two chapters of the Bible.

- Remember, the Holy City's size is 1400 miles x 1400 miles x 1400 miles. We calculated that if every floor is a mile high and your room has a ceiling that is a mile tall – the floor space in that Holy City would still be 13 times the land surface of this earth! It's big! And that city is, for now, up in Heaven! You are going one day soon to wherever that is!

One more curious question: Is the Marriage Feast of the Lamb a real feast? Will we actually be eating during those 18 or so earth months? The word used is γάμος – gamos. It means feasting, eating, a banquet, and wedding festivities. So if we are going to be eating all throughout that time, what in the world are we going to be eating? The only example we have in the Bible of food that people ate that was not earthly food, was the example of:

Exodus 16:2-4, 31: "There, too, the whole community of Israel complained about Moses and Aaron. 'If only the LORD had killed us back in Egypt,' they moaned. 'There we sat around pots filled with meat and ate all the bread we wanted. But now you have brought us into this wilderness to starve us all to death.' Then the LORD said to Moses, 'Look, I'm going to rain down food from Heaven for you.' The Israelites called the food manna. (*Mawn – what is it?*) (It was white like coriander seed, and it tasted like honey wafers.)"

Several more times in Scripture we are told that the Manna was "food from Heaven." What if Manna is just the tip of the Heavenly Cafeteria iceberg? What if once we get to Heaven with all our sin-cursed senses exploding open in glorified newness, the unlimited Heavenly food menu begins to be brought out for taste testing – and we discover that the food of Heaven makes our food here on earth seem like we're eating sawdust? I suspect that is exactly what we are going to experience!

Imagine taking one mouthful of the perfect recipes God makes without the attached curse of sin which destroys everything here on earth. Imagine, for a moment, what it might be like to experience (*thousands of times over*) foods that your palate has never even come close to savoring. If it sounds like I'm being symbolic, I'm not! I'm being dead literal! And speaking of dead literal – this coming banquet is definitely not a metaphor. It is a real happening!

Revelation 19:7: "Let us be glad and rejoice, and let us give honor to him. For the time has come, *(ἔρχω – ercho; a new real important never before done event is about to start)* **for the wedding feast of the Lamb, and his bride has prepared herself."** This is the same phrase Jesus used in the Garden of Gethsemane when he said to his disciples: Go ahead and sleep guys, "my time has come!" *(ἔρχω – ercho)* That was a real, humanity changing event, and so is this Feast!

- So Jesus raptures the Saints, then we are all presented to the Heavenly Father, probably in the Throne Room of God.

- A massive worship service like the one detailed in Revelation 4 and 5 will probably take place. Perhaps the four Hallelujahs take place in the Throne Room, but maybe not until we get inside the Banquet Hall of Heaven.

- At some point we are all called into the Marriage Feast setting, and millions of Saints from all the ages gather.

Before Jesus mounts up to descend to earth, with all of us accompanying him in His triumphal Second Coming. Before he takes on the antichrist and the armies of the world in the famous Battle of Armageddon. Before he finally, completely destroys the effects of sin in this world and throws the antichrist and the false prophet into the Lake of Fire and satan into the Abyss. That is just before "the sheep and goat judgment," at the end of Armageddon where the willfully wicked join the antichrist in the Lake of Fire. Just before any of that takes place, Jesus gathers all the Saints from all the ages – Abraham and Sarah, Moses, David, Mary of Nazareth and Mary Magdalene, and invites them/us to the Marriage Supper of the Lamb. Think of it; the thief on the cross may be sitting across the table from you! The widow who gave her last coin might be sitting right beside you!

Remember when Jesus said to the Church in Revelation 3 that **"To those who overcome He would write on them the name of His God,"** and then added, **"and I will write on them my new name"?** *(Revelation 3:12)*

I suspect that somewhere on a banquet table the size of the United States is a place setting with a card emblazoned with not only your earthly name, but a "special name" God has only for you, because you are His special invitee! But, there is one condition: You must embrace Jesus' redeeming gift of salvation!

So what is going to be happening inside the banquet room besides the new Heavenly food? *(Obviously I'm speculating here, but perhaps it is discerning speculation!)* Jesus will, I believe, spend some time during the introduction time, exploding our minds open to the real reality of God himself squeezing into a human embryo for the purpose of redeeming lost humanity.

With all the sin-curse washed out of our minds, we are going to say, "Oh my, I see it all so clearly now!" Imagine Jesus describing his own great sacrifice for us – as he shed every drop of his blood to wash away every drop of our sin!

Picture yourself sitting there around the heavenly banquet table as Jesus begins to explain all the things in this life that just didn't make any sense, all the things that brought you, and me, and millions of other people such pain and confusion. I don't know how much of what happened on earth we will remember, but if we do, *(at least through this finalization of us as Jesus' Bride)* imagine hearing Jesus' answer, once and for all, every anguished "Why?" question ever posed. Imagine Jesus patiently unveiling every tormented "If there is a loving God, then why, question?" And you will hear one after another after another of the redeemed Saints, *(including yourself)* begin to say, "Oh, now I get it! Now it all makes sense! It was so worth it all!"

But here is the core of any marriage celebration – the Groom and the Bride sharing their deep lasting love for one another. Imagine finally sitting in a room where Jesus personally assures us of his unconditional and eternal love, and probably for the first time in our existence, we completely believe him. I mean we read all the time that:

> **"God loved us so much that he gave his only begotten Son, that whoever believes in him will not perish but will have everlasting life."** *(John 3:16)*

> **"God showed his love for us in that while we were still sinners, Jesus died for us!"** *(Romans 5:8)*

We know what those Bible verses say, and we believe them *(sort of)*. But we are also painfully aware of how deep the stains of sin have etched us! How could God love you, knowing how stumbling your love for him really is? Imagine when we find ourselves, not only safely in Heaven, but sitting at the Wedding Feast with our Savior, while he reassures us of his relentless, unlimited, eternal love.

- "I loved you before the foundations of the world!" I pursued you even when you insisted in running in the other direction!

- I wouldn't let you go because my love was/is so deep. And now you are right here with me for all the endless ages of eternity, where I can shower my love into every crevasse of your everlasting life, without the curse of sin ever getting in the way again.

We've talked about how excited we will be... to be in the unclouded presence of Jesus. It's <u>a lot harder for us to understand that Jesus will be just as excited to be forever in our presence</u>! That's the whole symbolism of the "Bride."

Jesus is going to be more ecstatic to spend all of eternity with you – than you are to spend all of eternity with him!

And we look at our fallen stumbling selves and say, "How in the world can that be? Why would Jesus want to spend one moment with me?"

<u>But he does – oh he does! Because he loves you so, so much</u>! *(Have you put on your white wedding garment?)* Has your heart been transformed by first repenting of your sins, and then embracing the free gift of salvation that he paid for with his death on the cross? If not, you need to pray right now:

"Dear Lord Jesus, I know that I am a sinner, and I'm asking for your forgiveness. I believe you died for my sins and rose victoriously from the dead. I repent right now and turn from my sins and I invite you to come into my life and to cleanse my heart. I trust in your sin payment on my behalf right now and I will from this day forward serve you as my Savior and Lord." Amen.

CHAPTER 21

HEAVEN: Part VI

CHAPTER 21

Chapter 22

Studying the mystery and wonder of Heaven!

I told you several times that I purposely bought every book I could find, in print, written about Heaven in the last 100 years. *(500 years)* It is stunning, how few people used all of Scripture to write expository books about Heaven!

Just for comparison, I searched for books on wildebeests in Africa. I could instantly find more books on wildebeests than I could about Heaven – where all of us say we want to go and spend all of eternity in the presence of our Savior. This *Magnificent Migration* book description – *"The author takes readers on a staggering, emotional journey alongside the greatest land migration on the planet earth—that of the wildebeest across the Serengeti—to explore the mystery and wonder of migration in a sweeping story sure to leave its mark."* [16]

☺ There are more people studying "the mystery and wonder of the migration patterns of Wildebeests," than are studying the mystery and wonder of where we are going to spend all of eternity on the other side of our last breath! You say, Mr. Sarcastic Sam – that's because we don't really have much information about what Heaven is going to be like and what we are going to be doing there! No, that's not accurate!

We've already "cracked that nut" a lot in our discussion of the differences in us when we arrive there – with our sin nature gone, and our curse-clouded mind suddenly expanding open and our fogged-up earthly senses suddenly exploding open to experience what we were never able to here on earth. But before we go even further into what Heaven will be like – let me show you something I've never seen until studying this material, and I am seriously wrestling with this.

We *(in our church)* talk often about us Believers, here on earth, once our sins have been forgiven – God begins in us the process of sanctification. Our old sinful us begins to be replaced by a new righteous us. We begin to act less and less like the old sinful us, and more and more like Jesus shining through us.

> *That is the process of sanctification – and it is a process lasting right up till our last breath.*

But then we say <u>we are finally glorified</u>! I've been taught, and have taught others for many years – that at our last breath here, or at least when we rise in the rapture to meet Jesus in the air, we are then <u>instantly glorified</u>! That is a real biblical truth, and let me remind you again of the Scriptural basis of it all:

Philippians 3:20-21: "We are eagerly waiting for him to return as our Savior. He will take our weak mortal bodies and change them into glorious bodies *(δόξης)* <u>like his own</u>."

Colossians 3:1, 4: "Set your sights on the realities of Heaven where Christ sits in the place of honor at God's right hand. And when Christ, who is your life, is revealed to the whole world, you will share in all his glory." (δόξη)

Romans 8:17: "And since we are his children, we are his heirs. In fact, together with Christ <u>we are heirs of God's glory</u>." (δόξη)

But here is the issue that slammed into my thinking. I teach that <u>sanctification</u> for the Believer <u>is a process</u> that happens here on earth until our last breath. 1) Justification –Saved from the penalty of sin. 2) Sanctification- saved from the power of sin.   3) Glorification – saved from the presence of sin.

But what if <u>glorification</u> in Heaven <u>is a process</u> too? What if 'sharing in all God's glory" also unfolds over all the eons of eternity? *(I'm becoming convinced that is true!)* What if we are going to be learning more and more out of God's infinite storehouse of knowledge forever? I asked us a few pages ago, "What if the talents and spiritual gifts you are growing here continue on into your future in Heaven?"

What if the skills and spiritual gifts you developed on Earth continue expanding and pouring out through you into what you will be doing for the next 1000 "years" in Heaven? *(I'm now convinced that's true too – God doesn't waste anything!)*

So if this theory is right – when we arrive in Heaven for the presentation to the Father, then move on into the Marriage Supper of the Lamb – we will be free of the curse of sin, as we have discussed, but the beginning of our eternity-long learning process will have just begun. When Jesus clearly and logically expands our minds open to what really happened from his "It is finished" on the cross until our pulling up a chair and sitting down at the Marriage Supper table – we will probably fill our intellect more in that "18 months" than we did the whole time we spent on earth!

The curtain will be pulled back for us and we will see behind the veil at the massive "Conflict of the Ages" that has waged between God and satan, as God began to build his Church and forge his Bride into those people who would not only live with him forever in Heaven, but who would then carry on an expanding eternal ministry across the universe – something the Bible refers to as "ruling and reigning" with Christ! *(Whatever that means, we're getting to it!)*

Somewhere along the way, there is *(I suspect)* going to come a change in the agenda of the Marriage Supper of the Lamb. Biblically, at the end of the Marriage Feast in Heaven, something very momentous takes place. It's one of the most treasured passages in the Bible. Understand this is the very next thing *(after the Marriage Supper)* in Revelation 19.

> **Revelation 19:11-14, 16: "Then I saw Heaven opened, and a white horse was standing there. Its rider was named Faithful and True. His eyes were like flames of fire, and on His head were many crowns. He wore a robe dipped in blood, and His title was the Word of God. <u>The armies of heaven, dressed in the finest of pure white linen, followed Him on white horses.</u> On His robe at His thigh was written this title: King of all kings and Lord of all lords."**

Somewhere along the way, during that Marriage Feast, Jesus is *(perhaps)* going to say to his millions of glorified Saints – We now all have a job to do back on earth. All you "Saints" know exactly what it is, because you've all read Revelation 19.

"Yes, Jesus, we've all read Revelation 19, but we had a little bit of trouble understanding what we were reading, so could you please run us through those details again."

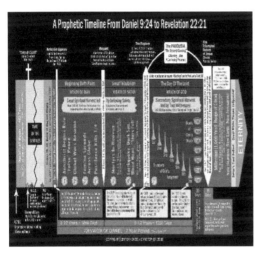

The period of the "Four Hallelujahs" in Heaven corresponds exactly to the mopping up of evil on this earth. The Marriage Supper of the Lamb is happening exactly as God is finalizing "planet Earth" for the return of Jesus. *(You can download this color chart free at samchess.com)*

I purposely don't usually tend to focus much on the "trumpet and bowl judgments" happening on Earth because the Believers *(both living and dead)* have been "raptured" into Heaven, and are celebrating the Marriage Supper of the Lamb. But, let's think about them for a bit, to see the sharp contrast to what we the Saints are experiencing in Heaven.

- It's hard to grasp the level of pure evil that is consuming the earth by this time. This is the period in the Bible called the "Day of the Lord" or the "Day of the Lord's wrath"– where an "antichrist" has risen to world power. Isaiah, Ezekiel, Daniel, Joel, Zephaniah, Amos, and Jeremiah all write about it. They prophesied in the Old Testament the horrors that Revelation spells out will be happening during that final "terrible day of the Lord," as Malachi called it!

- The Prophets seemed to know that God was going to eventually wipe out the curse of sin on earth! They knew that once he did so, the Messiah would set up an eternal earthly reign – which is exactly what he is going to do!

- The part they struggled with was that the Messiah had to come <u>first</u> to redeem humanity from their sins, by paying their sin debt – and then come a <u>second</u> time to set up his eternal reign!

At this point in our study, even though all Believers have been raptured into Heaven and are at the Marriage Feast table – there will still be people coming to Christ on earth during those awful days. There are still here on earth, as recorded in the book of Revelation, the two witnesses, the 144,000 sealed un-killable Jewish evangelists, the three flying evangelistic angels – flying, we are told, "all over the world," spreading the Gospel message. That sounds strange, Sam! Perhaps, but it is all right there in John's "unveiling." Those who are "saved" do not join us in Heaven. They join us when we return here with Jesus! <u>Who</u>

<u>do you think we Redeemed Saints are going to be reigning over after all</u>? *(We'll come to that?)*

After the horrible trumpet judgments, which last about 17 (IMO) months *(based on the time frame presented in Revelation)*, come the rapid-fire final bowl judgments *(we're now in the final 30 days)*. We need to see this to understand our coming role:

Bowl #1: "Horrible, malignant sores break out on everyone who has the mark of the beast and who worships his statue." *(Revelation 16:2)*

Bowl #2: "The sea becomes like the blood of a corpse, and everything in the sea dies." *(Revelation 16:3)*

Bowl #3: "The rivers and springs become blood." *(Revelation 16:4)*

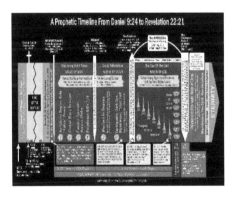

Bowl #4: The sun scorches everyone with its fire and "Everyone was burned by this blast of heat, and <u>they cursed the name of God</u>, who had control over all these plagues. <u>They did not repent of their sins and turn to God and give Him glory</u>!" *(Revelation 16:8-9) A vast gulf between sin and righteousness.* We're seeing that evil attitude grow more and more now, where very sinful people are calling their evil actions righteous – and they are developing a pure hatred for those who really are living righteous lives!

Bowl #5: "The fifth angel poured out his bowl on the throne of the beast, and his kingdom is plunged into darkness. His subjects grind their teeth in anguish, <u>and they cursed the God of heaven for their pains and sores. But they did not repent of their evil deeds and turn to God</u>." *(Revelation 16:10-11)*

By this time on earth, the antichrist as the world leader, must have terribly low favorability ratings. After he is assassinated and resurrected *(Revelation 13:14)*, the world believes in him. *(He is a counterfeit Jesus!)* He leads "the whole world" to worship himself, and satan – and all who follow him take satan's "mark" on their hand or forehead.

- But in the seven years since the "counterfeit-christ" came to power promising to right all the wrongs of the world, the earth has gone from a seemingly peaceful place to a seething ball of complete destruction! <u>All of this is happening while we are celebrating the Marriage Supper of the Lamb</u>!

- Well over half of the world's remaining population have died! Instead of economic recovery, the antichrist has ruled over a complete worldwide economic collapse. There is no money to buy the supplies that aren't available in stores anyway – no lights to turn on to cut through the pitch darkness outside day and night. Complete anarchy reigns everywhere. Temperatures are intensely hot at all times, and there is no clean water to take a bath or drinkable water to satisfy one's thirst.

Bowl #6: Revelation 16:12-14, 16: "Then the sixth angel poured out his bowl on the great Euphrates River, and it dried up so that the kings from the east could march their armies toward the west without hindrance. And I saw three evil spirits that looked like frogs leap from the mouths of the dragon, the beast, and the false prophet. They are demonic spirits who work miracles and go out to all the rulers of the world to gather them <u>for battle against the Lord on that great judgment day of God the Almighty. And the demonic spirits gathered all the rulers and their armies to a place with the Hebrew name Armageddon.</u>"

Let's put this picture together in our minds: As this 6th bowl is being poured out on the earth, Jesus, after an intense briefing about what is to come, is leading us all out of the Marriage Supper banquet hall, and we all gather at a staging area. *(the size of the US and Canada, who knows?)* Heading out toward this final mission is Jesus, all of us Redeemed Glorified Saints, and we find later – all of the angels of Heaven too!

Satan's demons are gathering the armies of the world to fight against the returning Jesus. **Revelation 19:19: "Then I saw the beast and the kings of the world and their armies gathered together to fight against the one sitting on the horse and his army."** *(us!)*

- But those godless armies are not purposely coming to fight Jesus *(IMO)*. They aren't exactly Sunday School kids. They know nothing, nor care anything, about a "returning Jesus."

- The armies are *(IMO)* coming to take down the antichrist! *(Their failed world leader!)* They've had enough of his awful leadership! What's left of the world's armies are coming from every direction to dethrone him!

These are not unified armies. They are going to fight each other too, until the last group standing becomes the new world leader. So they come, by the millions, from every direction toward Jerusalem where the antichrist has set up his headquarters. Notice – while these armies may *think* they are coming to fight the antichrist, that is *not why satan is assembling them.* Satan is bringing the remaining might of the world to take on the returning Jesus! How does satan know that Jesus is going to return at that point? Because he's read the same Book we're reading, and he well knows that God keeps his Word!

 Satan knows that as he is gathering the armies of the world at Har Megiddo, we Saints are mounting up with Jesus to return to earth. That's been part of the New Testament for the last 1900 years. Satan has heard it read more times than he can stand! *(Valley of Megiddo)* Satan knows exactly what God says He is going to do at the End. Yet he still foolishly believes that he can thwart God's plan! Like a moth drawn to a flame, he will walk right into the trap of setting the stage

for God's final judgment on himself, the antichrist, and the willfully rebellious.

The Jezreel Valley stretches 180 miles from the Mediterranean to the Jordan River. The returning Jesus is finally going to plant his feet sixty miles south on the Mount of Olives *(Zechariah says.)* exactly at the same place he ascended from! But clearly there is first going to be a massive confrontation 60 miles north at Har Megiddo/Armageddon! <u>You are literally going to be with Jesus when this final confrontation takes place!</u>

From all over the planet, like salmon instinctively called upstream, angry, hate-filled people migrate toward Jerusalem, stumbling in the darkness, burning from the heat, with the stench of diseased, sweat-pouring, filth-ridden bodies – a glut of pure evil and hatred filling the air, the monumental clash of wicked people killing everybody who did not think just like them.

And then, in the middle of that pounding chaos, out of the corner of their eye the <u>make-shift soldiers start to see a light way up in the heavens</u>. Although the sky is pitch black and they haven't seen a star in weeks, there is one there now! At dusk the next day the same light appears, but this time it's much larger.

Each night it gets bigger and brighter until it seems to fill the sky. The brightness seems to come from the center, extending outward for thousands of miles in every direction. The sun-like brilliance is bouncing off what looks like layers of clouds, but it cannot be clouds because there are none out there. *("He's coming on the clouds!" What looks like clouds is actually the angels and us!)*

Imagine if what is coming toward earth is brighter by far than any comet *(because it is lit from within)* and has a combined mass larger than the largest continent. Every time the earth turns, every eye is locked toward the east as this insanely bright spectacle *(that is Jesus' Triumphant Return to Earth)* draws closer and closer.

As this brilliant new threat fills the sky, obviously coming directly toward the earth, what is left of the hate-filled throngs lose interest in fighting the antichrist or each other, and position themselves and their weapons to take on this new, unknown enemy. Every remaining missile on earth is probably pointed in the direction of the center of the light.

> *What is it?* **Revelation 19:11-14, 16: "Then I saw heaven opened, and a white horse was standing there. Its rider was named Faithful and True. His eyes were like flames of fire, and on His head were many crowns. He wore a robe dipped in blood, and His title was the Word of God. <u>The armies of heaven, dressed in the finest of pure white linen, followed Him on white horses</u>.** *(You!)* **On His robe at His thigh was written this title: King of all kings and Lord of all lords!"**

Chapter 23

---

*Returning with Jesus in his Glorious
Second Coming.*

I purposely left us in the last chapter with a prophetic Biblical cliffhanger. We left off the storyline of Scripture just as Jesus is returning from Heaven with his Saints. That's us, and your Redeemed Grandma, and Mother Teresa, and Abraham Lincoln, and Peter the Apostle, and Moses the Jewish Deliverer and Red Sea Splitter. <u>All of us together are returning with Jesus</u> in his Glorious Second Coming, *(its the end of time as we know it)*. The curtain is falling on all of human history and getting ready to rise on what the Bible calls "eternity." We Saints have freshly finished up the Marriage Supper of the Lamb. *(Revelation 19:7-9)* Let's read this again:

> **Revelation 19:11-14, 16: "Then I saw Heaven opened,** *(twice this phrase shows up, once in 4:1 to let John (and us) begin looking into Heaven – and now here to let Jesus and us exit Heaven on our way back to earth)* **and a white horse was standing there. Its rider was named Faithful and True. His eyes were like flames of fire, and on His head were many crowns. He wore a robe dipped in blood, and His title was the Word of God. The armies of heaven, dressed in the finest of pure white linen,** *(that's us)* **followed Him on white horses. On His robe**

at His thigh was written this title: King of all kings and Lord of all lords."

By the way, it's not just us millions/billions of New Testament Redeemed Believers and Old Testament Saints returning with Jesus in his Second Coming. All of the angels come too. How in the world do you know that Sam?

Matthew 25:31: "When the Son of Man comes in his glory, and all the angels with him, then he will sit on his Glorious Throne." (That's not the Rapture, by the way. Jesus brings angels with him then too, but doesn't yet establish his eternal throne!)

2 Thessalonians 1:7-8 NASB: "To give relief to you who are afflicted, along with us, when the Lord Jesus will be revealed from Heaven with His mighty angels in flaming fire, dealing out retribution to those who do not know God, and to those who do not obey the gospel of our Lord Jesus." *(Again, that's not the Rapture, Jesus takes the Saints, living and dead, back to Heaven then, but he doesn't "deal out retribution on sin and satan" and establish his eternal throne, until his Second Coming!)*

We need to lock this picture in our minds of the hugeness of this Second Coming event – millions/billions of Saints, *(you included)* and millions/ billions of angels leaving Heaven and coming to this destroyed earth. Seeing that picture in our mind will help us fully understand what the Bible says comes next.

As Jesus, and us, approach the earth, the whole world is in the final throes of the judgments *(The Day of the Lord)* that have been raining down on sin, satan, the antichrist – in fact, on this whole sin-cursed planet, in the form of the Trumpet and Bowl judgments listed in Revelation 8,9,10, and 16.

I told you in the last chapter that I don't often focus on that final "wrath of God" on earth part, because we "Saints," both living and dead have been raptured. *(We aren't here when the Trumpet and Bowl judgments fall on this earth!)* But to get the full picture of what you are going to visually look out over when you return with Jesus in his Second Coming, we need to have in our minds, at least, that last 30 days of what is happening on this "writhing with sin, cursed" planet as we approach with Jesus.

Sidebar review: The antichrist, a world dictator, came to power seven years earlier. He won't come to power as a dictator. He comes to power as a political genius who can bring world peace. I suspect it happens after a cataclysmic world event, which I suspect is the battle described in Ezekiel 38-39, *(The Battle of Gog and Magog)* which almost certainly includes *(IMO)* "Russia" leading its allies to wipe out Israel. But Ezekiel says God answers with fire from Heaven! *(Ezekiel 39:6-8)*

The one we call the antichrist, the false Messiah, the counterfeit replacement for Jesus is the "first seal" Jesus opens in Revelation 6, *(It's the 1ˢᵗ white horse of the apocalypse.) Download this color chart free at samchess.com*

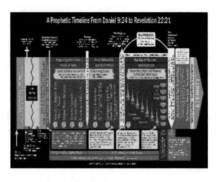

Everybody believes this counterfeit Messiah can save the world. Even Israel will sign a seven-year peace treaty allowing him to lead them, in spite of the fact he is almost certainly not Jewish.

John's Revelation reveals that a couple of years pass and violence breaks out across the world that is far worse than anything up to that time.

And then massive famine will sweep the earth and many will die from hunger. *(That's the second and third Horseman John sees, and also the second and third seal that Jesus is opening in Revelation 6.)*

The fourth seal is a little shocking to us now *(especially now)* because we are told that, added to the violence and famine will be "pestilence, a strange spreading disease" that will sweep through the world, and the death toll *(John records)* will reach to ¼ of the world population. Does that ring a bell with anybody? It rings a bell none of us had ever thought of before the Covid-19 plague!

When the Church is raptured "the world goes to hell," and I'm not saying that as a curse. When the presence of the Church, and the Believer's life witness, and all the righteous deeds that we do, and all our influence on this world disappears in a moment of time, the forces of hell will reign supreme! We always talk about the Rapture as a blessed event from our perspective as "rapture-es." But let your mind imagine what it will be like on this planet when every bit of righteousness is released from the world like air leaving a balloon.

I am convinced that others will come to Jesus after that time. There will be, after all, millions of unused Bibles lying around although I'm sure the antichrist will have whole units of his administration gathering them up for massive book burnings.

It's at that point, though, that God says, "This whole sin curse has gone on long enough. I am now entering the final, final stage where my prophesied 'Day of the Lord's Wrath' will begin to consume the reign of sin on this planet – ending in the judgment of the antichrist, and finally even satan himself. I will wipe the curse of sin off the planet and set up, right here on this earth, a New Heaven and New Earth."

As we already noted, the antichrist *(seven years before)* set out assuring everybody that he was going to save the world and make everybody's life a utopia, and instead, almost half of the world's population have now died. If you think gas is expensive now, only the world governments will have any then. People will be killing each other over a bucket of grain. Factories will be gone. Unemployment will be at 97%. GDP will be at zero.

Do you think it's unmerciful that some countries were quarantining massive cities because of finding just 50 active Covid-19 cases during the epidemic? Imagine what kind of forced quarantining will be happening then! You think Russia was being brutal in Ukraine, ruthlessly killing innocent women and children? Imagine a world where absolutely all godly influences are gone!

> **Bowl #6: Revelation 16:12-14, 16: "Then the sixth angel poured out his bowl on the great Euphrates River, and it dried up so that the kings from the east could march their armies toward the west without hindrance. And I saw three evil spirits that looked like frogs leap from the mouths of the dragon, the beast, and the false prophet. They are demonic spirits who work miracles and go out to all the rulers of the world to gather them <u>for battle against the Lord on that great judgment day of God the Almighty. And the demonic spirits gathered all the rulers and their armies to a place with the Hebrew name Armageddon.</u>"** *(Har Megiddo)*

Here's a current picture of the Megiddo valley and the Megiddo airport. Israel was just poised to build a huge international airport in that valley, but held off because air traffic fell so low during Covid-19.

1) Picture that huge airport built. Picture the whole world around it being pummeled with the "poured out wrath" in the form of the trumpet and bowl judgments.

2) Then armies from all over what is left of the nations in the world will use their last fuel to assemble their last weapons and gather in this valley beside Megiddo. Napoleon called this valley "the most natural battle ground on the whole earth."

3) It's a "bowl of a valley" 180 miles long. Fighting between the armies becomes so fierce that **Revelation 14:19-20** says: **"The angel swung his sickle over the earth and loaded the grapes into the great winepress of God's wrath. The grapes were trampled in the winepress outside the city, and blood flowed from the winepress in a stream about 180 miles long and as high as a horse's bridle."**

As Jesus, and us, approach this 180-mile blood-soaked valley crammed with all the armies of the world all fighting with each other – finally, through the almost complete darkness they look up and see a light approaching. Remember, in the last chapter, that "light" is Jesus with millions, perhaps billions of us Saints, and millions/billions of God's angels approaching earth as the evil minions stare in hate-filled disbelief and turn their final few weapons toward this new threat.

At that moment the 7th and final bowl of God's wrath slams into the earth <u>bringing an end to time as we know it and</u>

setting up for the beginning of eternity! Bowl 7 is the mother of all bowl judgments. Imagine the armies gathered in the Jezreel valley pausing as this final judgment shakes their world *(literally)*, like nothing anyone had ever experienced before.

> **Revelation 16:17-21: "Then the seventh angel poured out his bowl into the air. And <u>a mighty shout came from the throne in the Temple, saying, 'It is finished!'</u>"** *What is finished?* Sin's hold over the earth is finished! Satan's chokehold on the soul of humanity is finished! The curse of sin, going back to Adam is finished, and Jesus is going to mop up the mess and start to set up his reign **"Then the thunder crashed and rolled, and lightning flashed. <u>And a great earthquake struck—the worst since people were placed on the earth</u>. The great city of 'Babylon' split into three sections, and the cities of many nations fell into heaps of rubble. And <u>every island disappeared</u>, and <u>all the mountains were leveled</u>. There was <u>a terrible hailstorm, and hailstones weighing as much as seventy-five pounds fell from the sky</u> onto the people below. <u>They cursed God because of the terrible plague of the hailstorm</u>."**

Imagine 3 ½ of those twenty-pound bags of ice you buy at the grocery store, frozen together falling at what speed? A softball sized hailstone reaches 105 MPH. A seventy-five pounder would be falling at over 500 mph. Imagine a rainless storm, hitting the Megiddo valley with updrafts so fierce that it creates 75 lb. hailstones. Imagine these hate-filled minions shaking their fists in God's face, just before they take a 75 pounder on the noggin.

At that moment, Jesus himself arrives, *(with all of us behind him)* filling thousands of square miles of airspace! A brilliant light, in a super-dark world gives way to vague shapes. One of those shapes becomes very, very clear to all the remaining hate-filled warriors still alive. As Jesus appears over the Megiddo valley, I somehow suspect the warriors very much attach this mind-blowing picture in the sky above them to **"their cursing the God of heaven for their pains and sores. But they did not repent of their evil deeds and turn to God".** *(Revelation 16:11)* And they have no intention of repenting now. They set themselves to fight God with their last evil breath.

> **Revelation 19:19-21: "Then I saw the beast and the kings of the world and their armies gathered together <u>to fight against the one sitting on the horse and his army</u>.** Who's his army? Our immediate response might be to say angels, but the only group called an army in Revelation 19 – is us! **And the beast *(antichrist)* was captured, and with him the false prophet who did mighty miracles on behalf of the beast—miracles that deceived all who had accepted the mark of the beast and who worshiped his statue. Both the beast and his false prophet were thrown alive into the fiery lake of burning sulfur. Their entire army was killed by the sharp sword that came from the mouth of the one riding the white horse."** *Boom! Bam! Crash!*

OK, let me now crunch my foot on the brake and bring this vivid narrative to a grinding stop. There is something we have to deal with here.

There is absolutely no use of my going on talking about the angel binding satan and putting him in the abyss for 1000 years, the renovation of the Earth into a New *(Garden of Eden like)* Earth, and the coming of the Holy City, the New Jerusalem. There is absolutely no use talking about satan being bound and all of us Redeemed Saints taking part in "reigning with Jesus." *(That's all found in the first verses of Revelation 20-21.)*

> **Revelation 20:1-2: "Then I saw an angel coming down from Heaven with the key to the bottomless pit and a heavy chain in his hand. He seized the dragon — that old serpent, who is the devil, satan — and bound him in chains for a thousand years."** *(2nd to last chapter in the Bible)*

> **Revelation 21:1: "Then I saw a New Heaven and a New Earth, for the old heaven and the old earth had disappeared. And the sea was also gone. And I saw the holy city, the New Jerusalem, coming down from God out of Heaven."** *(Next to last chapter in the Bible)*

Some of you reading might be saying right about now – that Chess spins a good story, and yes, he seems to be keeping the story-line to what the Bible seems to be saying. But <u>don't</u>

<u>you realize, Sam, that the whole of Revelation is metaphorical,</u> it's allegorical, it's symbolic. <u>It was never intended to be taken literally</u>!

- Don't you realize, Sam, that there isn't really a 1000 year period coming where satan will actually be bound – and there isn't really a 1000 year period where the church will be back on this earth "ruling and reigning" with Jesus.

- The answer is: No, I don't know that at all! *(And it's not because I haven't studied it deeply.)*

- Hear me when I assure you of this: The Early Church did, really honestly did take the Bible very, very literally! When they read Paul's prophetic words in:

1 Thessalonians 4:15-17: "We tell you this directly from the Lord: We who are still living when the Lord returns will not meet him ahead of those who have died. For the Lord himself will come down from heaven with a commanding shout, with the voice of the archangel, and with the trumpet call of God. First, the believers who have died will rise from their graves. *(Don't mistake this for something that is actually going to happen – it is simply metaphorical?)* **Then, together with them, <u>we who are still alive and remain on the earth will be caught up in the clouds to meet the Lord in the air. Then we will be with the Lord forever</u>."** *(Really?)*

The Early Church read verses like this and they said; "we believe them exactly as written!" The Early Church Fathers wrote a lot on this subject. Hermes, Papias, Justin Martyr, and Irenaeus, all say with certainty that the Early Church took exactly what they were reading very, very literally – looking forward completely to Jesus' prophesied Second Coming, and their prophesied reigning with him in eternity.

That's what put the wind in their sails as they were being slaughtered for their faith! Generation after generation could take the thought of dying violently because they were so sure that they would rise in a Rapture *(1 Thessalonians 4:17)* to be with Jesus forever – and then they would return with Jesus in his Second Coming. Satan, and in fact all of evil, was going to get his clock cleaned, and they would rule and reign with Jesus forever!

- But then *(300 years after Jesus)* the killing stopped!

- Emperor Constantine signed the Edict of Milan in 313 AD "tolerating" Christianity and later that century Christianity became "the official religion of the Empire" *(but it was far more a political move than a spiritual revival)*.

- St. Augustine *(to his credit)* told the Christians not to get all cozy with their pagan Roman neighbors, but many did it anyway.

But then St. Augustine *(Bishop of Hippo, North Africa)* did something that blows my mind. As a former Bible literalist, he then declared that he had decided that all of the forward looking prophetic passages were metaphorical. They were not talking about real events that would one day happen in each of our lives.

Augustine taught that all the teachings about a Rapture of the Saints or a Second Coming of Jesus to destroy sin and satan, or a "future reigning with Christ in Heaven, or a coming 1000 year "millennium" where Jesus would be reigning on this earth and we will be reigning with him was metaphorical.

All of that, Augustine said, <u>was not intended to be literal – it is all symbolism</u>! Augustine was smarter in his little finger than I am in my whole egg-shaped head – but he *(IMO)* seriously blew this one. He wasn't the only one who took a metaphorical view of Scripture. Others applied that view to the whole Bible!

The "thousand years," he said, "denotes "the whole duration of time on this world." The "reign of the Saints" means nothing more than the victory the Saints have over evil on this earth right now. "The Church, even now is "the kingdom of Christ and the kingdom of Heaven." Accordingly, even now his Saints "reign with him." [17] The first resurrection is the spiritual resurrection of the soul from sin. *(Not some rapture where the dead in Christ rise first!)*

- Can you imagine how the Early Church would have handled this teaching, as they watched their families butchered in front of their faces, and then they were lit on fire themselves?

- What if they thought they would hear on the other side, Sorry, what you experienced on earth in "reigning with me" is all the reigning you are ever going to do.

- Don't be expecting some future reigning with Christ when you get to Heaven. *(Just line up to receive your harp and be assigned your cloud!)*

But this view quickly folded into the developing Roman Catholic Church's primary viewpoint *(there was no Protestant Church yet)* and for the next 1400 years became the predominate *(Only?)* view of the "Universal" Catholic Church.

It is interesting that once the Church was no longer under persecution, and once they lost the view of a future Second Coming of Jesus to defeat evil, and take us to an eternity communing with God in his presence – the Church backslid so badly that we entered a time in history called the "Dark Ages." *Is there any connection?*

I searched for every verse in the New Testament that seems to teach a literal Second Coming of Jesus. I lined them all up on several pages. I found 265 verses that directly teach a Second Coming! If you include all the surrounding context, it becomes hundreds and hundreds of verses!

7,957 verses in the New Testament.
265 direct references to Jesus' Second Coming.
That's "one out of every 30 verses" in the New Testament!
Jesus, himself mentions his Second Coming 21 times!

Hear this: The Early Church took every one of those verses as their personal promises! And yet we are now supposed to believe that all of those verses are just a "metaphor" describing something other than what they seem to be saying!

I want to ask a new question: Besides the Revelation passage we looked at earlier about Jesus coming back with us, his Saints, to bring judgment on sin and satan – are there other passages the Early Church would have been hanging their hat on, to prove to them that Jesus really was going to clean sin/satan's clock? Yes!

> **Jude 1:14-15:** "Enoch, who lived in the seventh generation after Adam, prophesied about these people. He said, 'Listen! <u>The Lord is coming with countless thousands of his holy ones to execute judgment on the people of the world</u>. He will convict every person of all the ungodly things they have done and for all the insults that ungodly sinners have spoken against him.'" *(Holy ones – angels or Saints, or both?)*

> **2 Thessalonians 1:7-10:** "And God will provide rest for you who are being persecuted and also for us when the Lord Jesus appears from heaven. <u>He will come with his mighty angels, in flaming fire, bringing judgment</u> on those who don't know God and on those who refuse to obey the Good News of our Lord Jesus. They will be punished with eternal destruction, forever separated from the Lord and from his glorious power. <u>When he comes on that day, he will receive glory from his holy people—praise from all who believe. And this includes you</u>, for you believed what we told you about him."

So when the Early Church finally got their look at Revelation 19, about Jesus *(and you, and the angels)* returning, arriving at the valley of Armageddon to take out the final hate-filled armies of the old antichrist administration – Did they say: We already knew that was going to happen because of what Jude and Paul wrote. We just didn't know all the details until now? <u>Yes</u>!

The "reformers" started to break ranks slightly – they were forging a new "protesting" Church built around "salvation by grace through faith," rather than "salvation by works." But it <u>wasn't until the mid-1700's that people began to theorize that Jesus really was going to come back and take his Saints to a real Heaven</u>. It was the late 1700's before the church started to turn in large numbers back to a literal view of prophesy.

- I have spent now more than 3500 hours digging and preaching and writing on End Times, Eternity, and Heaven and *(with respect to those who disagree)* the deeper I dig, the more convinced I am that every passage means exactly what it says.

- Remember, the very first rule of Bible interpretation is: <u>If the plain sense makes sense, seek no other sense</u>!

- If that's true, and this isn't all metaphorical, you are literally going to be with Jesus when he arrives at the Valley of Megiddo, when he destroys those armies with "the Word" of his mouth.

- You'll also be present when he lands 60 miles south on the Mount of Olives, and time as we know it comes to an end and eternity begins.

- If the literal sense is true – then there is a whole lot more coming for you and me following our re-arrival on this earth.

We'll continue this final narrative in the chapters ahead, but we need to weave it in with some other very important truths.

CHAPTER 23

Chapter 24

_____

A New Heaven and New Earth?

So I was very blunt in the last chapter in discussing part of the huge hiccup *(IMO)* that happened in Christianity. The Early Church seriously believed in a Second Coming of Jesus and in our promised future reigning with Jesus in Heaven. I printed out all the promise-of-a-second-Coming passages – and they filled 21 pages, single spaced! I also gathered quotes from Early Church Fathers and historians who wrote that for at least the first 200 years, the Church clearly believed those End Times passages were literal and real.

- Jesus would come back from Heaven to gather the Saints.

- Jesus was going to take us, both living and dead, up to Heaven in a Rapture.

- We would then return with him in his glorious Second Coming.

- After that we will begin to "reign with him" through the first 1000 years of eternity and on into our endless "forever"!

But as we already said, Saint Augustine came along three hundred years after Jesus and said those promises are not real. They are metaphorical! Our reigning with Jesus is not really some future event in Heaven, but is simply describing what we are doing right now on this earth.

I asked the stunned question several chapters ago, "How could I have read every page of John Calvin's *Institutes of the Christian Religion* in seminary *(which I did)* and have only read one page on Heaven?" Here's why! Calvin was Augustinian to the core! Every third page of his Institutes, *(on average,)* quotes St. Augustine! Neither of them believed in a literal Heaven as presented in the Bible. That is also true of many of the other illustrious commentary authors I used as illustrations earlier in this book.

- Thankfully *(IMO)* in the last 250 years, particularly inside much of evangelical Christianity, there has been a huge swing back to a literal understanding of prophetic Scripture.

- That was boosted enormously by Israel *(75 years ago – as of this writing)* again "re-forming" as a nation, just as Ezekiel and Jeremiah had prophesied. People, preachers, theologians began to say, "Wow – this thing really does seem to be unfolding in the exact direction described in the book of Revelation!"

I say all that as a necessary introduction to the next future event I am going to describe to you – one that will deeply affect every Believer as you pass on from this life and enter into eternity.

If you don't believe that future prophecy is literal, then you won't get very excited about this world-changing *(literally)* event that seems to be coming like a cosmic freight train in the direction of us all. That world-changing event is the

Biblical concept that this sin-cursed earth and the atmosphere above it, will one day be renovated into a New Heavens and New Earth.

- Abraham, the nomad, believed that 4000 years ago. *(I'll show you!)*
- Several of the OT prophets described this "remaking" of the earth in great detail.

The New Testament describes exactly how this mother-of-all "make-overs" is going to come about. And John, in the last two chapters of the Bible, lays it all out in high definition!

> **Revelation 21:1-3: "Then I saw a New Heaven and a New Earth, for the old heaven and the old earth had disappeared. And the sea was also gone. And I saw the holy city, the New Jerusalem, coming down from God out of heaven like a bride beautifully dressed for her husband. I heard a loud shout from the Throne, saying, 'Look, God's home is now among his people! He will live with them, and they will be his people. God himself will be with them.'"**

The rest of Revelation 21 and 22 *(the last two chapters in the Bible)* are going to describe in vivid detail what your future home in Heaven is going to look like. *Does that interest you?*

We don't tend to think of this small 7,917.5 mile-wide ball that we live on, as all that significant in the bigger picture. We can look at a picture of just our Milky Way galaxy and be shocked by how small our world is.

And of course, we now know that there are at least a billion more galaxies beyond our own, some much larger than ours. So most astronomers would say we are just one evolved speck in the middle of trillions of other evolved specks. But that is not what the Bible says at all. Scripture makes this less than 8000 mile wide orb the centerpiece of God's redemptive plan!

Did you ever notice that in the account of creation, it's on the first day that God creates the Earth and the light directly around it? He spends day two and three forming the seas and the land and the vegetation and seed-bearing plants. It's on day four that God creates the sun and moon and stars! Are you saying, Sam, that God actually created the Earth as the only thing in existence *(except Heaven, of course)* before he created the rest of the universe. <u>Yes</u>, that's exactly what Genesis 1 says!

And there's more! This is the one planet that God put his "in his image" human creation on. This is the one planet that once those humans rejected him, God himself incarnated here to this earth to take on himself the sins of humanity. Jesus didn't go die on Pluto!

This is the one place Jesus promised that he is going to come back to, and this is the one place in the whole universe that the Bible directly says Jesus will set up his everlasting reign and we Redeemed Earthlings will reign here with him. *(Right here!)*

But that creates a real dilemma. When Adam and Eve rejected their loving Creator and rebelled against his loving grace, they came under the curse of sin – and so did this earth!

We are living on a sin-cursed earth! We love our earth. It still has the fingerprints of God all over it. My wife Sue, and I, spend our vacations in West Virginia, in the woods, with lots of wildlife. But our walks in the woods will take us by dead and decaying plant life. The occasional rotting carcass will remind us that this planet is still very much under the curse of sin! We will even take care that we ourselves do not end up as lunch for an even larger mammal. And a quick check of the news will remind us just how far God's "in-his-image" humans have fallen.

- Is there really coming a day when everything on earth reverts back to a pre-cursed state?

- Is it possible that not only will the curse on our bodies and souls be gone – but the curse on this earth is going to be lifted too?

- And are you one day soon, going to find yourself, not just living in the New Jerusalem, *(which we will talk about a lot more)* but you'll find yourself thriving on a renewed, renovated planet that is free from sin's-curse, completely free from the presence of satan – with the whole world again becoming like the Garden of Eden was before the fall?

- Is that a literal prophesy coming in the future? Will you personally experience it?

Oddly, many people, who say they are so anxious to get to Heaven, have no clear picture of Heaven other than that absurd sitting on a cloud strumming a harp. The old Patriarch, Abraham, who didn't have any parts of the Bible yet, knew better than that!

> **Hebrews 11:9-10: "And even when he reached the land God promised him, he lived there by faith—for he was like a foreigner, living in tents. And so did Isaac and Jacob, who inherited the same promise. Abraham was confidently looking forward to a city with eternal foundations, a city designed and built by God."**

The only real estate that nomad Abraham seems to have ever bought was the tiny parcel to bury his wife Sarah. The forefather of all of the Jewish and Christian faith didn't seem to give a hoot about earth property. Why? Because back there, 4000 years ago, he knew there was more to this life than this life!

I have no idea how he knew *(God must have told him)* that his real inheritance was a city with foundations, whose architect and builder is God. Notice the "city with foundations" comment. Abraham lived his life in moveable tents with no foundations. The first real foundation he was ever counting on was a "foundation built by God."

He couldn't have imagined the Holy City described in Revelation 21 – a 1400 mile long by 1400 mile wide, by 1400 mile high city with streets of gold, and where each of 12 mountain-sized gates are made out of a single massive pearl. That is the New Jerusalem, by the way, the same place Jesus was talking about when he said, *(in John 14:2)* "I'm going to prepare a place for you!"

- God gave Abraham four covenant promises, the first of which was <u>land</u>. Abe wandered around on it, but never held title to it.

- And he didn't seem to care, because he was so sure that God was going to end up laying the foundations of his inheritance! And he was right!

- We will come back to that before this discussion is over, the fact that the size of the footprint of the New Jerusalem *(1400 miles by 1400 miles)* just "happens to be" about the exact same square miles that God's original promise of land to Abraham was! *That must be significant!*

- We all understand, don't we, that Israel is not living today on the entire Promised Land? The Genesis 15 "Promised Land" reaches over to the Euphrates River, up into Syria, and down into Saudi Arabia. *(That promise fulfillment is still on its way. It is not metaphorical, it will be literal!)*

I've never really caught onto this before now, in the rest of the Hebrews 11 "faith chapter," The other "Heroes of the faith," also had a forward looking gaze:

Hebrews 11:13-16: "All these people died still believing what God had promised them. They did not

receive what was promised, but they saw it all from a distance and welcomed it.(*What were they seeing at a distance and welcoming?*)

"They agreed that they were foreigners and nomads here on earth. (*Even the ones in the Bible who became rich landowners!*) **Obviously people who say such things are looking forward to a country they can call their own. If they had longed for the country they came from, they could have gone back. But** <u>**they were looking for a better place, a Heavenly Homeland**</u>**. That is why God is not ashamed to be called their God, for he has prepared a city for them."**

It's not just the people at the end of the first century who now had 27 inspired books, revealing huge amounts of information about what is coming at the end of this life – Old Testament Saints, with almost no Bible at all, were completely sure that they were headed toward a "Heavenly Homeland," and they even knew that it would include a God-built Heavenly City!

Scripture indicates that wherever Heaven is now – once the curse of sin is cleansed from the universe, Heaven will expand to absorb all of the universe and most importantly, absorb all of this earth! If God's "home" is right now in Heaven, and we saw that fact in many passages:

- If that's true, (*and it is*) Revelation 21 says that once there is a New Heavens and a New Earth, the New Jerusalem actually moves from wherever it is in the intermediate Heaven, down to this earth.

- Then; **"I heard a loud shout from the Throne, saying, 'Look, God's home is now among his people! He will live with them, and they will be his people. God himself will be with them.'"** *(Revelation 21:3)*

- If God's home is right now in Heaven, and in the next to last chapter of the Bible God says, "My home is now on earth" – what conclusions should you draw?

- If the Holy City inside of which is not just your future home, but Revelation 22 says the Throne of God is in there too – If the very Throne Room of God, inside the New Jerusalem, is coming to this earth to stay, what does that tell you about the future of this planet?

The great big stumbling block to all these prophecies is the fact that this earth is right now under sin's curse. If God is going to bring his Throne Room here, and God himself is going to make his home among *(us)* his people. If that is going to be true, then something is going to have to happen to the curse of sin reaching around the planet and into the very center of the earth.

We can't put a bin of heavenly strawberries on our "mansion counter" and find them rotting the next day. We can't be worried about our heavenly dog (*If there is such a thing*) biting our neighbor in the next mansion over in the New Jerusalem, can we? ☺ (*Please don't use this question to ask me if your pet is in Heaven – I don't know!*)

 We can't very well have a New Earth with hurricanes and tornadoes blowing it apart, can we? We can't have the earth opening up and belching out lava, covering one of the gates of the New Jerusalem, now can we?

We don't have to get to the last chapters of the Bible to know there is a New Earth coming. Back in Isaiah, we're told that this old cursed earth is one day going to pass away and a new earth is coming.

Isaiah 65:17-19: "Look! I am creating new heavens and a new earth, and no one will even think about the old ones anymore. Be glad; rejoice forever in my creation! And look! I will create Jerusalem as a place of happiness. Her people will be a source of joy. I will rejoice over Jerusalem and delight in my people. And the sound of weeping and crying will be heard in it no more."

Clearly none of that has happened yet. There is definitely not yet a "new earth," and there is unfortunately still a lot of weeping and crying in today's Jerusalem. But this was written 700 years before Jesus was born! These Old Testament Saints were looking forward to something that many modern Christians are still unclear about – even though we now have all of revealed Scripture!

Isaiah 66:22 NIV: "'As the new heavens and the new earth that I make will endure before me,' declares the LORD, 'so will your name and descendants endure.'"

We need to try to address two questions before this chapter is finished. 1) When is this going to happen, and 2) How is it going to happen? *(When does the New Heavens and New Earth arrive?)* These are not simple questions with simple answers. *(There is much disagreement)*

But if we turn our logical *(theological)* minds up to the "high setting," I think we can have an "A-HA" moment here. Let me take you back to the sequence of events we were at in the last chapter. We will join Jesus and millions/billions of other Redeemed Saints, along with millions /billions of angels in the Glorious Second Coming of Jesus to this earth.

Remember, as this massive group approaches the planet – the completely God-forsaking world *(by this time)* is just finishing experiencing the horrifying "Trumpet and Bowl judgments" on sin, and satan, and the curse, and the last armies of the world are gathered to fight the final battle of Armageddon.

We tried to imagine that in a purely dark, intensely hot world, with no water, and no food – this brilliant light of Jesus' Second Coming approaches and the remaining evil armies turn and stare at us approaching. At that moment the 7th Bowl judgment falls on the earth and we read that it is so severe that <u>every island fell under the sea and every mountain was flattened</u>!

We need that utterly "destroyed-earth" picture in our minds as we ask ourselves when the New Earth arrives. Added all together, the "trumpet and bowl judgments" have completely destroyed the planet!

So what happens next? Zechariah prophecies that the whole massive entourage *(Jesus, the angels, all the Redeemed Saints)* makes its way 60 miles south, and Jesus lands on the Mount of Olives. *(It's the exact same place from which Jesus ascended.)*

> **Zechariah 14:4, 6-7, 9: "On that day his feet will stand on the Mount of Olives, east of Jerusalem. And the Mount of Olives will split apart, making a wide valley running from east to west. On that day the sources of light will no longer shine, yet there will be continuous day! Only the LORD knows how this could happen. There will be no normal day and night, for at evening time it will still be light. And the LORD will be king over all the earth. On that day there will be one LORD—his name alone will be worshiped."**

- Now here is where this gets a bit muddy, because if you read all of Zechariah 14, it sounds like from the moment Jesus *(and us)* land back on earth, there are changes that instantly begin to happen to the earth.

- The phrase "on that day – there will be continuous light" makes you think something starts changing right then and there, doesn't it? *(And I have come to believe that is exactly right!)*

- But if you try to match that to Revelation 20-21 you hit a "chronological snag," which causes the differences in viewpoints.

The last part of Revelation 19-20 gives us a fast series of events.

1) 19:20: The beast *(antichrist)* and false prophet are captured, and thrown into the fiery lake of burning sulfur.

2) The Armageddon armies are "neutralized" by the sword that comes from the mouth of the one riding the white horse.

3) 20:1-2: "Then I saw an angel coming down from heaven with the key to the bottomless pit and a heavy chain in his hand. He seized the dragon—that old serpent, who is the devil, satan—and bound him in chains for a thousand years."

4) Saints begin to rule with Jesus for 1000 years. Tribulation martyrs come alive and rule with the Saints and Jesus for 1000 years.

5) We all "will be priests of God and of Christ and will reign with him a thousand years."

6) 21:1: The New Heaven and New Earth arrives.

7) 21:2: The New Jerusalem comes down out of Heaven.

Several modern authors, who are far smarter than me, use that exact lineup. 1) The antichrist destroyed, 2) satan bound, 3) Saints reign with Jesus on earth for 1000 years, 4) Then comes the New Heavens and New Earth.

- And everything inside of my somewhat logical head is yelling "Whoa, stop the presses!" Do we not remember what shape the earth is in after months of Trumpet and Bowl judgments?

- The sky has been rolled up like a scroll. There are no lights. The sea and rivers have turned to blood. Every thing is dead. Every mountain is reduced to a pile of rubble. Every city is turned into a lifeless ghost town. *(And on and on)*

How in the world would we be reigning with Jesus on earth for 1000 years, when the whole earth looks like a nuclear bomb just went off every 50 miles or so? Do you see the dilemma?

I think there is a way to coordinate Revelation 20-21 running parallel without ignoring the *"Kai eidons"* that start both chapters. There is no chance *(IMO)* that we are going to be reigning with Jesus over this earth before the purifying fire of God has purged out all the effects of the curse! *(Please refer to Appendix C in the back of the book entitled, "A Chronology of Revelation 20 and 21.)*

So, let's talk for a few pages about the second question: The earth is going to be renovated, but how? How is that going to happen?

Besides the Revelation 21 passage, do we get other clues in the New Testament as to how this is going to unfold, Yes! Actually Peter gives us far more than "little clues." But first:

Hebrews 1:10-12: "He *(God)* **also says to the Son,** *(Jesus)* **'In the beginning, Lord, you laid the foundation of the earth and made the heavens with your hands. They will perish, but you remain forever. They will wear out like old clothing. You will fold them up like a cloak and discard them. But you are always the same; you will live forever.'"** *(The earth and the heavens will "perish.")*

Peter though really gets into the inspired task of telling us about the destruction of the old sinful cursed planet earth. It's a little shocking – but let's read it, and then I'll try to explain.

2 Peter 3:7, 10-13: "And by the same word, the present heavens and earth have been stored up for fire. They are being kept for the Day of Judgment, when ungodly people will be destroyed. Then the heavens will pass away with a terrible noise, and the very elements themselves will disappear in fire, and the earth and everything on it will be found to deserve judgment. Since everything around us is going to be destroyed like this, what holy and godly lives you should live, looking forward to the day of God and hurrying it along. On that day, he will set the heavens on fire, and the elements will melt away in the flames. But we are looking forward to the new heavens and new earth he has promised, a world filled with God's righteousness."

- Our minds probably should be coming up with questions like: If we come back with Jesus, and then he purifies sin off the planet with melting flames – isn't that going to get a little toasty, even to our glorified bodies?

- Good question, because there will also be Believers (*a lot*) who come to faith in Jesus even as the "Judgments" are falling those last two years – they will be among us and they will not be raptured and glorified. *(They are in fact the people you are going to be "reigning over.")*

- But a "holy conflagration" could get very toasty for them. *(One old author said God will have us all in the New Jerusalem while this burning off of sin and the curse takes place.)* Huh? If we look hard at the actual text, it might look a bit different than some of our Bible versions present it.

2 Peter 3:10: "Then the heavens will pass away with a terrible noise, and the very elements themselves will disappear in fire, *(Καυσούμενα λυθήσεται)* and the earth and everything on it will be found to deserve judgment."

Καυσούμενα *(burn off)* λυθήσεται – to loose, to break up, to release, lay bare, expose, unbind so something no longer holds together.

It is more the idea of purifying! In my mind it's more like a Holy Shock Wave, because actual fire *(the way we picture it)* would burn across the surface of the earth – but this "fire" needs to go deep into the crust of the earth and out into the atmosphere and across the universe, "burning" away everything associated with sin, and the curse, and death, and decay. It's not meant for the purpose of destroying the earth. It's for the purpose of regenerating and re-creating the earth. One more key word is in Revelation 21:5:

Revelation 21:5: "And the one sitting on the Throne said, 'Look, I am making everything new!'" *(not Neos – new in time; Kainos – new in quality.)*

- It's the exact same term Paul uses when he says we are *"new creations in Christ Jesus!"*

- God doesn't obliterate us and start over. He just completely remakes us from inside out! That is what he is going to do to this earth. *(IMO)*

It has become my strong belief that the "Holy Shock Wave" "burning" away everything associated with sin, and the curse, and death, and decay, happens right after we have come back to the earth with Jesus and before the 1000 year reign with him formerly begins.

If you would like to study further how to correlate that view with what we read in Revelation 20 and 21 – *Please refer to Appendix C in the back of the book entitled, "<u>A Chronology of Revelation 20 and 21</u>.)*

CHAPTER 24

Chapter 25

I can't wait to get to Heaven!

Lets' start to ask this question: What will you actually see when you arrive in Heaven? We've reveled often in Jesus' promise:

> **John 14:2-3 NIV: "My Father's house has many rooms; if that were not so, would I have told you that I am going there to prepare a place for you? And if I go and prepare a place for you..."**

I heard somebody talking about a loved one going to Heaven and how great it would be to get there themselves. I asked them a couple of questions, and it was soon clear they had no idea what Heaven was like. And that's very common – I can't wait to go to Heaven! *Why*? Why is Heaven so attractive to you? I don't know, but I can't wait to get there!

- What is going to be so different about Heaven, than what you are already experiencing here on earth? "I have no idea, but I'm going to love it!"

- What are you going to be doing forever in Heaven? I don't know, but I can't wait to spend all eternity doing it!

That may sound a little sarcastic ☺, but you have to admit, it is one of the oddities about human life. We believe we are going to spend 80, or so years on this planet, and then we're counting on spending all of eternity in Heaven. But we are so utterly fixated on what these 70-90 years can offer – and so oddly "uncurious" about what the next million years or so hold in store for us.

I've officiated 100+ funerals and I am increasingly stunned by the 85 year olds in the room that can't wait till the service is over so they can get on to the party. Why? There may be a reason why we are so disconnected from truths about Heaven:

> *Again:* **John 14:2-3, 4-6: "My Father's house has many rooms; if that were not so, would I have told you that I am going there to prepare a place for you? And if I go and prepare a place for you, I will come back and take you to be with me that you also may be where I am."** *(But watch what Jesus then says in the often overlooked verses 4-6.)*
>
> **"You know where I'm going."** *(What?)* **Thomas said to him, 'Lord, we don't know where you are going, so how can we know the way?' Jesus answered, 'I am the way and the truth and the life. No one comes to the Father except through me.'"**

- We get so focused on verse 6 *(and rightly so)* It's one of the most power-packed verses in the Bible!
- Or we focus one sentence earlier on Thomas' "doubting."
- But do we ever focus on what Jesus said to make Thomas doubt? "You know where I'm going," Jesus said! *What*?

Remember, they didn't have the book of Revelation yet. One of the disciples sitting there, right next to Jesus, *(his young first cousin John)* would handwrite Jesus' Revelation 65 years later!

They didn't have any of the New Testament yet! Several of the disciples sitting there *(or people they directly influenced)* would become the authors. Peter, who was perhaps sitting on the other side of Jesus, would one day write startling things about the end of this world and the beginnings of a New Heaven and a New Earth – but at this point, he's still a rough fisherman who can't keep his foot out of his mouth!

You know the way to the place where I am going!

How? Remember, out of the 913 verses in the Bible *(NLT)* that use the word Heaven and the hundreds more verses that describe Heaven without using the actual word, the majority of those verses are in the Old Testament! That was the disciple's Bible!

- The disciples knew those Scriptures. The Early Church would have pin-pointed every single verse that had anything to say about their future in Heaven – and they would have consumed those verses week after week.

- As we have noted, they were captivated by the coming prophesied return of Jesus, and their promise to spend all of eternity with him in the place he was preparing for them!

- If you are bored after studying this subject for 400+ pages, *(so far)* you should know that the Early Church poured over these verses for the next 300 years! *(We know that's true, because the Early Church Fathers wrote about it.)*

This is important: When young John eventually writes the last two chapters of the Bible, *(that we are going to be unfolding in the next few chapters)* he is not exposing new theology. He is completing theology that starts back in the Old Testament! That's what Jesus assumed the disciples should have been studying! *John would eventually write:*

Revelation 21:1-3: "Then I saw a new heaven and a new earth. And I saw the holy city, the New Jerusalem, coming down from God out of Heaven. I heard a loud shout from the Throne, saying, 'Look, God's home is now among his people!'"

If we were to pick 100 people at random out of churches in our town, and tell them that Heaven *(wherever it is now)* is one day going to expand to include the whole universe and absorb this whole earth as well! And one day this earth will be completely refashioned back into a new Garden of Eden, and that the Holy City is going to one day leave wherever it is and come here to a newly renovated earth, and that God's home, and his Throne Room, will one day be centered right here on this planet.

If you were to say those things to 100 random Christians in your town – a good percentage of them would look at you like you have three heads, even though God clearly spells that all out in graphic detail in the last two chapters of the NT.

Thomas didn't have the last two chapters of the Bible yet *(or even the first two chapters)* but when Jesus said to Thomas, "You know where I'm going!" and Thomas responds, "We don't know where you are going!" He's not just doubting, he's telling a big fat fib. The rest of the disciples are sitting there thinking, "You are a lying dipwad."

A handful of days later, after watching Jesus die, then rise from the dead – Jesus invited him to cure his plaguing doubts by sticking his fingers into the hole in his side. Thomas screams out; *"My Lord and My God!"* The truth all came crashing in. Not just the truth that Jesus was in fact the Messiah, God incarnate, who had come to this earth to die for his sins and the sins of all humanity, but also to rise triumphantly from the dead to bring eternal life to all who believe! *(That is the Gospel message they then taught to the growing Early Church, and that we still teach today.)* There is a piece of this Redemption message that I think we might be missing – that I really don't think Thomas and those early Believers were overlooking – especially the disciples who were directly taught by Jesus for three years. Here it is:

God, at Creation, formed this planet and repeatedly said every step along the way, "that's good!" When he created his best masterpiece – in-his-image humanity, he added one more descriptive word about them – they're "very good!"

Wherever Heaven existed before that first day, we need to understand that God invested that same "Heavenly" kind of perfection here! This earth was a newly created "piece of

425

what Heaven must be like." *(God would not, and could not have created anything less.)*

And then he invested the same kind of perfection into his "in-his-own likeness" children, Adam and Eve, creating them on an even higher level than the angels. And he gave Adam and Eve "dominion over the earth." He delegated to them ruler-ship over this planet. It was the ultimate delegation of God's power. That, as we said earlier, was what must have so angered satan and the point the evil one was so obsessed with – he'd been tossed out of Heaven, he wanted ruler-ship of earth! When Adam and Eve rebelled and fell under the curse of sin, it completely wrecked their souls. That story, of God coming to save us all by becoming human and paying our sin penalty is the "Gospel" message of Scripture.

Here's the problem: we modern Christians tend to apply "the redemption principle" only to humanity's sinfulness. We don't tend to apply it to the rest of God's creation. *But God does!* God's whole eternal mindset is one of redemption, restoration, and resurrection. Whatever God formed initially as part of his *"that's good"* creation, is how God is one day going to restore this cursed planet!

> 1) Since God made our original home here a Garden of Eden, when God is finally done wiping out the effects of the curse, this earth is going to return to that original Eden-like state. It's God's principle of restoration.

> - Several of the Old Testament prophets, prophesy a time when the earth will once again be "uncursed."

The vegetation will grow as if it's in a worldwide greenhouse.

- Zechariah says the light would never cease day or night, the lion and the wolf would lay side by side in perfect peace – and even the curse of human death will fade.

2) God originally made this planet as the one place in the universe that would be home to his "in-his-image-beloved" creation, and he himself would be here on this globe fellow-shipping with them. So now this very earth is where God will set up our eternal home, and his eternal home. This is where he will commune with us for all eternity. Picture it as the completion of a circle. Whatever God started on this planet, before the fall, he is going to bring back to perfect completion by the time the clock runs out and timeless eternity begins.

3) God originally gave Adam and Eve "dominion" over this earth. By the time *(in Revelation 20:1-2)* one angel takes a chain and binds satan into the Abyss – the redeemed Saints, *(we are told six times in Scripture)* will be *(again)* ruling on this earth!

Do you see the completion of a circle? It's God's timeless principle of regeneration, redemption, resurrection. It applies to everything God made, including you, but not just you. This is the bigger picture of redemption that I am convinced the disciples knew about, probably because Jesus had shared it with them. *(But also because it's in the Old Testament!)*

They knew that the earth was one day going to be restored and that somehow their expected "Heavenly Homeland," the Heavenly City they were all waiting on (*going back to Abraham and the ancient patriarchs*) was somehow going to be connected to a restored earth. Remember Isaiah's prophesy 700 years before Jesus was born?

> **Isaiah 65:17-19: "Look! I am creating new heavens and a new earth, and no one will even think about the old ones anymore. Be glad; rejoice forever in my creation! And look! I will create Jerusalem as a place of happiness. Her people will be a source of joy. I will rejoice over Jerusalem and delight in my people. And the sound of weeping and crying will be heard in it no more."** (Compare that to what John would write 800 years later. Notice, John wasn't coming up with brand new truth – he was completing the picture of what had been prophesied centuries before!)

> **Revelation 21:1-4: "Then I saw a new heaven and a new earth, for the old heaven and the old earth had disappeared. And I saw the holy city, the New Jerusalem, coming down from God out of heaven I heard a loud shout from the throne, saying, 'Look, God's home is now among his people! He will live with them, and they will be his people. God himself will be with them. He will wipe every tear from their eyes, and there will be no more death or sorrow or crying or pain.'"**

The idea that this cursed earth, as we now know it, has a clock ticking toward its demise is woven throughout Scripture.

Psalmist: **Psalm 102:25-26 NIV: "In the beginning you laid the foundations of the earth, and the heavens are the work of your hands. They will perish, but you remain; they will all wear out like a garment. Like clothing you will change them and they will be discarded."**

Isaiah 51:6 NIV: "Lift up your eyes to the heavens, and look at the earth beneath; for the heavens vanish like smoke, the earth will wear out like a garment, and they who dwell in it will die in like manner; but my salvation will be forever, and my righteousness will never be dismayed."

See that? The people in the Old Testament, long before Jesus ever came as a Baby in a manger, knew that there was coming a day when this planet as we know it, was going to wear out like an old set of clothes and be "discarded."

- But they also had the Isaiah 65 promise that they would not need to remember the "old heavens and the old earth" anymore – because God was going to create a new heavens and a new earth!

- They didn't have the foggiest idea how, or when that was going to happen, but they knew it somehow had to be connected to the Heavenly Home/ Heavenly city that the Ancients had looked for, and spoken of.

You can imagine that after Jesus arrives, starts his ministry, chooses his disciples, and performs thousands of humanly impossible miracles – they finally, *at the end of his ministry,* start to figure out that this Messiah is exactly who Isaiah prophesied he would be: *Immanuel, Mighty God, the Father of Eternity*. Jesus had created the universe. *(John 1)* They must have pummeled him with questions about how the old cursed earth would once again become an un-cursed Garden of Eden, and I have a strong sense that he carefully told them. You can see the idea showing up in Jesus' public teaching:

> *Jesus:* **Matthew 19:28: "Jesus replied, 'I assure you that when the world is made new and the Son of Man sits upon his glorious throne, you who have been my followers will also sit on twelve thrones.'"**
>
> **Mark 13:31: "Heaven and earth will disappear, but my words will never disappear."**

Somehow, the "world being made new" was going to be connected to Jesus, the Messiah, finally taking his place as the ruler of this planet. They may not have understood, for sure, that Jesus was going to die, or that he would rise again, or that he would go back to Heaven – but they did know at some point Jesus was going to finally set up an eternal reign on this earth. They were going to be part of it, and it would not happen until the old earth had been wrapped up like an old T-shirt, and a new uncursed world had emerged.

- It's the principle of regeneration, and while Jesus' listeners seemed to not understand a lot of stuff he told them – they did seem to catch on to this.

- A case in point is brash, arrogant, "foot in the mouth" Peter. After the day of Pentecost, the old unlearned, but now "Spirit empowered" fisherman, gets up and lays out one of the best sermons anybody ever preached. He calls people to repent, he promises them the Second Coming of Jesus, but he carefully adds in the circumstances around Jesus' return.

Acts 3:19-21: "Now repent of your sins and turn to God, so that your sins may be wiped away. Then times of refreshment will come from the presence of the Lord, and he will again send you Jesus, your appointed Messiah. For <u>he must remain in heaven until the time for the final restoration of all things</u>, as God promised long ago through his holy prophets."

What exactly is the <u>final restoration of all things</u>? It's exactly what we were talking about earlier. Anything God began before the fall, he is going to restore, as part of the final "restoration of all things." Only the things sin has irreparably destroyed, including satan, and his minions, and those who have willfully rejected God's gift of grace will not get restored.

- Don't imagine God saying, "Wow I saved humanity, but too bad about the sin-cursed earth. Satan unexpectedly got his slimy paws in that one and made it un-restorable." No, this restored earth is where Jesus plans to set up his everlasting reign!

- *I will repeat this essential truth again:* This earth is where Jesus' Redeemed Saints will once again exert "dominion" over the earth. It is where the Holy City, the New Jerusalem is going to come down to. The Holy City is where your Jesus-prepared home is! The Holy City is where the very Throne Room of God is, where he will live and commune with his children for eternity!

Revelation 21:5-7: "The One sitting on the Throne said, 'Look, I am making everything new!' And then he said to me, 'Write this down, for what I tell you is trustworthy and true.' And he also said, 'It is finished! I am the Alpha and the Omega—the Beginning and the End. To all who are thirsty I will give freely from the springs of the water of life. All who are victorious will inherit all these blessings, and I will be their God, and they will be my children.'"

Imagine the sinlessness of Heaven, the curse-less state of God's Home, as it begins to enlarge across the universe.

The "Holy Shock wave" Peter describes travels as fast as the speed of light across the universe, purging sin out of every molecule. Imagine as the "holiness of Heaven" touches anything in the universe that is infected by the curse – it "purifies it," burning off the curse of sin.

When the shock wave of Heaven reaches this earth, the very hotbed of sin and the curse – you can imagine what it would have looked like to Peter in a vision – as pure holiness meets pure sin, and what it will probably look like to us, as we watch holiness burning up sin and its effects, first hand, with our newly glorified eyes.

And once that purification has cleansed the earth then the Holy City of God containing the home that Jesus has prepared for you, is settling down onto this very planet. And at some point you will be ushered into the New Jerusalem, stopping for a few hours/days to worship in the

Throne Room. And then you will finally set your glorified feet inside your eternal residence. I want to describe that to you in the next chapter!

CHAPTER 25

HEAVEN: Part VII

CHAPTER 25

Chapter 26

"On that day, life-giving waters will flow out from Jerusalem."

By way of review: *(Again Sam – yes, again.)* Jesus, with millions/billions of us Redeemed Believers, and millions/billions of angels move in over Jerusalem and the Mount of Olives for Jesus' Second Advent. We will probably fill all the skies from the valley of Megiddo to Jerusalem – but then Zechariah sees this:

> **Zechariah 14:4-9: "On that day his feet will stand on the Mount of Olives, east of Jerusalem. And the Mount of Olives will split apart, making a wide valley running from east to west. Half the mountain will move toward the north and half toward the south. Then the LORD my God will come (Jesus!), and all his holy ones with him.** *(QADOSH – sacred – holy ones – that's us!)*
>
> **"On that day the sources of light will no longer shine,** *(remember during the horrific trumpet and bowl judgments the "stars have fallen from the sky" and the world is plunged into darkness)* **yet** *(now)* **there will be continuous day! Only the LORD knows how this could happen. There will be no normal day and night, for at evening time it will still be light.**

From the day Jesus' feet land back on this earth, <u>the lights come back on</u>! Not from the sun or stars, not light from huge electric generators. *(they've all been turned into rubble.)* The entire earth was reduced to almost complete darkness, and now light is radiating everywhere again. It is radiating from one Source, in Jerusalem, and it finds its way out across the once dark planet.

"On that day life-giving waters will flow out from Jerusalem, *(remember, the waters had turned to blood and everything in them had died)* half toward the Dead Sea and half toward the Mediterranean, flowing continuously in both summer and winter. And the LORD will be king over all the earth. On that day there will be one LORD—his name alone will be worshiped."

Ok, Sam, you say, that sounds like Zechariah is ejecting us full speed into the New Heavens and New Earth that you were describing in the last chapter. This must be exactly where that transformation begins! Yes, I believe it is!

In John's great "unveiling" in Revelation 21, he describes in high definition a New Earth, replacing the old earth, and a New Jerusalem, a Heavenly City will replace the Old. Remember, Abraham looking forward to that very city, "with foundations whose builder and architect is God?" – This is it!

John doesn't mention the landing on the Mount of Olives, or the "on that day" change in world lighting and life-giving water.

John doesn't mention the changes in the Earth, "from sin-cursed to God-blessed" until chapter 21. Without Zechariah's prophecy, we wouldn't yet know about that, but that is why we always balance Scripture with Scripture. John used, I believe, a literary technique we still use today, called a "parenthetical insert." He used the same technique back in chapter 12 when he mentions a long past "war in Heaven." *Please refer to Appendix C in the back of the book titled, "A Chronology of Revelation 20 and 21.)*

Isaiah has specific things to say about what is one day coming. Clearly God was eventually going to clean up the mess that satan had made of the earth!

> **Isaiah 11:6-9: "In that day the wolf and the lamb will live together; the leopard will lie down with the baby goat. The calf and the yearling will be safe with the lion, and a little child will lead them all. The cow will graze near the bear. The cub and the calf will lie down together. The lion will eat hay like a cow. The baby will play safely near the hole of a cobra. Yes, a little child will put its hand in a nest of deadly snakes without harm. Nothing will hurt or destroy in all my holy mountain, for as the waters fill the sea, so the earth will be filled with people who know the LORD."**

But there was even more truth prophesied than just that the wolf would not be making the lamb into its afternoon snack, or that we could quit worrying about poisonous snakes. There is more:

> **Isaiah 2:2-3: "In the last days, the mountain of the LORD's house will be the highest of all— the most important place on earth. It will be raised above the other hills, and people from all over the world will stream there to worship. People from many nations will come and say, 'Come, let us go up to the mountain of the LORD, to the house of Jacob's God. There he will teach us his ways, and we will walk in his paths.'"** *By the way;*

> **Zechariah 14:10, 16 NIV: "All the land from Geba, north of Judah, to Rimmon, south of Jerusalem, will become one vast plain. But Jerusalem will be raised up in its original place. Then the survivors from all the nations that have attacked Jerusalem will go up year after year to worship the King, the LORD Almighty."**

The point is, in the Old Testament, those Ancients knew there was coming a day when:

Jerusalem will became the spiritual center of the earth, but not just the spiritual center of the earth – it will become the literal, physical center of the earth. We haven't seen that yet! But that, for sure, is still coming!

And it is never presented as some metaphorical symbolism. The ancients all knew, the First Century Church knew, we should all now know – that there is a real time coming when on the way to the new Capital City of the earth, the New Jerusalem, you will not only pass the occasional boy leading his pet lion around – but Jerusalem would be "raised up higher than any city on earth," perhaps higher than any point on earth. You say, Sam, how do you know that can possibly be true? I can because it's right here in the Bible!

- Do we remember the last bowl judgment to land on this sin-cursed earth, just as Jesus and us, and the angels are making our way here, in Jesus' Glorious Second Coming?

Revelation 16:17-20 "Then the seventh angel poured out his bowl into the air. And a mighty shout came from the throne in the Temple, saying, 'It is finished!' *(This is the last of the last before Jesus takes over the reigns of earth!)*

"Then the thunder crashed and rolled, and lightning flashed. And a great earthquake struck—the worst since people were placed on the earth. The great city of Babylon split into three sections, and the cities of many nations fell into heaps of rubble. And every island disappeared, and all the mountains were leveled."

So this highest building on Earth, in Dubai, makes the skyscrapers beside it look like matchboxes – according to Revelation 16:19 they all come crashing to earth in piles of rubble. The highest mountain on the planet, Mount Everest, is "leveled."

The unsolvable problem of lowly Jerusalem becoming the "highest point on earth" that everyone sees for hundreds of miles as they approach it – becomes far better understood when you look at it through the lens of what else the Bible says is happening right then. Every other city and mountain has crashed into rubble. The New Jerusalem will be 1400 miles high. That's 7,392,000 feet tall. That's 254 times higher than Mount Everest. No wonder people coming to Jerusalem to worship the Lord the Almighty can see the city from horizons one third of the way around the earth. And wait until you see what the city is made of, and how unbelievably bright it will be from thousands and thousands of miles away!

So you return with Jesus in his glorious Second Coming. You land on the Mount of Olives or in the vicinity. The land around Jerusalem *(Zechariah 14 says)* becomes a vast plain. "How big will that new 'vast plain' be," you ask?

It will be the same size as the first floor dimensions of the New Jerusalem! *(1400 miles x 1400 miles!)* Because as land structure shifting is taking place – the New Jerusalem, the place that houses the Throne Room of God – the place where the "room" that Jesus said he was going to prepare for you, is coming! That Holy City is already, by the time Jesus plants his feet on the Mount of Olives, on its way here!

Revelation 21:3-7: "I heard a loud shout from the Throne, saying, 'Look, God's home is now among his people! He will live with them, and they will be his people. God himself will be with them. He will wipe every tear from their eyes, and there will be no more death or sorrow or crying or pain. All these things are gone forever.'

Do we understand that this entire conversation from God to his Redeemed is being announced from the Throne Room? You will be there for this event! You will be bubbling over with joy when you hear this loud shout coming from the Throne!

> **"And the one sitting on the throne said, 'Look, I am making everything new!' And then he said to me, 'Write this down, for what I tell you is trustworthy and true.' And he also said, 'It is finished! I am the Alpha and the Omega—the Beginning and the End. To all who are thirsty I will give freely from the springs of the water of life. All who are victorious will inherit all these blessings, and I will be their God, and they will be my children.'"**

Presumably, many millions of us redeemed, glorified Saints will be at this orientation speech together. When you step outside and raise your eyes up, up, and up – what you see will be beyond all human comprehension.

Note: the Holy City is not all of Heaven. This is just its capital. All of Heaven is undoubtedly massive even now, but by this time, Heaven will have expanded to absorb all the universe, and all of this planet – turning absolutely everything, *(except the lake of fire/abyss, wherever that is)* into a new Heavens and a New Earth.

Speaking of massive, *again,* when you see the Heavenly Capital for the first time from outside, your eyes will go up and up. You'll be able to see the top, perhaps from 100 miles away, but not from just outside the "gates of pearl." Here are the city's measurements up against a relief of the United States. If you want to walk across the city one day, it would be the distance from Miami to Buffalo, or westward to San Antonio, Texas.

The biggest city *(by area)* in the US is Anchorage, Alaska. I've been there, Sue and I walked around it in one afternoon. But they list their square footage as four times the size of Los Angeles.

- The New Jerusalem is 4,500 times bigger than Los Angeles, and that's just on the floor level! It goes up into the sky, the same distance. If every floor is 1/2 mile there are 2800 floors. That's 26 times the entire land surface area of the whole earth. If each floor is ¼ mile tall – that is 52 times the land surface area of the earth.

- Remember, Heaven will eventually become as large as the whole universe, but just the Capital City would be big enough to house every human who has ever lived on just a handful of the floors. *(Sadly, they won't all be there!)*

- Well, what about trying to get to the Heavenly grocery store on market day clear across the City. Won't that be hard? And won't standing, waiting for those elevators on the 1389th floor become a real pain. ☺

- Remember, after Jesus' resurrection in his glorified body, Jesus was in a room – and then instantly, he wasn't! He was in one place, and then suddenly he was in another.

- Someone asked me if we will have the ability to move around all of Heaven *(the whole universe)* with just a thought from our glorified mind? I think the answer, is probably yes!

Enough on how big the city is. What does it look like?

Revelation 21:10-11, 15-18: "So he took me in the Spirit to a great, high mountain, and he showed me the holy city, Jerusalem, descending out of heaven from God. It shone with the glory of God and sparkled like a precious stone—like jasper as clear as crystal. The angel who talked to me held in his hand a gold measuring stick to measure the city, its gates, and its wall. When he measured it, he found it was a square, as wide as it was long. In fact, its length and width and height were each 1,400 miles. Then he measured the walls and found them to be 216 feet thick (according to the human standard used by the angel).

"The wall was made of jasper, and the city was pure gold, as clear as glass." Imagine the pure light of God reflecting through 216 feet of translucent walls, and then reflecting outward – so people a thousand miles away can see it as clear as if it were next door.

The third noticeable element of the city is the foundations. Some writers say the city will just hover above the earth. Then why, I would ask, the need to describe such extravagant foundations? Remember, tent-dwelling Abraham was looking for a city "with foundations," whose Builder and Architect is God.

> **Revelation 21:19-20: "The wall of the city was built on foundation stones inlaid with twelve precious stones: the first was jasper, the second sapphire, the third agate, the fourth emerald, the fifth onyx, the sixth carnelian, the seventh chrysolite, the eighth beryl, the ninth topaz, the tenth chrysoprase, the eleventh jacinth, the twelfth amethyst."**

Every conceivable color, but not faked color or forced color like we come up with. This is pure color – as the light of God refracts through perfect, flawless, divine gemstones.

You know how high-end jewelry stores will have bright lights reflecting on their counters from every direction to make the jewels sparkle. That will be like "matchsticks in a dark room" compared to what you will see the first time you lay eyes on the Heavenly City.

And you will be seeing them, with glorified eyes. Remember how we talked earlier in this book about us, now only being able to see a tiny part of the available light spectrum. When the scales of the curse of sin fall off, and you really, really <u>see</u> for the first time! Imagine walking up and touching those foundations and then laying your hands on the gates of pearl and standing on the streets of gold.

Revelation 21:21: "The twelve gates were made of pearls—each gate from a single pearl! And the main street was pure gold, as clear as glass."

Many have joked about us not caring much about gold in Heaven since "gold is just pavement," but I have a feeling the awe at what we are actually going to see is going to be a million times greater than anything we can imagine now! Is there a deep longing for Heaven growing inside of you? It is in me!

CHAPTER 26

Chapter 27

Ruling and reigning with Jesus!

So we now have the final battle on earth, the battle of Armageddon in the rear view mirror. Jesus, with his redeemed Saints *(us),* and his numberless army of angels in tow defeats the hate-filled armies of the earth with the sword *(Word)* from his mouth. The antichrist is dropped into the Lake of Fire. Zechariah 14 records that Jesus lands back on the Mount of Olives exactly where he had ascended to Heaven.

 **Zechariah 14:4-5, 8-9: "On that day his feet will stand on the Mount of Olives, east of Jerusalem. And the Mount of Olives will split apart, making a wide valley running from east to west. Half the mountain will move toward the north and half toward the south. Then the LORD my God will come (Jesus!), and all his holy ones with him.** *(QADOSH – sacred – holy ones – that's us!)* **On that day life-giving waters will flow out from Jerusalem. And the LORD will be king over all the earth. On that day there will be one LORD—his name alone will be worshiped."**

- I was reading an article where the author was very forcefully showing how the whole book of Zechariah repeatedly snaps one prophetic picture after another of the coming Messiah. Including:

- The facts that he would ride into Jerusalem on a donkey in chapter 9, that the price for his betrayal would be exactly 30 pieces of silver which would then buy a potter's field. *(Remember this is being written 500 years before Jesus would be born.)*

- The fact that every eye would see him as he comes in the clouds in chapter 12 – but that first he would be pierced. The fact that his followers would scatter after his death in chapter 13. All dead-on fulfilled prophecies!

And then this particular author came to chapter 14 and just wrote the word "conclusion," and said: "Do not under any circumstances believe that chapter 14 is actually, literally describing the Second Coming of Jesus. This chapter is purely allegorical and in no way can be thought to be a literal coming event! *What?*

I had some strong out-loud words to say to the author. Because, as I dug through "hundreds and hundreds" of passages on Heaven over a period of eight months. I increasingly became sure that most of these end-times verses are meant to be taken as literally as possible!

Zechariah does indeed finish his flourish of prophecies about the returning Jesus in chapter 14 – by snapping a vivid snapshot of Jesus returning back to the very place he ascended from! He splits the mountain, brings light radiating back to a world that had gone completely dark, and sends new life-giving waters flowing out to a dead water world. But watch this new morsel: *(new to this book – not to Scripture!)*

Zechariah acknowledges, 500 years before Jesus is born, that this "Returning One" is going to be "his Lord and his God!" And that he will bring his *Qadosh* – his holy ones – back with him *(Us)*, and that "on that day" he will begin setting up an eternal ruler-ship right here on this planet and he will be king over all the Earth!

This principle of Jesus returning as "ruler of the world" is very important to what we are going to unfold next!

> **Zechariah 9:9-10** says: **"Rejoice, O people of Zion! Shout in triumph, O people of Jerusalem! Look, your king is coming to you. He is righteous and victorious, yet he is humble, riding on a donkey— riding on a donkey's colt.   I will remove the battle chariots from Israel and the warhorses from Jerusalem. I will destroy all the weapons used in battle, and your king will bring peace to the nations. His realm will stretch from sea to sea and from Ephraim** *(northern tribe)* **to the ends of the earth."**

- If Zechariah got the "riding on a donkey's colt" part right – one would/should assume he's going to get the part about the donkey-riding "King" reigning to the ends of the earth right too! Yes? It's clearly the same person!

- Revelation 19:16 says when Jesus returns, he will come as the King of all kings and the Lord of all lords!

But that part hasn't happened yet! Neither has Israel's battle chariots been removed, and all the battle weapons destroyed from Israel. They will be one day!

The angel Gabriel told Mary when he was announcing Jesus' birth:

> **Luke 1:31-33: "You will conceive and give birth to a son, and you will name him Jesus. He will be very great and will be called the Son of the Most High. The Lord God will <u>give him the throne of his ancestor David</u>. And he will <u>reign over Israel forever; his Kingdom will never end!</u>"** Jesus is not just a coming Savior – he is coming back as a forever reigning King!

We can use the same logic we used with Zechariah. Clearly Gabriel got the first part right. Mary did conceive, gave birth to a son and named him "Jesus-The Saving One." But when exactly did the second part of that prophecy happen, the forever reigning king part? It hasn't, yet – but it will!

Pilate at the trial asked Jesus if he was a King. Jesus said yes, "I am a king. But my kingdom is not of this world." He could have added the word "Yet." Because we have scores of Scriptures that tell us Jesus is indeed going to set up an earthly kingdom – where he will reign forever. He wasn't, at his trial, ready to focus on his coming earthly kingship yet. He needed to goad Pilate into killing him, so he could pay humanity's sin penalty.

I already noted that I preached a series a few years ago where I pulled out every use in the Bible of the words "eternity, eternal, everlasting." It became clear that God's promise to David was a "forever Throne." God's covenant promises to Israel were forever promises. God's relationship with his chosen people would never, ever end!

There are those who would try to spiritualize this and say Israel's time in history is over, and any perceived prophecy of Jesus eventually "sitting on the Throne of David" should be spiritualized, because God's not going to give Israel another chance to be saved, and David's kingdom was dissolved years ago – but you literally *(IMO)* have to stomp over top of scores of passages to hold that view. Isaiah's famous prophecy of the coming Messiah/Savior was:

> **Isaiah 9:6-7: "For a child is born to us, a son is given to us. The government will rest on his shoulders. And he will be called: Wonderful Counselor, Mighty God, Everlasting Father, Prince of Peace. His government and its peace will never end. He will rule with fairness and justice from the throne of his ancestor David for all eternity."**

Seriously, where is the Throne of David located? It's not in Heaven! It never was. It was right here on earth. So if the coming Messiah is going to reign on David's Throne – where is he going to be reigning from? And how long will he be reigning for?

God has a future plan for this earth, a future plan for the Children of Israel, and a future plan for Jerusalem. His plan involves <u>an actual kingdom over which the Second Coming Messiah will reign</u> *(forever)* <u>and over which his people, the Redeemed Saints, will reign with him</u>. Multiple passages *(which we will look at)* say the Redeemed Saints will return to this earth with Jesus, and we will somehow take part in his "ruling and reigning." What does that mean? Is that literal or is it figurative?

If you ask many Christians what they are going to be doing in Heaven for all of eternity, not too many of them will respond, <u>I'm going to be reigning with Jesus</u>, because that sounds like arrogance, or narcissism, and then there is the whole issue of who you would be reigning over? "We're going to heaven to worship God! When we are not worshipping God, in the Throne Room, we are going to be sitting on a cloud playing a harp." No!

Besides ruling with Jesus for all of eternity sounds like work and everybody knows that we are going to Heaven so we can leave work behind, because "doing nothing" is the reward for having to have been so busy all our years. When we get to Heaven we are going to enjoy the first few "years" just doing nothing, sucking in the Heavenly atmosphere, meeting those who have gone before.

And then "500 years" in, we are going to be doing the same thing, and "1000 years" in we are going to be still at it, still enjoying that "doing nothing" part. Somewhere along the way somebody is going to say – "my, if only there were some Little Debbie wrappers laying around on the Golden Streets to be picked up."

That "doing nothing" theme is not the picture Scripture paints of your Heavenly future at all. It paints a picture of the Redeemed Saints busy doing eternal things that bring them amazing fulfillment – and brings peace and harmony to the entire planet and perhaps the entire universe. We are apparently going to be doing those eternal things right alongside of our "ruling and reigning" Savior.

I found something that I had never seen before in Daniel's vision in chapter 7.

> **Daniel 7:2-3, 8: "In my vision that night, I, Daniel, saw a great storm churning the surface of a great sea. Then four huge beasts came up out of the water.** (He describes four beasts which are later identified as the four major empires that have ruled the earth.) **As I was looking suddenly another small horn appeared. This little horn had eyes like human eyes and a mouth that was boasting arrogantly."** *(Many/most would say that is the antichrist at the end of time.) Then this happens. I've often quoted this – but missed the ending of it all:*

> **Daniel 7:9-10, 13-14: "I watched as thrones were put in place and the Ancient One sat down to judge. His clothing was as white as snow, his hair like purest wool. He sat on a fiery throne with wheels of blazing fire, and a river of fire was pouring out, flowing from his presence. Millions of angels ministered to him; many millions stood to attend him. Then the court began its session, and the books were opened.** *(We looked at this as one glance inside the Throne Room.)*

> **"As my vision continued that night, I saw someone like a Son of Man coming with the clouds of heaven. He approached the Ancient One and was led into his presence. He was given authority, honor, and sovereignty over all the nations of the world, so that people of every race and nation and language would**

obey him. His rule is eternal—it will never end. His kingdom will never be destroyed."

As I already stated, I've quoted that so many times, showing that when Jesus called himself "the Son of Man" *(his most-used name for himself)*, every Jewish person listening knew that he was pointing to himself as the one described by Daniel. They expected an eternal ruler. They just missed the fact that their long-awaited Messiah would first come to save them from their sins, and then return a second time to take over the reign of planet Earth, <u>forever</u>! <u>His rule will be eternal</u>! <u>His kingdom will never end</u>!

This next part totally escaped me. It is the very next part of the end-times package that Daniel is seeing in his vision;

> **Daniel 7:21-22, 27: "As I watched, this horn** *(antichrist)* **was waging war against God's holy people and was defeating them, until the Ancient One—the Most High—came and judged in favor of his holy people. <u>Then the time arrived for the holy people to take over the kingdom. Then the sovereignty, power, and greatness of all the kingdoms under heaven will be given to the holy people of the Most High</u>. His (Jesus) kingdom will last forever, and all rulers will serve and obey him."** *(What?)* That's not talking about angels; <u>that's talking about us</u>! The sovereignty, power, and greatness of all the kingdoms under heaven will be given to us – the holy people of the Most High.

- Right after the feeding of the 5000, the first century followers of Jesus tried to force him into defeating Rome and they tried to make him their King – this is what they were basing it on. The Messiah King would take control over sin and satan. *(Represented most to them as the Roman Empire. Rome was, after all, the last "beast" Daniel saw.)*

- They wanted Jesus to defeat Rome and set up his Kingdom right then, knowing that Daniel promised that they themselves as followers of the Messiah would become "rulers" on the earth. They weren't totally wrong – they just missed the "die on a cross first" part!

- So when Zechariah sees Jesus landing on the Mount of Olives and becoming King of the whole earth, his readers knew what that signaled was coming next, and sure enough John in Revelation 20 gives that exact sequence.

1) One angel binds satan in the abyss for 1000 years. (vv. 1-3)

2) John sees "thrones and people sitting on them" with authority to judge. Who? (v. 3?)

3) The martyrs since the Rapture come back to life and join "the throne sitters" in reigning for 1000 years. (vv. 4-5).

4) Verse 6 fills in the info that **everybody** who was part of the "first resurrection/rapture" will be "priests of God and Christ and will reign for 1000 years."

5) Satan is released after the 1000 years to gather those who still rejected Jesus' 1000 year rule. (vv. 7-10)

6) The Great White Throne Judgment arrives, where the unbelieving dead finally rise at the end of the 1000 years and are judged and condemned. (vv. 11-15)

Let's focus on two parts of that for the rest of this chapter. After satan is bound for 1000 years, which presumably happens right as Jesus *(and us)* return to this planet. <u>The Saints are placed on Thrones with the authority to judge</u>!

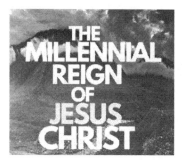

Daniel has already said that the Saints are going to rule for all of eternity, but there is extra emphasis here placed on the first 1000 years. *Why?*

What is so important about the first 1000 years, out of all of eternity? It's a time we often refer to as "the Millennium." *Note this:* The glorified Saints who return with Jesus and reign, and the martyrs who come back to life and reign are not the only humans left on the planet. Many Believers come through the Tribulation/Judgment period still very much alive. We often think of the antichrist as chasing down every Believer on the planet who hasn't taken his mark on their hand or forehead – but this planet is a very big place and the antichrist has his hands increasingly full in and around Jerusalem.

- I envision millions of people turning to Jesus as their Savior, including a lot of Jews, even as the Trumpet and Bowl judgments finish crashing down. ·

- Those Tribulation Believers, and their new babies and young children, make their way alive into the first 1000 years. They are not part of the raptured, glorified Saints – which means they are still reproducing!

- In fact, they reproduce a lot – replenishing a decimated population. With satan gone, with Jesus and his saints ruling, the earth becomes a renewed green house with vast resources. Several Old Testament passages describe the earth during the millennium.

- Isaiah says the human lifespan returns to a pre-flood stage, with the man who lives past 100 being as a young child. *(Isaiah 65:20)* So the world fills right back up with people.

Most of them, we are told, worship the King of Kings. Our job, as rulers with Christ for the first 1000 years, will apparently be to encourage that process.

Amazingly, with satan bound, and the world finally a peaceful place, with no wars and no/little crime, and most everyone following the laws established by the King of all Kings and the Lord of all Lords – Stunningly, the sin nature buried deep within humanity still manages to rise to the surface, and when satan is finally released at the end of the 1000 years, what John sees is kind of shocking.

Revelation 20:7-8, 10: "When the thousand years come to an end, satan will be let out of his prison. He will go out to deceive the nations in every corner of the earth. He will <u>gather them together for battle—a mighty army, as numberless as sand along the seashore.</u>

Q: How in the world can satan gather a "numberless throng" to fight Jesus? It's stunning to see how much sin still lurks in the human heart even with satan bound and Jesus reigning in truth.

Q: After just one angel locks satan up for 1000 years, does he actually still believe he has the slightest chance of winning? *(Yes! satan is the father of lies, he lies all the time, even to himself! Revelation 20:10)*

"Then the devil, who had deceived them, was thrown into the fiery lake of burning sulfur, joining the beast and the false prophet. There they will be tormented day and night forever and ever." *That's the end of the end* – except for "the Great White Throne Judgment," which comes next, recorded in the last 5 verses of Revelation 20.

- All of the unbelieving dead, all of the remaining living unbelievers – all are brought before God for their final sentence. *(That's the end of the end of the end.)*

- **And that's the end of sin on this world**! Everyone left on the planet has placed their faith in Jesus. But they are still going to need ruling over. Remember Daniel said we will be reigning for all of eternity.

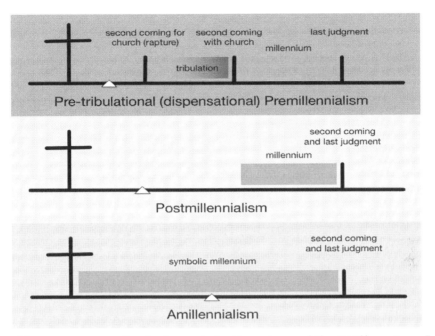

Now, not everybody buys into the view of the Millennium I just presented. I presented a very literal view. There are, however, three main views:

Post millennialism: This view, started in early 1700's by Daniel Whitby, says that the 1000 years is not a future event and it is not necessarily 1000 years. It represents the period of time we are living in right now where "we are taking part in reigning with Jesus every day as we live out our Christian lives." As we influence our world with the Gospel – the world will become a better and better place until we are living in a utopian world which will usher in the Return of Jesus, followed by the eternal state.

- That view was popular in the early 1900's when inventions were exploding onto the scene, with cars and radios, and TV's, and airplanes.

- The world seemed to be moving toward a utopia, and then came WWI and the great Depression and then Hitler and WWII and the Cold War with threats of nuclear annihilation – and the belief that the world was getting better and better largely vanished.

Amillenialism – "No millennium": There is no coming 1000 year reign of Christ and all the teachings about it need to be seen as allegorical or symbolic. The symbolic millennium can be seen happening throughout the last 2000 or even 6000 years. When Jesus returns we will simply join him in the "eternal state" without all this "ruling" hullabaloo. ☺

As I've stated, the more I study these passages, the more entrenched I become in believing that these passages are talking about a real Second Advent of Jesus to set up a real 1000 year reign, followed by an eternal reign. And we Redeemed Saints have in our coming future – actually ruling and reigning beside Jesus *(as Daniel prophesied)* for all of eternity. Let me take that view a step deeper:

> **Romans 8:16-17 NIV: "The Spirit himself testifies with our spirit that we are God's children. Now if we are children, then <u>we are heirs—heirs of God and co-heirs with Christ</u>, if indeed we share in his sufferings in order that we may also share in his glory."**

So you are an **heir of God** and **a co-heir with Jesus** when this thing is all over – what does that mean?

1 Peter 1:3-4: "It is by his great mercy that we have been born again, because God raised Jesus Christ from the dead. Now we live with great expectation, and <u>we have a priceless inheritance—an inheritance that is kept in heaven for you</u>, pure and undefiled, beyond the reach of change and decay."

So what is your inheritance in Heaven – the undiluted presence of God? Yes. Being able to worship God at 1000+% in Heaven? Yes. Finally being without the curse of sin in your soul that has held you down all your life? Yes. Having a place/room/mansion in the New Jerusalem that Jesus has prepared for you? Yes.

- But none of those four things would apply to Jesus, and Romans 8 says – you are <u>co-heirs</u> with him!

- Jesus isn't waiting for a home in Heaven. He's the one who made your home there! Jesus doesn't need the undiluted presence of God – He is God!

- So <u>what is Jesus going to inherit that you are going to inherit with him</u>? What does Jesus not have now, that he is going to receive, and you are going to receive alongside of him – and share it with him as a co-heir?

Daniel 7:13-14: "As my vision continued that night, I saw someone like a Son of Man coming with the clouds of heaven. He approached the Ancient One and was led into his presence. He was given authority, honor, and sovereignty over all the nations of the world, so that people of every race and nation and

language would obey him. His rule is eternal — it will never end. His kingdom will never be destroyed."

- There is the one thing Jesus does not have yet, but is going to receive from the Father at the end of the age. and you are a joint-heir, a co-heir with him in that coming inheritance!

- Remember, when God created this earth he gave Adam and Eve, dominion, ruler-ship, not just over naming animals and planting a garden – They were in charge of their world. They exercised "dominion."

- But they fell. The rulership of earth was transferred to satan who had already tried to gain rulership in Heaven and failed. In the End, when satan is finally defeated, bound into the abyss for a thousand years. Creator Jesus will once again assume rulership over the Heavens and earth – and you and I will pick up where Adam and Eve left off. We will inherit their dominion rule, as co-heirs with Jesus! What do we think these verses mean?

1 Corinthians 6:2-3: "Don't you realize that someday we believers will judge the world? And since you are going to judge the world, can't you decide even these little things among yourselves? Don't you realize that we will judge angels? So you should surely be able to resolve ordinary disputes in this life." (Guys, we better learn to deal with the little dust-ups in this life, because we are on our way to ruling over the world – including even the angels!)

2 Timothy 2:11-12: "This is a trustworthy saying: If we die with him, we will also live with him. If we endure hardship, <u>we will reign with him</u>." *(joint-heirs)*

Revelation 5:9-10: "They sang a new song with these words: "You are worthy to take the scroll and break its seals and open it, for you were slain and your blood has ransomed people for God from every tribe and language and people and nation. You have caused them to become a Kingdom of priests for our God. <u>And they will reign on the earth</u>." This is so specific! They/<u>we, the blood bought</u> – <u>will reign</u>! Where – <u>on the earth</u>! So will Jesus! You will be his co-heir!

Revelation 20:6: "Blessed and holy are those who share in the first resurrection. For them the second death holds no power, but <u>they will be priests of God and of Christ and will reign with him a thousand years</u>."

Again: **Daniel 7:22, 27:** "Then the time arrived for the holy people to take over the kingdom. Then <u>the sovereignty, power, and greatness of all the kingdoms under heaven will be given to the holy people of the Most High</u>."

Whoa, Sam, I didn't sign up as a Jesus-follower, to join with him in "ruling" over the earth, and maybe the whole universe in the future. I just want to go to Heaven and do nothing for the next 1000 years.

- I want to stop by the Throne Room for my morning devotions then go back to my mansion that Jesus went to prepare for me. Well – you might just be disappointed!

- Actually, you won't. You are going to find the activities you get to do for/with Jesus in the future so absolutely satisfying, so eternally fulfilling – that you will relish leaving your "mansion" each morning to do your part in "co-ruling" with Jesus.

Let me reinforce this "reigning theme" a little bit more. Look at the words Jesus closed with to the Seven Churches:

Revelation 2:10: "But if you remain faithful even when facing death, <u>I will give you the crown of life</u>." *Crown? Why didn't he say ball cap or cowboy hat? What do you do with a crown?*

Revelation 3:11: "I am coming soon. Hold on to what you have, so that no one will<u> take away your crown</u>." *(Huh?)*

Revelation 2:26: "To all who are victorious, who obey me to the very end, To them <u>I will give authority over all the nations</u>."

Revelation 3:20-21: "Behold! I stand at the door and knock. If you hear my voice and open the door, I will come in, and we will share a meal together as friends. Those who are <u>victorious will sit with me on my throne</u>, just as I was victorious and sat with my Father on his throne."

Chapter 28

Getting ready to reign with Jesus!

When I was five years old, our family moved from Pennsylvania. My parents had been song evangelists, but my dad had lost his singing voice, so we moved to Findlay, Ohio where he became a meat-cutter. One of the first things we did was visit the church we were going to attend. I still have memories of arriving in front of that church parsonage. My little blonde head with the bowl haircut *(administered by my grandfather)* was peering out the rear window and seeing three boys on the front porch. Our families became inseparable for the next few decades.

Ten years later when the boys' dad, my pastor, was killed in a horrific auto accident, his family moved to Hobe Sound, Florida and not too long after, my family followed.

 *Fast forward.* The oldest boy on that porch, Rick Addison and myself – have both now pastored churches on the Treasure Coast of Florida for more than four decades. The week I wrote this chapter – Rick Addison died. He was two years older than me. He lived a life of faithful service to God. That sure makes this whole subject matter very real.

After eight months of studying Heaven, I can now picture Rick arriving. I can picture the massive difference in who he is, without the curse of sin on his body *(and soul)*. I can see him walking into the New Jerusalem on streets of pure clear gold with the light of God refracting in every direction. I can see him stepping into the Throne Room of God and falling on his face in worship.

But keep this in mind, The Throne Room where Rick is falling in worship now – is coming here! The New Jerusalem is coming here! The very Home of God is coming here. And your eternal home *(the place Jesus left to prepare for you)* will be centered right here on Earth!

This Earth is going to become the centerpiece of God's forever rule!

That Holy City, pictured in the last two chapters of the Bible, measuring 1400 miles long, by 1400 miles wide, by 1400 miles high – if you look at God's original promise of land to Abraham in Genesis 15,  reaching over to the Euphrates River in Iraq – if you square it off, it's about the same square footage as the promised New Jerusalem.

I'm assuming the Holy City will cover that same area. And whatever it is that you are going to be doing for all of eternity, it will be headquartered right there in the New Jerusalem, because God says his home will be among his people.

> **Revelation 21:2-5: "And I saw the Holy City, the New Jerusalem, coming down from God out of Heaven like a bride beautifully dressed for her husband. I heard a loud shout from the Throne, saying, '<u>Look, God's home is now among his people! He will live with them, and they will be his people. God himself will be with them</u>. He will wipe every tear from their eyes, and there will be no more death or sorrow or crying or pain. All these things are gone forever.' And the One sitting on the Throne said, 'Look, I am making everything new!'"**

And from that very place, for all of eternity, Jesus will set up his eternal rule – from right here on this earth, extending outward across the universe. As the angel Gabriel said to Mary when announcing Jesus' birth.

> **Luke 1:31-33: "You will conceive and give birth to a son, and you will name him Jesus. He will be very great and will be called the Son of the Most High. The Lord God will give him the throne of his ancestor David. And he will reign over Israel forever; his Kingdom will never end!"**

Question: How can I be so absolutely certain that the prophecies about the Second Coming of Jesus (*and all that is said to happen afterward*) are to be taken literally?

Logical answer: Because all of the prophecies about Jesus' First Coming were meant to be taken literally, and **every one of them happened exactly as predicted!**

There is no doubt *(in my mind)* that Jesus believed he was coming back to earth, a second time, to set up a forever kingdom – reigning here on this earth. *Watch this:*

> **Acts 1:6-8: "So when the Apostles were with Jesus, they kept asking him, 'Lord, has the time come for you to free Israel and restore our kingdom?' He replied, 'The Father alone has the authority to set those dates and times, and they are not for you to know. But you will receive power when the Holy Spirit comes upon you. And you will be my witnesses, telling people about me everywhere—in Jerusalem, throughout Judea, in Samaria, and to the ends of the earth.'"**

We get very focused on verse 8 about the Holy Spirit and power *(and rightly so),* but we tend to gloss over verses 6-7. Now that Jesus had died and risen from the dead, the disciples knew that one of the next things on the coming prophetic calendar would be the "Jesus' reigning" part. And *(remember from the last chapter)* they knew that when Jesus started reigning, they would reign with him! Jesus had told them so!

- Notice in Acts 1, Jesus doesn't say, "No you've got it all wrong, I'm not going to set up an earthly reign after all." Clearly, He was indeed going to. He was sure of it. The disciples were sure of it!

- What the disciples surely didn't understand was the need to first grow Jesus' Church around the world.

They sure didn't know the process was going to take 2000+ years!

- So Jesus says: Focus on what you need to focus on right now. My Holy Spirit is going to empower you to take the Gospel message to the world.

- My/Your Heavenly Father knows the dates when I will set up my earthly rule, and you will begin to reign with me. I'm sure, pounding in the back of all their heads was the amazing prophetic promises in Daniel 7:

Daniel 7:9, 13-14: "I watched as thrones were put in place and the Ancient One sat down to judge. His clothing was as white as snow, his hair like purest wool. He sat on a fiery throne with wheels of blazing fire. As my vision continued that night, I saw someone like a Son of Man coming with the clouds of heaven. He approached the Ancient One and was led into his presence. He was given authority, honor, and sovereignty over all the nations of the world, so that people of every race and nation and language would obey him. His rule is eternal—it will never end. His kingdom will never be destroyed."

The disciples' risen Savior was indeed going to, one day, be given authority, honor, and sovereignty over all the nations of the world. Every race, nation, language would obey him, right here on a renewed planet earth! His rule will be eternal! Where, on Pluto? No, right here on this Earth!

The Early Believers weren't getting all excited about God ruling in Heaven, he already does that now! They were excited about him ruling on this earth. That part hadn't/hasn't started yet! They believed with all their hearts that the Messiah would one day bring Heaven to Earth! They were right! They understood that part better than many Christians today. When we pray the Lord's Prayer: May your will be done on earth as it is in Heaven, we need to understand that, prophetically, the whole fulfillment of that prayer hasn't quite, completely happened yet, but it will!

 We need to all grasp the Biblical foundational fact that there is not a square inch of this whole universe God doesn't own. He made it! Every molecule came "out of his being" at Creation. He is sovereign over every atom. So when the Creator God *(who owns all that is in existence)* <u>starts talking about you, as a Believer being his heir</u> – that's kind of a big deal! Actually it's a massive deal!

> **Romans 8:16-17 NIV: "The Spirit himself testifies with our spirit that we are God's children. Now if we are children, then <u>we are heirs—heirs of God and co-heirs with Christ</u>."**

> **Galatians 3:29: "And now that you belong to Christ, you are the true children of Abraham. <u>You are his (God's) heirs</u>, and God's promise to Abraham belongs to you."**

We all know what the word heir or heiress means. If you are the heir of a very rich father, what your Father owns he is going to share with you. What the wealthy father owns, he entrusts to the management of his heirs.

> Creator God made this planet, the centerpiece of his creation. In fact **Hebrews 1:2 NIV** says: **"In these last days he has spoken to us by his Son, <u>whom he appointed heir of all things</u>, and through whom also he made the universe."**

Jesus, the heir of all things created this earth and he gave Adam and Eve rulership – they were in charge of this world. They exercised "dominion." The owner of the universe gave ownership of this "centerpiece" planet to his "in his image" children. Adam and Eve were once already "ruling and reigning" over this world, before they rebelled against their loving Creator. When they fell, the rulership of earth, the dominion of this one planet, was transferred to satan. That's why Paul calls satan "the god of this world, the prince of the power of the air." *(2 Corinthians 4:4, Ephesians 2:2)*

But in the End, when satan is finally defeated, bound into the abyss for a thousand years, *(and then finally thrown into the lake of fire forever)* Creator Jesus will once again assume rule over this Earth – and you and I *(and all the Redeemed)* will pick up where Adam and Eve left off. We will inherit their dominion role as co-heirs with Jesus! **Romans 8:17: "Now if we are children, then we are heirs—heirs of God and co-heirs with Christ."**

What does it mean that in the eternity to come you will be an "heir of God" and co-heirs with the one God *"appointed heir of all things, and through whom also he made the universe?" (Hebrews 1:2)*

- On the spiritual side, we inherit the results of Jesus' First Coming in a cleansed-from-sin soul. His death and resurrection assures us of eternal life with God in Heaven, if we repent and believe.

- But on the physical side, we also inherit the results of Jesus' Second Coming when he destroys the effects of sin and the curse on this earth and sets up his everlasting rule. As the now legal children of our Heavenly Father, forever adopted into his family, we become the legal heirs to all that our infinite Father possesses.*(which is every molecule in the universe).* Our Savior is not just our Redeemer from sin – but he is the heir of all things and we will become "co-heirs with him."

So what is Jesus going to inherit that you are going to inherit with him?

Once again, this is so important: What does Creator Jesus *(John 1)* not have now, that he is soon going to receive – and you are going to receive it alongside of him, and share it with him as a co-heir? RULERSHIP!

We read familiar scriptures like **Ephesians 1:9-10: "God has now revealed to us his mysterious will regarding Christ—which is to fulfill his own good plan. And this is the plan: At the right time he will bring everything together under the authority of Christ— everything in heaven and on earth."** We love those verses, but we often don't quite realize that <u>hasn't happened yet</u>! It's going to!

Colossians 1:19-20: "For God in all his fullness was pleased to live in Christ, and through him God reconciled everything to himself. He made peace with everything in heaven and on earth by means of Christ's blood on the cross." Jesus' blood on the cross provided for him to "make peace with everything in Heaven and Earth," but that hasn't quite been fulfilled yet!

We love to refer to Jesus as the King of all kings and the Lord of all Lords, and spiritually that is true in our hearts. But remember that is the phrase that is inscribed on Jesus' robe as he returns in his Glorious Second Coming. That's a part of Jesus' inheritance that is yet to be fulfilled.

Did you know that there is a specific place in the book of Revelation where the switch is flipped, and Jesus takes over the reign of the whole universe? As the last trumpet, the seventh trumpet is blown, the final bowl judgments start reigning down on sin, satan, and the curse on this earth. *(Which by my calculations happens in that last 30 days of "time" just as Jesus, and we Redeemed, are mounting up for the Second Coming.)*

Revelation 11:15-17: "Then the seventh angel blew his trumpet, and there were loud voices shouting in heaven: <u>'The world has</u> *now* <u>become the Kingdom of our Lord and of his Christ, and he will reign forever and ever.</u>' The twenty-four elders sitting on their thrones before God fell with their faces to the ground

and worshiped him. And they said, 'We give thanks to you, Lord God, the Almighty, the one who is and who always was, for now you have assumed your great power and have begun to reign.'"

That's the exact point-in-time, when Jesus receives his inheritance from the Father as the eternal ruler of this earth! The stunning part is that you are said to be a co-heir and the "co-heir-ship" can only apply to this one point – because this is the only part Jesus has yet to inherit. *(Does that make sense?)* There are a number of passages that describe your "co-heiring" with Jesus for all of eternity. Let's look at, and talk about what they might mean.

2 Timothy 2:11-12: "This is a trustworthy saying: If we die with him, *(embrace his death for us by faith)* **we will also live** *(eternally)* **with him. If we endure hardship,** *(remain faithful)* **we will reign with him."** *(joint-heirs)*

Revelation 5:9-10: "And they sang a new song with these words: 'You are worthy to take the scroll and break its seals and open it, for you were slain and your blood has ransomed people for God from every tribe and language and people and nation. And you have caused them to become a Kingdom of priests for our God. And they will reign on the earth.'" (They, the blood bought, will reign! Where? On the earth! So will Jesus. You will be his co-heir!)

Revelation 3:20-21: "Look! I stand at the door and knock. If you hear my voice and open the door, I will come in, and we will share a meal together as friends. Those who are victorious will sit with me on my

throne, just as I was victorious and sat with my Father on his throne." When are we specifically told that Jesus is going to sit on a throne? It's when he gets back here! So when are you going to sit on a throne with him? It'll be when you get back here on this earth!

How many of us even imagine that as we are being faithful Christians in this life, that God is actually grooming us for leadership in the next life? And faithfulness is the key! The Type A person who "demands and commands" in this life may not be the one leading in the next. The little lady, who quietly "prays Heaven down" in this life, may be the one ruling "five cities" in the next. I'm not making that five cities part up.

> **Luke 16:10-11: "If you are faithful in little things, you will be faithful in large ones. But if you are dishonest in little things, you won't be honest with greater responsibilities. And if you are untrustworthy about worldly wealth, who will trust you with the true riches of heaven?"**

Remember the parable of the ten talents. Watch the way Jesus words this:

> **Luke 19:15-19: "After he was crowned king, he returned and called in the servants to whom he had given the money. He wanted to find out what their profits were. The first servant reported, 'Master, I invested your money and made ten times the original amount!' 'Well done!' the king exclaimed. 'You are a good servant. You have been faithful with the little I entrusted to you, so you will be governor of ten cities**

as your reward.' The next servant reported, 'Master, I invested your money and made five times the original amount.' Well done!' the king said. 'You will be governor over five cities.'" *(What cities – where?)*

We kind of toss that "five cities" part aside, once again imagining that Jesus is speaking metaphorically. What if he isn't? The disciples certainly believed he was being 100% literal.

Jesus is not just preparing a place for us – He is also preparing us for that place!

You – "But I don't want to rule over cities!" – Good! Jesus said, "It is the meek who will inherit the earth." "He meant that the meek now – will inherit the earth then!"

- Whatever he had planned for you to do – whether it is ruling over an earthly city or orchestrating the creation of whole new galaxies,

- Remember God loves to create! One has to assume he may keep on creating – and you may be a part of something he is forming light years away, eons in the future.

- You are going to be reigning with Jesus, and you are going to love every Heavenly second of it!

Conclusion

Hebrews 13:14: "For this world is not our permanent home; we are looking forward to a home (πόλιν/city) yet to come." I said earlier in this book that if we get the idea that this is HOME and going to Heaven is <u>taking us away from our home</u> – we aren't going to ever want to leave!

But if we truly start to understand that <u>this is all temporary</u>! Our real home is already being prepared on the other side of this life – only then can we get a proper perspective on this world around us.

Philippians 3:20-21: "But we are *(right now)* citizens of Heaven, where the Lord Jesus Christ lives. And we are eagerly waiting for him to return as our Savior. He will take our weak mortal bodies and change them into glorious bodies like his own."

Colossians 3:1-2: "Since you have been raised to new life with Christ, set your sights on the realities of Heaven, where Christ sits in the place of honor at God's right hand. Think about the things of heaven, not the things of earth."

I promise you this *one more time*: One earth hour after we arrive in Heaven we are going to say, **"Why in the world was I so intent on staying on the Earth!"**

HEAVEN

Appendix A

Four key passages on satan in the Bible

We don't want to magnify satan and his minions in any way. We talk about them only from the standpoint of how they are defeated by Jesus, and we are promised to "overcome" them through the power of Jesus in us.

There are a limited number of Old Testament passages that talk directly about satan himself. There are disagreements about what these passages teach. Some say they are just discussing bigger-than-life evil humans who lived in ancient times. But as we read them, we know there has to be more to them.

Prophetic passages in the Old Testament are sometimes difficult to spot. Many of the Messianic passages are buried inside other texts. It's only when we see quotes in the New Testament that we discern the Old Testament was actually prophesying Jesus' arrival. So it is with passages about the evil one.

The following are four classic passages describing satan in Scripture: *(IMO)*

Passage #1.

> **Isaiah 14:1-4: "But the LORD will have mercy on the descendants of Jacob. He will choose Israel as his special people once again. He will bring them back to settle once again in their own land. And people from**

many different nations will come and join them there and unite with the people of Israel. The nations of the world will help the people of Israel to return, and those who come to live in the LORD's land will serve them. Those who captured Israel will themselves be captured, and Israel will rule over its enemies. In that wonderful day when the LORD gives his people rest from sorrow and fear, from slavery and chains, you will taunt the <u>king of Babylon</u>. You will say..."

*Q: You are going to find people who say, "The following passage is just talking in an exaggerated way (**hyperbolic**) about a human king in Babylon." Is it?*

Isaiah 14:12-17: "How you are fallen from heaven, O shining star, son of the morning! *(Lucifer = light-bearer)* You have been thrown down to the earth, you who destroyed the nations of the world. For you said to yourself, 'I will ascend to heaven and set my throne above God's stars. I will preside on the mountain of the gods far away in the north. I will climb to the highest heavens and be like the Most High.'

"Instead, you will be brought down to the place of the dead, down to its lowest depths. Everyone there will stare at you and ask, 'Can this be the one who shook the earth and made the kingdoms of the world tremble? Is this the one who destroyed the world and made it into a wasteland? Is this the king who demolished the world's greatest cities and had no mercy on his prisoners?'"

Q: Is that a description of the "fall of satan" or is it just a human example? I fully believe God has inserted here a high definition description of satan's fall. What do you think? Can the above words be describing a human king or is there only one being in the universe that this could describe?

Passage #2.

> **Ezekiel 28: 1-2, 11-13, 14-17: "Then this message came to me from the LORD: 'Son of man, give the <u>prince of Tyre</u> this message from the Sovereign LORD...' Then this further message came to me from the LORD: 'Son of man, sing this funeral song for the king of Tyre. Give him this message from the Sovereign LORD:'**

Q: Who in the world was the prince/king of Tyre? Do the following words fit any human king?

> **'You were <u>the model of perfection</u>, full of wisdom and exquisite in beauty. <u>You were in Eden, the garden of God</u>. Your clothing was adorned with every precious stone— red carnelian, pale-green peridot, white moon-stone, blue-green beryl, onyx, green jasper, blue lapis lazuli, turquoise, and emerald— all beautifully crafted for you and set in the finest gold. They were given to you on the day you were created.'**

Q: Many say we can't apply this to a description of satan because the text says it's addressed to a human king. Do these words sound like they apply to a pagan king from a Phoenician town 12 miles north of Israel in modern day Lebanon?

'I ordained and anointed you as the mighty angelic guardian. You had access to the holy mountain of God and walked among the stones of fire. You were blameless in all you did from the day you were created until the day evil was found in you.'

'Your rich commerce led you to violence, and you sinned. So I banished you in disgrace from the mountain of God. I expelled you, O mighty guardian, from your place among the stones of fire. Your heart was filled with pride because of all your beauty. Your wisdom was corrupted by your love of splendor. So I threw you to the ground and exposed you to the curious gaze of kings.'"

Q: You see how the text seems to wind its way back and forth from an earthly king to someone who couldn't possibly have been human? Of what human would God ever say, "I ordained and anointed you as the mighty angelic guardian? He wouldn't!

Q; If the above passages are describing satan before and after his fall, what all can we learn about him here?

Passage #3.

Luke 10:17-20: "When the seventy-two disciples returned, they joyfully reported to him, 'Lord, even the demons obey us when we use your name!' 'Yes,' he told them, '<u>I saw satan fall from heaven like lightning</u>! Look, I have given you authority over all the power of the enemy. But don't rejoice because evil spirits obey you; rejoice because your names are registered in heaven.'"

Q: Some say that that is just a figurative way of Jesus saying while you guys were out casting out demons – it was as if I was seeing satan fall down over and over – as opposed to Jesus actually saying: "I was there when satan was cast out of Heaven"! What do you think?

Passage #4.

> **Revelation 12:7-9: "Then there was war in heaven. Michael and his angels fought against the dragon and his angels. And the dragon lost the battle, and he and his angels were forced out of heaven. This great dragon—the <u>ancient serpent called the devil, or satan, the one deceiving the whole world</u>—was thrown down to the earth with all his angels."**

Q: I have read some authors who make this out to be a future battle that is yet to take place. Is there any theological possibility that satan and his minions are going to return to Heaven to fight against God and be thrown out of Heaven again? After the original fall of Lucifer and 1/3 of the angels – is there any point where sin will once again be present in Heaven?

Q: Some use the argument that in the book of Job satan appeared before God in Heaven. But if you look closely, there is nowhere in that text that says such a meeting took place in Heaven, is there?

Q: Is the passage in Revelation 12 (in fact the whole chapter) not simply a flashback in time to fill in missing details? Don't we commonly use the same technique in novels today – to be telling a story and then suddenly pause and flashback in time to fill in missing details in the reader's mind? I am totally convinced that

Revelation 12 is a "parenthetical insert," and that the "war in heaven" is describing an event that took place at the beginning of recorded time. What do you think?

Appendix B

Do Believers go straight to Heaven when they die?

1 Thessalonians 4:13-14: "And now, dear brothers and sisters, we want you to know what will happen to the Believers who have died so you will not grieve like people who have no hope. For since we believe that Jesus died and was raised to life again, we also believe that when Jesus returns, <u>God will bring back with him the Believers who have died</u>."

Q: Do we realize what huge news this is to the Thessalonians?

<u>Not only were the Believers who had died going to make it to Heaven – they were already there</u>! To understand why this was such a shock, we need to understand a bit more of their thinking. The entire Old Testament taught the concept of SHEOL – the <u>holding place for the dead</u>. It wasn't just a "hole in the ground."

<u>65 times</u> in the Old Testament it teaches a state of consciousness. But in <u>some instances, the people were in a place of punishment, and in some instances they were in a place of reward</u>.

- The idea that dead people were in a holding place, some headed toward reward and some headed toward punishment carried right on into the New Testament. *(Hades)*

- And there is no doubt that the Thessalonians had this whirling around in their minds even from the teachings of Jesus himself.

The Rich Man and Lazarus! **Luke 16:19-29: "Jesus said, 'There was a certain rich man who was splendidly clothed in purple and fine linen and who lived each day in luxury. At his gate lay a poor man named Lazarus who was covered with sores. As Lazarus lay there longing for scraps from the rich man's table, the dogs would come and lick his open sores.**

Q: Is this a parable or a true story?

'Finally, the poor man died and was carried by the angels to sit beside Abraham at the heavenly banquet. (κόλπος – be with, lap, side, bosom) The rich man also died and was buried, and he went to the place of the dead. *(Hades)* There, in torment, he saw Abraham in the far distance with Lazarus at his side. The rich man shouted, "Father Abraham, have some pity! Send Lazarus over here to dip the tip of his finger in water and cool my tongue. I am in anguish in these flames." (Φλόξ – phlox)

Q: What truths can you draw from Jesus' true story?

> **'But Abraham said to him, "Son, remember that during your lifetime you had everything you wanted, and Lazarus had nothing. So now he is here being comforted, and you are in anguish. And besides, there is a great chasm separating us. No one can cross over to you from here, and no one can cross over to us from there." Then the rich man said, "Please, Father Abraham, at least send him to my father's home. For I**

have five brothers, and I want him to warn them so they don't end up in this place of torment." But Abraham said, "Moses and the prophets have warned them. Your brothers can read what they wrote.""

Q: So, are Lazarus and the Rich man in separate parts of the same place called Sheol? (NT Greek – Hades)

Q: What do we do with Old Testament examples like Enoch who walked with God and was no more because God took him? (Genesis 5:21-24)

Q: Who showed up with Jesus at his transfiguration? How did that happen?

Matthew 17:1-8: "Six days later Jesus took Peter and the two brothers, James and John, and led them up a high mountain to be alone. As the men watched, Jesus' appearance was transformed so that his face shone like the sun, and his clothes became as white as light. <u>Suddenly, Moses and Elijah appeared and began talking with Jesus</u>. Peter exclaimed, 'Lord, it's wonderful for us to be here! If you want, I'll make three shelters as memorials—one for you, one for Moses, and one for Elijah.' But even as he spoke, a bright cloud overshadowed them, and a voice from the cloud said, 'This is my dearly loved Son, who brings me great joy. Listen to him.' The disciples were terrified and fell face down on the ground. Then Jesus came over and touched them. 'Get up,' he said. 'Don't be afraid.' <u>And when they looked up, Moses and Elijah were gone</u>, and they saw only Jesus."

Q: So where did the old dead dudes come from?

Q: When Jesus spoke to the <u>thief on the cross</u>, what exactly was Jesus promising him?

> **Luke 23:38-43: "A sign was fastened above him with these words: 'This is the King of the Jews.' One of the criminals hanging beside him scoffed, 'So you're the Messiah, are you? Prove it by saving yourself — and us, too, while you're at it!' But the other criminal protested, 'Don't you fear God even when you have been sentenced to die? We deserve to die for our crimes, but this man hasn't done anything wrong.' Then he said, 'Jesus, remember me when you come into your Kingdom.' And Jesus replied, 'I assure you, today you will be with me in paradise.'"** παραδείσῳ.

Q: What exactly is Jesus promising the thief?

The only other times this word (παραδείσῳ) is used in the New Testament:

> **2 Corinthians 12:4: "I was <u>caught up to paradise</u> and heard things so astounding that they cannot be expressed in words, things no human is allowed to tell."**

> **Revelation 2:7: "Anyone with ears to hear must listen to the Spirit and understand what he is saying to the churches. To everyone who is victorious I will <u>give fruit from the tree of life in the paradise of God</u>."**

490

Q: Where are these two places referring to?

When Stephen was being martyred, where did he expect to end his day? **Acts 7:54-59: "The Jewish leaders were infuriated by Stephen's accusation, and they shook their fists at him in rage. But Stephen, full of the Holy Spirit, gazed steadily into heaven and saw the glory of God, and he saw Jesus standing in the place of honor at God's right hand. And he told them, 'Look, I see the heavens opened and the Son of Man standing in the place of honor at God's right hand!'**

"Then they put their hands over their ears and began shouting. They rushed at him and dragged him out of the city and began to stone him. His accusers took off their coats and laid them at the feet of a young man named Saul. As they stoned him, Stephen prayed, <u>'Lord Jesus, receive my spirit.</u>'"

Q: Where did Stephen believe Jesus would be when he "received his spirit?

Q: Where did Paul think he was going to end up when he breathed his last breath?

Philippians 1:21-25: "For to me, living means living for Christ, and dying is even better. But if I live, I can do more fruitful work for Christ. So I really don't know which is better. I'm torn between two desires: <u>I long to go and be with Christ, which would be far better for me</u>. But for your sakes, it is better that I continue to live. Knowing this, I am convinced that I will remain

alive so I can continue to help all of you grow and experience the joy of your faith."

2 Corinthians 5:6-8: "So we are always confident, even though we know that as <u>long as we live in these bodies we are not at home with the Lord</u>. For we live by believing and not by seeing. Yes, we are fully confident, and <u>we would rather be away from these earthly bodies, for then we will be at home with the Lord</u>."

NIV: We are confident, I say, and would prefer to be away from the body and at home with the Lord.

NKJV: to be absent from the body and to be present with the Lord.

ESV: we would rather be away from the body and at home with the Lord.

Q: So where exactly is Paul thinking he will be right after his last breath?

- It was common in the Old Testament and on into the New Testament to refer to dead people as "sleeping."

Acts 13:36: "Now when David had served God's purpose in his own generation, <u>he fell asleep;</u> he was buried with his ancestors and his body decayed."

- "Koimao – to sleep" (koimeterion to the latin – *coemeterium* – to the French *cimetiere*, to the English?

Q: Some teach <u>"soul sleep,"</u> that no part of us will raise until the Trumpet blast from Jesus, but what do we know about our bodies once we die from what Paul said in I Thessalonians?

1 Thessalonians 4:13-14: "And now, dear brothers and sisters, we want you to know what will happen to the Believers who have died so you will not grieve like people who have no hope. For since we believe that Jesus died and was raised to life again, we also believe that when Jesus returns, <u>God will bring back with him the Believers who have died</u>."

Q: Doesn't that create a dilemma?

Q: Doesn't the same passage say:

1 Thessalonians 4:16-17: "For the Lord himself will come down from heaven with a commanding shout, with the voice of the archangel, and with the trumpet call of God. First, the believers who have died will rise from their graves. Then, together with them, we who are still alive and remain on the earth will be caught up in the clouds to meet the Lord in the air. Then we will be with the Lord forever!"

Q: How can "already dead" Believers come back with Jesus, but raise to meet Jesus in the air when he returns?

1 Corinthians 15:52: "In a moment, in the twinkling of an eye, at the last trumpet. For the trumpet will sound, and the dead will be raised imperishable, and we shall be changed."

Ephesians 4:8-9: "Therefore it says, 'When he ascended on high he led a host of captives, and he gave gifts to men.' *(anthropoi – men and/or women)* **(In saying, 'He ascended,' what does it mean but that he**

had also descended into the lower regions, the earth?"
(lower parts of the earth)

Q: In Paul's letter to the Ephesians is he teaching that when Jesus died and rose again, he emptied the "reward side of Hades" – directly into the presence of God in Heaven?

Q: And that from Jesus' resurrection on, every Believer who dies goes straight to Heaven?

Appendix C

A Chronology of Revelation 20-21

Q: Is Revelation 20 a "<u>parenthetical insert</u>" like Chapter 12 was about the long past "war in heaven" where satan and his minions are thrown out?

Q: Is the story line in Revelation 19 and Revelation 21 the account of what happens to God, Heaven, and the Earth as time comes to an end and eternity starts?

Q: Is Revelation 20 a "parenthetical insert" that breaks away and defines what is happening to satan and unbelievers (vs. Believers) at the same time Revelation 19 and 21 are unfolding?

First <u>looking backward</u> as time on this earth is ending: **Revelation 19:19-20: "Then I saw** *(Kai eidon)* **the beast and the kings of the world and their armies gathered together to fight against the One sitting on the horse** *(Battle of Armageddon!)* **and his army. And the beast was captured, with him the false prophet. Both the beast and his false prophet were thrown alive into the fiery lake of burning sulfur. Their entire army was killed by the sharp sword that came from mouth of the One riding the white horse."** *(Zechariah 14 says Jesus and us, then land on the Mount of Olives. On that day the Lord will be King over all the Earth!)*

Now <u>looking forward</u> to the beginning of the events of eternity:
Notice the<u> numbers 1-7</u> that I have inserted to show what I believe to be the actual Biblical timeline. *(Notice numbers 1-7 are out of order on purpose.)* I do believe they show Revelation 20 is a "parenthetical insert" as in Revelation 12.

See #1 below,

> **#2) Revelation 21:1-7:** *(What happens to God, Heaven and the Earth for the next 1000 year+)* **"Then I saw** *(kai eidon)* **a new heaven and a new earth, for the old heaven and the old earth had disappeared. And the sea was also gone.**
>
> **#3) "And I saw** *(kai – one flowing event!)* **the Holy City, the New Jerusalem, coming down from God out of heaven. I heard a loud shout from the Throne, saying, 'Look, God's home is now among his people! He will live with them, and they will be his people. God himself will be with them. He will wipe every tear from their eyes, and there will be no more death or sorrow or crying or pain.'**
>
> **"And** *(kai)* **the one sitting on the Throne said, 'Look, I am making everything new!'** *(kainos – new in quality – not new in time!)***And he also** *(kai)* **said, "It is finished! I am the Alpha and the Omega—the Beginning and the End. To all who are thirsty I will give freely from the springs of the water of life. All who are victorious will inherit all these blessings, and I will be their God, and they will be my children.'"**

Revelation 20:1-8, 10, 12-15: *(What happens to satan and unbelievers vs. the Believers for the next 1000 years?)* **"Then I saw** (*kai eidon)* #**1) An angel coming down from Heaven with the key to the bottomless pit and a heavy chain in his hand. He seized the dragon—that old serpent, who is the devil, satan—and bound him in chains for a thousand years.** #**4) Then I saw** *(kai eidon)* <u>thrones, and the people sitting on them</u> *(us!)* **had been given the authority to judge.** #**5) And** *(kai)* **I saw the souls of those who had been beheaded** *(martyrs)* **for their testimony about Jesus.** <u>They all came to life again,</u> *(martyrs)* <u>and they reigned with Christ for a thousand years.</u>

"This is the first resurrection. *(The rest of the dead "unbelievers" did not come back to life until the thousand years had ended.)* **Blessed and holy are those who share in the first resurrection** *(Rapture + martyrs)* **They will be priests of God and of Christ and will reign with him a thousand years.**

#**6)** *satan is released temporarily:* **"When the thousand years come to an end, satan will be let out of his prison. He will go out to deceive the nations—** *(What? Why?)* **Then** *(finally)* **the devil, who had deceived them, was thrown into the fiery lake of burning sulfur, joining the beast and the false prophet.**

#**7)** *The Great White throne Judgment,* **"I saw the dead standing before God's throne. The books were opened, the dead were judged according to what they had done.**

The sea gave up its dead, and death and the grave gave up their dead. *(Unbelievers)* And all were judged. Then death and the grave were thrown into the lake of fire. And anyone whose name was not found recorded in the Book of Life was thrown into the lake of fire."

Appendix D

A Theology of the Rapture of Jesus Christ

Matthew 24 is Jesus' last public sermon before going to his trial. This is the right place to start. This is the <u>longest and most thorough list of what to expect before Jesus' Rapture</u> in the whole Bible, <u>and it comes right from Jesus' mouth</u>. The same sermon is also recorded by Mark in Mark 13 and by Luke in Luke 21. We will compare those two accounts to make sure the main points match Matthew's account.

> **Matthew 24:1-8: "As Jesus was leaving the Temple grounds, his disciples pointed out to him the various Temple buildings. But he responded, 'Do you see all these buildings? I tell you the truth, <u>they will be completely demolished</u>. Not one stone will be left on top of another!'** *(He's prophesying the destruction of Jerusalem and the destruction of the Temple in 70 AD by Roman General Titus.* Since Nehemiah's small beginnings – Jerusalem had become massive.)*

> **"Later, Jesus sat on the Mount of Olives. His disciples came to him privately and said, 'Tell us, when will all this happen? What sign will signal your return** *(parousia)* **and the end of the world** *(age)*?'**

"Jesus told them, 'Don't let anyone mislead you, for many will come in my name, claiming, "I am the Messiah." They will deceive many. And you will <u>hear of wars and threats of wars, but don't panic</u>. Yes, these things must take place, but the end won't follow immediately. Nation will go to war against nation, and kingdom against kingdom. There will be famines and earthquakes in many parts of the world. But all <u>this is only the first of the birth pains, with more to come</u>."

So far everything Jesus is prophesying can be applied to what they were going to be experiencing in the first century.

- It would take a long time for Rome to lose control and **"nations to go to war against nations and kingdoms against kingdoms."**

- Famines and earthquakes in many parts of the world would mean more, once they figured out they were on a "round planet," and there were several more continents they knew nothing about!

- But as Jesus said: **Those things would be only "the first of birth pains."**

Matthew 24:9-13: **"Then you will be arrested, persecuted, and killed. You will be hated all over the world because you are my followers. And many will turn away from me and betray and hate each other. And many false prophets will appear and will deceive many people. Sin will be rampant everywhere, and the love of many will grow cold. But <u>the one who endures to the end will be saved</u>."** *(Ok – what's the end?)*

Jesus' answer to "what signs will signal your return and the end of the age" is not done. He starts to add "happenings" that could not possibly be fulfilled in the 1st  century! **Matthew 24:14: "And the Good News about the Kingdom will be preached throughout the whole world, so that all nations will hear it; and then the end will come."** *(They had no idea what the words "whole world" meant!)*

- We are just now in the last five years that Wycliffe Bible Translators says it will have the <u>Bible translated into every readable language</u>!

- I sometimes hear preachers talk about **"<u>the sign-less return of Jesus.</u>"** Jesus could come back at any moment. There are absolutely no signs waiting to be fulfilled.

- The problem with that is – you have this unfinished list right from Jesus' mouth <u>telling us what signs have to happen</u> *(in chronological order)* before his return.

- In order to call Jesus expected return "sign-less" *(imminent return),* <u>you would have to simply eliminate *(or ignore)* the rest of the things on Jesus' list</u>.

Before we look at the rest of this list as recorded in Matthew 24, and Mark 13, and Luke 21, let's jump down to <u>the extremely important climax of this passage</u> just to make sure we are headed toward the same focal point!

Entry #1. Matthew 24:30-31: "And then at last, <u>the sign that the Son of Man is coming will appear in the heavens,</u> and there will be deep mourning among all the peoples of the earth. And they will see the Son of Man coming (ἔρχομαι – erchomai; Leaving one place and arriving at another) on the clouds of heaven with power and great glory. And <u>he will send out his angels with the mighty blast of a trumpet,</u> and they will gather his chosen ones from all <u>over the world</u>—from the farthest ends of the earth and the heavens."

Entry #2. **Mark 13:26-27: "Then everyone <u>will see the Son of Man coming on the clouds</u> with great power and glory. And he will send out his angels to <u>gather his chosen ones from all over the world</u>—from the farthest ends of the earth the and the heavens."**

Entry #3. **Luke 21:27-32: "'Then <u>everyone will see the Son of Man coming on a cloud with power and great glory.</u> So when all these things begin to happen, stand and look up, for your salvation is near!' Then he gave them this illustration: 'Notice the fig tree, or any other tree. When the leaves come out, you know without being told that summer is near. In the same way, when you <u>see all these things taking place</u>** (*All what things?*)**, you can know that the Kingdom of God is near. I tell you the truth, <u>this generation</u>** (*What generation?*) **will not pass from the scene until all these things have taken place.'"** (*The generation that <u>sees all these things take place!</u>*)

Are the above "finale points" of all three synoptic Gospels describing the Rapture?

Q: Are these passages describing the same thing Paul describes in 1 Thessalonians 4?

1 Thessalonians 4:15-18: "We tell you this directly from the Lord: We who are still living when the Lord returns will not meet him ahead of those who have died. For the <u>Lord himself will come down from heaven with a commanding shout</u>, with the voice of the archangel, and with the trumpet call of God. First, <u>the believers who have died will rise from their graves. Then, together with them, we who are still alive and remain on the earth will be caught up in the clouds to meet the Lord in the air</u>. Then we will be with the Lord forever. So encourage each other with these words."

Q: How do we know these verses are not the "<u>Glorious Second Coming</u>" when Jesus finally returns to earth to clean up sin, and antichrist, and bind satan in the abyss?

#1) Because **in one case the Saints are still on the earth**, or their bodies are in graves, waiting to be raptured. In the other case, the Saints are already in Heaven, coming back with Jesus to earth.

#2) **In one case <u>the unbelievers on earth are completely unsuspecting</u>** *(just as it was in the days of Noah).* On the other hand – the earth has been through the horrors of the Trumpet and Bowl judgments. A large percentage of the earth population is dead, electricity and water and food are almost nonexistent, the earth has been twisted by massive earthquakes and the atmosphere above the earth is upended. And the final God-hating armies of the world are gathered for the battle of Armageddon.

So, if the three Synoptic Gospel writers are all describing the Rapture, <u>then we cannot simply ignore the rest of what they tell us Jesus says, before the finale verses</u>! Matthew records several more significant points before Jesus says:

Matthew 24:30: "And then at last, <u>the sign that the Son of Man is coming will appear in the heavens</u>, and there will be deep mourning among all the peoples of the earth. And they will see the Son of Man coming (ἔρχομαι – erchomai; *Leaving one place and arriving at another*) on the clouds of heaven with power and great glory."

- If we believe that Matthew 24:30 is describing the Rapture of the Saints, we must, then, take time to <u>study the rest of what Jesus himself says comes before the rapture</u>! *(The word "rapture" is a later Latin word coming from the Greek word "harpazo – to snatch away; to seize," coming from* ἁρπαγησόμεθα- "caught up" *in 1 Thessalonians. 4:17.)*

- If we take the Bible literally and believe it exactly as it is presented, we must not *(IMO)* take Matthew 24 or Mark 13 and acknowledge they are written in direct response to the disciple's question, "What are the signs of your coming?" – Then jump to verse 30 and teach about the rapture, simply choosing to ignore the verses directly in front of the rapture verses that lay out additional signs of Jesus' coming!

- We do not get to choose what we do and do not accept as "signs of his coming"!

We do not look at a list of "signs of Jesus' coming" right from Jesus' mouth – and then say "his coming is sign-less!"

So what are some other "signs" listed *(presumably in Chronological order)* that Jesus himself says precede the verses describing the Rapture? *(Back in v. 15)*

> *Entry #1.* **Matthew 24:15-22: "'The day is coming when you will see what Daniel the prophet spoke about— the sacrilegious object that causes desecration standing in the Holy Place.' (Reader, pay attention!) 'Then those in Judea must flee to the hills. A person out on the deck of a roof must not go down into the house to pack. A person out in the field must not return even to get a coat. How terrible it will be for pregnant women and for nursing mothers in those days. And pray that your flight will not be in winter or on the Sabbath. For there will be greater anguish than at any time since the world began. And it will never be so great again. In fact, unless that time of calamity is shortened, not a single person will survive. But it will be shortened for the sake of God's chosen ones.'"**

> *Entry #2.* **Mark 13:14-20: "'The day is coming when you will see the sacrilegious object that causes desecration standing where it should not be.' (Reader, pay attention!) 'Then those in Judea must flee to the hills.**

A person out on the deck of a roof must not go down into the house to pack. A person out in the field must not return even to get a coat. How terrible it will be for pregnant women and for nursing mothers in those days. And pray that your flight will not be in winter. For there will be greater anguish in those days than at any time since God created the world. And it will never be so great again. In fact, unless the Lord shortens that time of calamity, not a single person will survive. But for the sake of his chosen ones he has shortened those days.'"

Entry #3. Luke 21:20-24: "And <u>when you see Jerusalem surrounded by armies</u>, then you will know that the time of its destruction has arrived. Then those in Judea must flee to the hills. Those in Jerusalem must get out, and those out in the country should not return to the city. For <u>those will be days of God's vengeance</u>, and the prophetic words of the Scriptures will be fulfilled. How terrible it will be for pregnant women and for nursing mothers in those days. For there will be disaster in the land and great anger against this people. They will be killed by the sword or sent away as captives to all the nations of the world. And <u>Jerusalem will be trampled down by the Gentiles until the period of the Gentiles comes to an end.</u>"

Q: Do we have any idea what "the abomination of desolation" is, and when it shows up in prophetic history?

Daniel 9:26-27: "After this period of sixty-two sets of seven, <u>the Anointed One will be killed,</u> *(that's Jesus' crucifixion) appearing* **to have accomplished nothing, and a ruler will arise whose armies will destroy the city and the Temple.** *(That's the fall of Jerusalem in 70 AD.)* **The end will come with a flood, and war and its miseries are decreed from that time to the very end.** *(That's the list Jesus gives us in Matthew 24.)* **The ruler will make a treaty with the people <u>for a period of one set of seven,</u>** *(that's the antichrist!)* **but <u>after half this time</u>, he will put an end to the sacrifices and offerings. And <u>as a climax to all his terrible deeds, he will set up a sacrilegious object that causes desecration</u>, until the fate decreed for this defiler is finally poured out on him."**

Q: Do we know exactly when the antichrist will reveal himself to be a satanic monster? Yes! 3 ½ years into the final seven! (Revelation 11-12 even lists it as 1260 days.)

Q: If the revealing of the antichrist as an evil monster doesn't happen until halfway through the final seven years of Tribulation – why does Jesus (in Matthew 24) include it in verse 15 before the verse about the rapture in verse 30?

We have another passage from the Apostle Paul to the Thessalonians that tackles this subject head on:

2 Thessalonians 2:1-4: "Now, dear brothers and sisters, let <u>us clarify some things about 1) the coming of our Lord Jesus Christ and 2) how we will be gathered to meet him</u>. Don't be so easily shaken or alarmed by those who say that the day of the Lord has already begun. Don't believe them, even if they claim to have had a spiritual vision, a

revelation, or a letter supposedly from us. Don't be fooled by what they say.

"<u>For that day will not come until there is 3) a great rebellion against God and</u> 4) <u>the man of lawlessness is revealed—the one who brings destruction.</u> He will exalt himself and defy everything that people call god and every object of worship. He will even sit in the temple of God, claiming that he himself is God."

- Paul clarifies some things about 1) the coming of our Lord Jesus Christ and 2) how we will be gathered to meet him. He says that day will not come until there is 3) a great rebellion against God and 4) the man of lawlessness is revealed—the one who brings destruction.

- There is another section in <u>Jesus' "line-up of expected signs"</u> that is almost completely ignored.

- Not only does every Synoptic Gospel writer emphasize it, but we have a direct link describing it in detail in Revelation 6.

- When the Early Church in the 2nd century read their new letter of Revelation, <u>there is not a chance in the world that they did not make the connection!</u> *(IMO)*

Entry #1. **Matthew 24:27-30: "For as the lightning flashes in the east and shines to the west, so it will be when the Son of Man comes.** *(parousia)* **Just as the gathering of vultures shows there is a carcass nearby, so these signs indicate that the end is near.** <u>Immediately after the anguish of those days, the sun</u>

will be darkened, the moon will give no light, the stars will fall from the sky, and the powers in the heavens will be shaken. And then at last, the sign that the Son of Man is coming will appear in the heavens, and there will be deep mourning among all the peoples of the earth. And they will see the Son of Man coming on the clouds of heaven with power and great glory."

Q: How many times do you ever hear anybody teach that the sign just before Jesus comes *and raptures his Saints – is going to be a huge disruption in the heavens?* And yet those are the exact word that come from Jesus' mouth – in all three Synoptic Gospels!

> *Entry #2.* **Mark 13:24-27: "At that time, after the anguish of those days, the sun will be darkened, the moon will give no light, the stars will fall from the sky, and the powers in the heavens will be shaken. Then everyone will see the Son of Man coming on the clouds with great power and glory. And he will send out his angels to gather his chosen ones from all over the world —from the farthest ends of the earth and heaven."**

> *Entry #3.* **Luke 21:25-28: "And there will be strange signs in the sun, moon, and stars. And here on earth the nations will be in turmoil, perplexed by the roaring seas and strange tides. People will be terrified at what they see coming upon the earth, for the powers in the heavens will be shaken. Then everyone will see the Son of Man coming on a cloud with power and**

great glory. So when all these things begin to happen, stand and look up, for your salvation is near!"

Now notice the direct correlation to the above three passages that John then writes into the end of Revelation 6:

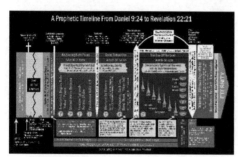

Revelation 6:12-17: "I watched as the Lamb broke the sixth seal, and there was a great earthquake. The sun became as dark as black cloth, and the moon became as red as blood. Then the stars of the sky fell to the earth like green figs falling from a tree shaken by a strong wind. The sky was rolled up like a scroll, and all of the mountains and islands were moved from their places. Then everyone—the kings of the earth, the rulers, the generals, the wealthy, the powerful, and every slave and free person—all hid themselves in the caves and among the rocks of the mountains. And they cried to the mountains and the rocks, 'Fall on us and hide us from the face of the one who sits on the throne and from the wrath of the Lamb. (Clearly, for the first time this isn't something humans are producing – and even the sinners know it!) **For the great day of their wrath has come, and who is able to survive?'"** (Wrath of man vs. the Wrath of God!)

- The standard default answer from many modern day preachers is that the whole of the seven years of Tribulation is the outpoured wrath of God.

- But here, **the "wrath of God" is specifically defined as happening after the Lamb breaks the 6th seal**!

Notice: God did give us three "inspired assurances" that **we Believers are not going to be the direct recipients of God's final wrath** on sin and satan. *(The question we all must wrestle with is – when does God's wrath on sin and satan begin?)*

1 Thessalonians 1:10: "and to wait for his Son from heaven, whom he raised from the dead—Jesus, who rescues us from the coming wrath."

1 Thessalonians 5:9-10: "For God did not appoint us to suffer wrath but to receive salvation through our Lord Jesus Christ. He died for us so that, whether we are awake [alive] or asleep [dead], we may live together with Him."

Revelation 3:10: "Because you have obeyed my command to persevere, I will protect you from the great time of testing that will come upon the whole world to test those who belong to this world."

The next event on God's prophetic calendar as stated in Matthew 24, Mark 13, and Luke 21 is the return of Jesus to take his Saints with him back to Heaven. *(Except the "sealing of 144,000 Jews"– who won't be raptured, but will stay on Earth to lead a revival.* IMO)

Revelation 7:9-10: "After this I saw (μετὰ ταῦτα εἶδον) **a vast crowd, too great to count, from every nation and tribe and people and language, standing in front of the Throne and before the Lamb. They were clothed in white robes and held palm branches in their hands.**

And they were shouting with a great roar, 'Salvation comes from our God who sits on the Throne and from the Lamb!'" *(That's us! And that's hugely significant!)*

Then One Of The Elders Asked Me, "These In White Robes--who Are They, And Where Did They Come From?"

Revelation 7-13

Revelation 7:13-17 NLT: "Then one of the twenty-four elders asked, 'Who are these who are clothed in white? Where did they come from?' And I said to him, 'Sir, you are the one who knows.' *(Because you are one of them!)* **Then he said to me, 'These are the ones who died in** [a] **the great tribulation.** (ἐρχόμενοι *ek – erchomai ek – came out from)* **They have washed their robes in the blood of the Lamb and made them white.'"**

If you say, "Wow there is an alternate reading there, I really want to know what the [a] stands for." (Footnote a. 7:14 [a] – Greek for *who came out of.)*

"That is why **they stand in front of God's throne** and serve him day and night in his Temple. And he who sits on the throne will give them shelter. They will never again be hungry or thirsty; they will never be scorched by the heat of the sun. For the Lamb on the throne will be their Shepherd. He will lead them to springs of life-giving water. And God will wipe every tear from their eyes."

I looked up every reference in the NLT where they translated the word *erchomai.* There are **256 times the word is used**.

- **255 of those times they translate the word, "to come, coming, came**." *(which is the root meaning of the word.)*

- **One time in Revelation 7:14, they translate the word, "to die!"** *(which is in no way ever the meaning of the word!)*

- This is the other word *(erchomai)* often used to describe Jesus' Second Coming. It's the word used in Revelation 22 when Jesus says, **"I am coming soon!"** It is the same word used when Jesus says: "If anyone is thirsty let him/her come!" It's the phrase at the end of the Bible that says: "**Come Lord Jesus!**"

Simply put – it always, always means "to come, to leave one place and arrive at another." **"So why, why would the translators translate the word, 'to die'?"**

- That has lead generations of Believers down a false trail declaring that those "clothed in white" are all "martyrs."

- Remember, this comes soon after the revealing of the antichrist as an evil monster, halfway through the Tribulation. That would mean he would be revealed as evil, and then have to instantly kill enough people all over the planet to immediately present "**a vast crowd, too great to count,** *(of martyrs)* **from every nation and tribe and people and language, standing in front of the Throne and before the Lamb.**" *(That timeline is not believable. IMO)*

By this time, the antichrist is working out of Jerusalem. He now has a favorability rating of about zero. The armies of the world are massing to come to Jerusalem and bring his reign crashing down *(IMO.)* *(They certainly don't know they are going to arrive there to meet a returning Jesus with all his Saints and all his angels.)*

We picture the antichrist running all over the world in the last 3 ½ years killing everyone who hasn't taken the Mark of the Beast. I suspect though, that with the Trumpet and Bowl judgments of God's Wrath raining down on him and the earth during that time, his ability to demand anything or kill people in the remote parts of the planet will be largely limited.

- Don't forget, there are still thousands/millions *(IMO)* rejecting the antichrist in that last 3 ½ years who will enter the millennium. *(1000 year reign of Jesus and us.)*

- They will not be raptured or glorified. Who did we think we were going to be reigning over?

- It's them, the fruit of a world-wide revival during the Tribulation! *(IMO)*

ENDNOTES

1. Randy Alcorn, *Heaven* (Wheaton, IL: Tyndale House Publishers, Inc., 2004), Pg. 11-12.

2. Isaac Asimov, https://www.brainyquote.com/quotes /isaac_asimov_122403, 12.

3. Randy Alcorn, *Heaven* (author paraphrased), 6.

4. John Eldridge, *The Journey of Desire* (Nashville, TN: Thomas Nelson Publishers, 2000), 14-15.

5. Robert Roy Britt, "Huge Hole Found in the Universe," *Space.com, August 23, 2007*, https://www.space.com/4271-huge-hole-universe.html, 24.

6. David Berg, *Top 100 David Berg Quotes (2023 Update) - Quotefancy.com* https://quotefancy.com/david-berg-quotes, 30.

7. Mark Twain, *The Adventures of Huckleberry Finn* (New York, NY: Fawcett Columbine, 1996), 32.

8. Randy Alcorn, *Heaven* (Eternal Perspectives Ministries, 2004),Pages 20-22, 37.

9. Anton S. Levey, *The satanic Bible* (New York, NY: Avon Books,1969), 121.

10. L. Stafford Betty (Stanford Encyclopedia of Philosophy, 2017), 146.

11. David Jeremiah, *Revealing the Mysteries of Heaven* (San Diego, CA: Turning Point, 2017), 146

12. Joni Eareckson Tada, (*Quotes by Joni Eareckson Tada*),

https://gracequotes.org/author-quote/joni-eareckson-tada/, 197.

13. Information we forget, World-skills *Global Industry Partners*, 207.

14. *"Curve of Forgetting,"* (University of Waterloo, Waterloo, ON, Canada, 2010) available online:
http://www.adm.uwaterloo.ca/infocs/study/curve.html, 207.

15. *"How Do We See Color?"* (Pantone.com, September 27, 2020), available online: https://www.pantone.com/articles/color-fundamentals/how-do-we-see-color#, 299.

16. Sy Montgomery, *The Magnificent Migration* (New York, NY: Clarion Books, 2019), 338.

17. St. Augustine, Bishop of Hippo, North Africa, *De Civitate Dei XX 7-9* (early 5th Century AD), 360.

ACKNOWLEDGEMENTS

God nudged **Cass Everett**, after her retirement, to sell her home in Pennsylvania and move to the "unknown land" of South Florida. In God's providential plan she ended up just a few miles from our church. Cass' use of her spiritual gifts has become invaluable at Grace Emmanuel Church, but she has become, to me, a gift from God.

Who, but God, could have planned an ADD pastor linking up with a gentle "do it by the book" editor. This book literally would not have been in print without the time Cass has invested in it.

She has poured so, so many long hours into repeatedly editing and reviewing and re-editing the manuscripts for this book, "What Scares Demons," and "Unmasking Revelation." No one but God will ever know the long evenings she sat up late into the night finding the phrase that didn't quite communicate, finding the exclamation mark before the quotation mark rather than after it, finding the underline extending under the period. She also tirelessly worked through the use of every Scripture, culminating in the Scripture index at the end of this book.

Penny Worley, the administrative secretary at Grace Emmanuel Church, designed the cover of this book. She is also a special gift from God in my life. In spite of the already huge demands on her time at the church, when I walk into Penny's office with a personal project, she never fails to give away her free time, and always with excellence beyond measure.

A special thanks to **Sara Talbacka, Holly Jochum, Helen Rhoades** and **George Waddy**, for their "beta" reading and editing of the manuscript and their priceless suggestions.

SCRIPTURE BY CHAPTER INDEX

HEAVEN

HEAVEN

SCRIPTURE VERSIONS

Additional Scripture Versions used:

ABOUT THE AUTHOR

Sam Chess has served as a Pastor on the Treasure Coast of Florida, for more than 40 years. He presently serves as the Senior Pastor of Grace Emmanuel Church *(EFCA)* in Port Saint Lucie. *(See graceemmanuel.com)* He and his wife Sue founded the church in 1990.

Grace Emmanuel has four radio programs called "GRACE ALIVE" on the regional Christian radio station WCNO. *(WCNO.com)* These four programs reach from Ft. Lauderdale to Melbourne, FL – halfway across the state, and into the Bahamas.

Sam serves on the board of the Treasure Coast Christian Alliance, which brings together local government officials, business leaders, and Church leaders in unity and purpose.

Sam and Sue have three grown children and nine wonderful grandchildren. Sue Chess serves as the Executive Director of Care Net Pregnancy Services of the Treasure Coast.

Sam holds a Bachelor's degree from Hobe Sound Bible College and a Master's degree from Trinity International University.

Sam is also the author of two other books, _What Scares Demons_ and _Unmasking Revelation_.

OTHER BOOKS BY SAM CHESS

Unmasking Revelation

The Book of Revelation was meant to ignite awe and worship.

There is a special blessing promised to all who read and obey the words of Revelation (1:3). Yet many Christians slam their Bible shut before reading because they find the end times prophecy to be confusing, weird, and even scary. Revelation was never meant to be feared or skipped over. In *Unmasking Revelation*, Sam Chess walks through how Jesus left first century Christians with the hope of His return, and how the letter of Revelation was given as a guide to how it all would end. Jesus was going to victoriously win and satan, and death, and hell, and even the curse of sin itself (22:3) would be purged off this planet!

Through *Unmasking Revelation*, the difficult parts of Revelation become understandable, and the weird and frightening are "unmasked" to simply unfold the storyline of Jesus' (and Christians') final triumphant victory.

What Scares Demons

1 John 3:8: "The Son of God came to DESTROY the works of the devil."

In *What Scares Demons*, Sam Chess shows us that Jesus left Heaven and came into this world, as a Savior, as OUR SAVIOR, to forgive and cleanse our sins! But Jesus also came into this world as a HEAVENLY WARRIOR to do fatal damage to "satan's kingdom of darkness"!

> **Hebrews 2:14-15: "…he too shared in their humanity so that by his death he might break the power of him who holds the power of death — that is, the devil…**
>
> o   Jesus didn't come to this earth to have a word spat with satan. He came to destroy him! Jesus didn't just come to save us from sin – He came to save us from satan!
>
> **Colossians 1:12-14: "…For he has rescued us from the kingdom of darkness and transferred us into the Kingdom of his dear Son."**

What you see and hear from demons when come in contact with Jesus and scream out in fear in the Gospels should make you never fear them again in your life! The truth is – demons are scared to death of your God, they are scared to death of your Savior and they are scared to death of YOU, a Redeemed Saint, and the presence of God that lives in you!

> **James 2:19: "You believe that there is one God. Good! Even the demons believe that — and they tremble/shudder. (φρίσσω) in terror!"**

They know something that they hope you never find out: They know that all the power is on your side! You are a Son or Daughter of the Most High God! And they are scared to death of what you will do with your life when you figure that all out!

Made in the USA
Monee, IL
16 February 2024

b779507a-fd1c-4715-89d7-d3040a9394ffR01